Published by
Rajneesh Foundation International
Rajneeshpuram, Oregon 97741 U.S.A.

Bhagwan Shree Rajneesh

Philosophia Ultima

Discourses on the Mandukya Upanishad

Editor: Ma Yoga Anurag
Design: Swami Dhyan Abhudaya
Direction: Ma Yoga Pratima, M.M.,D.Phil.M. (RIMU), Arihanta
Copyright: © 1983 Rajneesh Foundation International
Published by:
   Ma Anand Sheela, M.M.,D.Phil.M.,D.Litt.M.(RIMU), Acharya
   Rajneesh Foundation International, President
   P.O. Box 9, Rajneeshpuram
   Oregon 97741 U.S.A.

First Edition: December 1983 — 10,000 copies

Translations copyright © Alistair Shearer and Peter Russell from
THE UPANISHADS published by Wildwood House Ltd., London,
1978.

Printed in U.S.A.
ISBN 0-88050-617-2
Library of Congress Catalog Number 83-043216

CONTENTS

INTRODUCTION

"If you cannot laugh, you cannot understand life.
If you cannot laugh, you are not open . . .
you are closed;
your doors, your windows are all closed.
In laughter, heartfelt laughter . . .
you experience life entering you,
touching you at the deepest core."
Bhagwan Shree Rajneesh

If you can read this book without experiencing at least one deep belly laugh, there is no hope for you; your doors and windows are not only closed but nailed shut. Within these pages, the uniqueness, beauty, penetrating insight and crystal clarity of the enlightened Master, Bhagwan Shree Rajneesh, is revealed. His compassion and loving acceptance is demonstrated time after time as He helps us to see the world, reality, ourselves, with the blinders removed. Bhagwan doesn't apologize or compromise nor does He ask for our acceptance or respect. He simply says what He has to say, pointing out that tomorrow He might contradict Himself completely. Some of His statements are so totally new and unexpected, you may feel your whole perspective shifting:

> *"Man can be a mother, woman can be a*
> *mother; the moment you are creative, you*
> *are a mother."*

And that is one of the effects of coming in contact with a Master; He changes our perspective, He challenges us to risk, to look at and experience life with a totally new awareness.

As you enter into these sutras of the Mandukya Upanishad and read the responses to disciples' questions, don't be surprised to find your traditional beliefs shaken. If you find tears in your eyes, know that He has touched your heart, for above all, Bhagwan is a Master of the Heart. You may feel hurt, but if you look a little deeper, you may come to see that only one who loves unconditionally cares enough to make you look at the rubbish of life as well as the diamonds. And if you'll put aside your rational mind and open your heart, just a little, maybe you'll recognize the gifts Bhagwan is offering—deep communion with the Master, and a glimpse of what is possible.

"We are very close to the sunrise.
Just a little effort
and the earth can be transformed,
totally transformed into a beautiful place—
it has never been,
but man has always dreamt about it."
Bhagwan Shree Rajneesh

Swami Anand Madyapa

These discourses,
based on the sutras of
the Mandukya and Isa Upanishads,
were given at Shree Rajneesh Ashram,
Poona, India
December 11-26, 1980

माण्डूक्योपनिषद्

शांति-पाठः

ॐ भद्रं कर्णेभिः शृणुयाम देवाः
भद्रं पश्येमाक्षभिर्यजत्राः।
स्थिरैरंगैस्तुष्टुवां सस्तनूभिर्व्यशेम
देवहितं यदायुः॥
स्वस्ति न इन्द्रो वृद्धश्रवाः
स्वस्ति नः पूषा विश्ववेदाः।
स्वस्तिनस्ताक्ष्र्यौ अरिष्टनेमिः
स्वस्ति नो वृहस्पतिर्दधातु॥
ॐ शांतिः शांतिः शांतिः॥

Māndūkyopaniṣad
Śānti-pāṭhaḥ

Om bhadraṁ karṇebhiḥ śṛṇuyāma devāḥ
Bhadraṁ paśyemākṣabhir yajatrāḥ,
Sthirair aṅgais tuṣṭuvāṁsas tanūbhir vyaśema
Deva-hitaṁ yad āyuḥ.
Svasti na indro vriddhaśravāḥ
Svasti naḥ pūṣā visvavedāḥ,
Svasti nastākṛṣyo aristanemiḥ
Svasti no vrhaspatirdadhātu
Om śāntiḥ śāntiḥ śāntiḥ

Discourse 1

December 11, 1980

THIS IS THE BRIDGE TO THAT

ओमित्येतदक्षरमिदं सर्वं
तस्योपव्याख्यानं भूतं
भवद्भविष्यदिति सर्वमोङ्कार एव।
यच्चान्यत् त्रिकालातीतं
तदप्योङ्कार एव॥
सर्वंह्येतद्
ब्रह्मायमात्मा ब्रह्म

Om ityetad akṣaram, idaṁ sarvaṁ
Tasyopavyākhyānam, bhūtaṁ
Bhavad bhaviṣyad iti, sarvam oṅkara eva.
Yac cānyat trikālātītaṁ
Tad apyoṁkāra eva.

Sarvaṁ hyetad
Brahma, ayam ātmā brahma

AUM,
The imperishable sound,
is the seed of all that exists.
The past, the present, the future,
—all are but the unfolding of AUM.
And whatever transcends
the three realms of time,
that indeed is the flowering of AUM.

This whole creation is ultimately Brahman.
And the Self,
this also is Brahman.

ॐ पूर्णमदः पूर्णमिदं पूर्णात् पूर्णमुदच्यते।
पूर्णस्य पूर्णमादाय पूर्णमेवावशिष्यते॥

AUM
Pūrnamadah
Pūrnamidaṃ
Pūrnāt pūrnamudachyatē
Pūrnasya pūrnamādāya
Pūrnamēva vashisyatē.

AUM
That is the Whole.
This is the Whole.
From wholeness emerges wholeness.
Wholeness coming from wholeness,
wholeness still remains.

THIS IS ONE OF THE MOST significant statements ever made anywhere on the earth at any time. It contains the whole secret of the mystic approach towards life. This small sutra contains the essence of the Upanishadic vision. Neither before nor afterwards has the vision been transcended; it still remains the Everest of human consciousness. And there seems to be no possibility of going beyond it.

The Upanishadic vision is that the universe is a totality, indivisible; it is an organic whole. The parts are not separate, we are all existing in a togetherness: the trees, the mountains, the people, the birds, the stars, howsoever far away they may appear—don't be deceived by the appearance—they are all interlinked, all bridged. Even the smallest blade of grass is connected to the farthest star, and it is *as* significant as the greatest sun.

Nothing is insignificant, nothing is smaller than anything else. The part represents the whole just as the seed contains the whole. The seed contains the past—because all the trees that have preceded it are contained in it. And the seed also contains the whole future—all the trees that may happen through it are potentially there. And of course the seed contains the present. The seed looks so small, but it is not as small as it looks. If you dissect it you will not find the flowers and the colors and the fragrance, and then you may decide that the seed is empty, but in fact your method was wrong.

That's what science has been doing with reality—dissecting it, analyzing it. Analysis is destructive. What is needed is a unifying vision, a synthesis. And that is the Upanishadic approach: the part becomes the whole, the whole becomes the part. There is no hierarchy in the Upanishadic vision of life. Nothing is lower, nothing is higher, nothing is mundane and nothing is sacred—all is one.

This vision remained the vision of a few mystics. It never became part of human consciousness. That's why there is so much misery in the world, so much ugliness, insensitivity. People are not flowering; their hidden splendor, their imprisoned splendor is not freed. People are living imprisoned lives, chained. They contain infinity in them but they are not even aware of it.

First the so-called religions, the organized religions of the world, destroyed humanity. Then came science. Science is nothing but an organized materialistic approach to life. Just as religion is an organized approach as far as man's subjectivity is concerned, science is also a church, a priesthood, and as superstitious as any religion has ever been. Of course, the dimensions are different: religions are organized superstitions about the inner, and science is organized superstitions about the outer.

The Upanishad and its approach is individual. The word *upanishad* means: sitting in deep communion with the Master. It has nothing to do with the church. No church can ever be religious, all churches are basically political. You have to understand the definition: politics means society, collectivity; religion means individuality.

Religion is a rebellion against the collective. Anything that depends on the collectivity, on tradition, on dogma, on ideology, is bound to be against the individual. And the individual is the only reality, the collective is only a word. You never come across the society, you always come across the individual. You never come across humanity, you always come across human beings. You never come across love, you always come across two lovers. You come across loving but never across love.

But we have been conditioned to live with abstractions: society, humanity, love, God. These are all abstractions, empty concepts with no concrete reality behind them.

The Upanishad is very realistic, very pragmatic. It is communion from heart to heart. That's the meaning of *upanishad*, a very strange meaning—sitting by the side of a Master, just sitting by the side of a Master . . . and then something transpires. Something like a flame jumps from the heart of the Master to the heart of the disciple.

The Master has come home, the Master has experienced the truth. The disciple is seeking, but the seeker has to be silent, utterly silent. It is not a question of asking questions, because the ultimate questions can neither be asked nor answered. They are only transmitted—without asking, without answering. That transmission beyond words is the meaning of the word *upanishad*. And before we enter into these sutras of the Mandukya Upanishad, this has to be understood.

My whole effort here is to revive the spirit of the Upanishads again. You all sitting in silence with me . . . this pause, this rest, this relaxed attitude . . . this silence in which all dualities disappear . . . I am not here, you are not there, but something pervades, permeates, overwhelms . . . *that* overwhelming experience is contained in these sutras.

This *mangal* sutra—

AUM
Purnamadah
Purnamidam
Purnat purnamudachyate
Purnasya purnamadaya
Purnameva vashisyate—

—can be said to contain the whole approach, the vision.

That means the beyond, the invisible. *This* means the within, the visible. *That* means the hidden, *this* means the manifest. *That* means the infinite, *this* means the finite. *That* is the whole, of course, but the insistence of the Upanishads is: *this* too, is the whole.

One is not supposed to renounce life. Renunciation is against the spirit of the Upanishads. The Upanishadic seers were not renunciates, they had not escaped away from life—because where can you escape to? Wherever you go you will be in the whole as much as you are in the whole here. The marketplace and the monastery, both are part of the whole. To be with your wife, your husband, your children, your friends, is as sacred, as holy, as to go to the Himalayas and to live in a cave in absolute solitariness. Both belong to the same existence.

It is Jainism and Buddhism and their emphasis on renunciation that destroyed the Upanishadic flight—the flight from this to that, the flight of the part to the whole. Jainism and Buddhism are rooted in renunciation; they are life-negative, they are *against* life. Their attitude is that of condemnation: *this* is wrong and *that* is right. Leave this for that. If you want to attain to *that*, then you have to renounce this. And the Upanishad says:

> *Purnamadah*
> *Purnamidam*
> *Purnat purnamudachyate*
>
> *That is the Whole.*
> *This is the Whole.*

There is *no* difference at all. It is *one* reality. The without and the within are not two, but two aspects of the same phenomenon. Matter and spirit are not to be put in antagonism against each other, they are not opposites. And we know they are not opposites because in you the meeting is happening. Even this very moment your body and your soul are not two, they are one. Your body affects your consciousness, your consciousness affects your body. Your body is only the outermost part of your consciousness, and your consciousness is nothing but the innermost core of your body. The body is the dimension that spreads outwards, and the consciousness, the soul, is the dimension that goes inwards. But it is one spectrum. You are already *living* the unity of this and that.

But Jainism and Buddhism both created a great calamity; the calamity was that they condemned life. And it appealed to the people—for the simple reasonthat people don't know the art of living. Hence they are miserable, they are living in suffering; their life is a continuous drag from one suffering to another. And they don't see any hope—everything seems to be a hopeless despair. So when Buddhism and Jainism started saying that life itself is wrong, it appealed to the people.

People are always ready to throw the responsibility on others' shoulders. Nobody wants to say, "I don't know how to live—that's why I am suffering." Everybody would like to shirk the responsibility. And this was a beautiful way, and very logical, very appealing, very rational: that life itself is suffering. Buddha says, "Life is suffering, birth is suffering, death is suffering, everything is suffering." And it corresponded with the people's experiences. But the reason is not that *life* is suffering, the reason is that you don't know how to play the game, you don't know the art of living it.

Of course it is a suffering if you don't know how to play the flute; it will be a suffering to you and to the neighbors and to everybody. And sooner or later you will get fed up and you will want to renounce this flute because it is simply creating trouble for you and for others. But the flute is not at fault. It is simply that you don't know how to play, otherwise it is capable of creating beautiful music. It can nourish you and others.

Life is a very complex phenomenon, far more complex than a flute. Life is the whole orchestra, thousands of musical instruments together. And you have to learn to play all of them in such a way that you can create a harmony. That's the whole art . . . and life is an opportunity to learn it. It is not to be renounced, it is to be rejoiced.

I belong to the Upanishadic world, the Upanishads belong to me. Their vision is my vision too. I would like to destroy this life-negative approach, to uproot it completely. It has made you suffer and it has helped you to rationalize your suffering—then the only way is to escape. But do you know the people who have escaped? Are they really blissful? Just look at your so-called saints and mahatmas. Are they really blissful? They look so sad, so serious, so dead. They talk about bliss; that does not mean that they are blissful. In fact, whenever a person talks too much about bliss that simply shows that he is trying to compensate. He is suffering deep down; talking about bliss he is trying to create an illusion for himself.

It is almost always the people who have failed in love who write poetry about love; otherwise, who has time to write poetry about love? One should love, rather. When you know how to cook, you cook; you don't go on writing about how to cook beautiful foods. You simply prepare beautiful food, nourishing food. It is always the people who have missed the train who talk about love and who talk about bliss and who talk about truth. Otherwise there is no need—one simply lives it. One's life becomes a message! And that is the only true message.

Just look at your saints. They cannot be blissful, they are so egoistic. Their whole mind is full of nothing but ego. If you look into their eyes you will find only one message written in thousands of ways: holier-than-thou, a deep condemnation for you, a deep condemnation for all people, a deep condemnation for everything that exists.

"What a dust I raise!" said the fly on the chariot wheel.

Look into the eyes of your so-called saints and you will see only that: "What a dust I raise!" Just flies raising much dust, making much fuss, much ado about nothing. Yes, they are full of words, theories, hypotheses, but a blind man can be very much acquainted with all the theories about light—that does not help him to see.

A flea sits down on the flap of a box of corn flakes, takes out a deckchair, sunglasses and suntan lotion, and begins to sun himself.

Suddenly he sees another flea run quickly past him. He settles down into his deckchair when out of nowhere the flea races past from the other direction. This scene—the flea running past from one direction then the other—goes on for a while.

Unable to contain his curiosity the first flea grabs the second one as he is running past. "Hey! What's your hurry? What are you doing?"

Gasping for breath the second flea mutters, "Can't stop now. It says, 'Tear across the dotted line.'"

Yes, your saints are full of words, scriptures. They have read much, studied a great deal, but that does not make them knowers. Knowing is a totally different phenomenon. It is seeing, it is not believing. They are all believers, and believers always behave foolishly, because a blind man can learn too much about light and then he may start believing that he knows what light is. And then the trouble begins. He may throw his walking-stick; he may stop asking others, "Where is the door?" or, "Where is the way?" because he thinks that he knows himself. "Now enough, there is no need to ask and inquire." He is bound for trouble; the trouble is inevitable.

A South American style dictatorship has taken over in the United States: Ronald Reagan, John Anderson, and Jimmy Carter are lined up to be shot. As the firing squad gets ready, Reagan yells, "Earthquake!" and escapes in the commotion. As the executioners ready themselves again, Anderson yells, "Flood!" and he escapes in the confusion. As the firing squad lines up for a third time, Jimmy Carter decides to try the same idea and he yells, "Fire!"

The pundits are the greatest fools in the world. They may talk about great things but they have not even known the little things of life. They may talk about the beyond, about that, but they know nothing about this. And without knowing this you cannot know about that —this is the bridge to that. This world has to be lived with such joy that you can discover God in it, because there is no other way to find him. This is the message of the Upanishads.

> *From wholeness emerges wholeness.*
> *Wholeness coming from wholeness,*
> *wholeness still remains.*

One very important thing to be remembered: the Upanishads don't believe in perfection, they believe in totality. The perfectionist is a neurotic type of person.

In fact, every perfectionist is insane; he is bound to be insane. If he is not yet insane that means he is not yet really a perfectionist. To be a real perfectionist and not to be insane is impossible.

Life is perfect in only one sense: it is perfectly imperfect. That's why there is evolution, that's why there is movement, that's why life is possible. If it is perfect that means the dead end has come. Life remains flowing, always moving from one peak to another peak. There is no end . . . no full point ever comes. The goal is never achieved, remember. Life is not goal-oriented, it is *journey*-oriented. Life is a pilgrimage.

Enjoy each moment because each moment is a goal unto itself. Don't sacrifice it for another goal. Don't sacrifice this for that, otherwise you will miss both. Live this and the miracle happens: living *this* totally, you find *that* hidden behind it. Each moment lived totally brings you closer and closer to God. The more total you are, the more intense and passionate your approach towards life is, the closer you are to paradise. When nothing is being held back, when each act becomes total . . . when you are dancing you are simply dancing, so much so that the dancer disappears into the dance. Even that division between the dancer and the dance disappears—there is only dance and no dancer. The merger, the melting is absolute. You have found the truth, you have found *that*.

When the musician has completely forgotten himself, when he is no more self-conscious, when he becomes selfless—or to put it more exactly, when he becomes unself-conscious, when he is almost not—when only the music is there: that totality, that passionate state . . . and you will discover *that*.

And it is also significant to remember that all the Upanishads start with AUM. AUM simply represents the musical approach towards existence, not the mathematical approach.

The scientific approach is mathematical, the mystic's approach is musical. The musician is very close to mysticism, far closer than the philosopher. In fact, music comes closest as far as expressing the truth is concerned, because music is meaningful without any words; it is meaningful simply because it rings some bells in your heart. The great music is that which creates a synchronicity between you and itself, when your heart starts resonating in the same way, when you start pulsating in the same way.

I have heard a beautiful story:

It happened in Lucknow in the time of Vajid Ali Shah. . . .He was the king of Lucknow, a very crazy man, a drunkard, but a lover of music, art, sculpture, painting, a lover of beauty. He used to invite all kinds of dancers, singers, musicians, poets, to his court.

One musician was constantly refusing to come. Vajid Ali Shah went to him—that was a rare gesture from him, he had never gone to anybody. His invitation was enough, and he was ready to pay as much as demanded or more. But the musician was reluctant to come.

When Vajid Ali Shah went to him he said, "I can come, but you will have to fulfill my condition. I have only one single condition and that is: when I am playing or singing, nobody can move his head."

Vajid Ali Shah said, "That is not a difficult thing, don't be worried. I will inform the people who are going to come to listen that 'If you move your head, your head will be chopped off!'" He was a crazy man—he could have done that, and he actually prepared for it. He informed the whole capital of Lucknow: "Those who want to come, they should be aware that it is risky. Soldiers will be standing with naked swords and whoever moves his head, nods his head in appreciation, his head will be chopped off!"

Lucknow had at least ten thousand music lovers—only one hundred people turned up. It was dangerous! You may be simply moving your head because a mosquito has been torturing you, or for some other reason . . . you may forget because the musician is great and to remember it continuously will be difficult. Even snakes start moving, dancing—it will be difficult. So people avoided, but a hundred people came. They were real lovers of music, they risked their lives—it was worth it. And the people were standing with naked swords. It was a strange gathering!

The musician started playing, and he was such a great musician that within fifteen minutes' time a few heads started moving. Vajid Ali Shah became very much worried because it was not only one head: a few heads, then a few more joined in, then a few more. Then he became very much concerned: "Is he going to kill all these one hundred people? And these are the most appreciative people in the whole capital!" He knew them; they were lovers of music.

By the time the musician finished in the middle of the night, all the hundred people were swaying. Vajid Ali asked, "Now what do you say? Should I cut these people's heads? My soldiers are ready, and because I have given you my promise I am ready to fulfill it."

The musician laughed and he said, "Don't be worried! This condition was made only so that people who are real lovers would come. One who is ready to risk his life must be a passionate lover. Now these are the people I would like to sing and play for. Withdraw your soldiers! I was waiting: if there had been a few people whose heads had not moved, then those people would have had to be removed from the gathering. Now I will play because all the heads have moved; this is the right gathering I have waited for my whole life. These are the people who forgot completely, forgot even the question of life—it was a question of life and death."

All the Upanishads begin with AUM; AUM means the primordial sound. The *Rig Veda* says—the most ancient scripture of the world—"First the absolute, the Brahman, then *waak*, the sound, the vibrating energy which becomes the universe." The Bible also says the same thing, but has missed the point in translation. It says: In the beginning there was the Word and the Word was with God, and the Word and the God were one. 'The word' is not the right translation, it cannot be. I don't know what the original Hebrew or Aramaic word for 'word' is, but one thing I know, it cannot be 'word', it can only be 'sound'; it can only be a musical sound. It will be something like AUM, because 'word' means sound with meaning and the moment meaning comes in it brings a limitation, it brings a definition. Sound is unlimited; it is simply vibration.

Now scientists, physicists particularly, have discovered that existence consists only of vibrations. They call it 'vibrations of electricity'. It does not matter what name you give, what jargon you use, but vibration means sound. That is the meaning of AUM.

AUM is the primordial sound of which the whole universe consists; we are made of music. Hence if we move into anything totally, only the music is left and everything else disappears because music is the stuff we are made of; all else is arbitrary, artificial, invented. Only the music hidden in our souls is not invented; it is part of God. God is the musician and we are his music. He is the dancer and we are his dance. He is the poet and we are his poetry. He is the singer and we are his song. This is the meaning of AUM.

But the pundits, the scholars have been constantly missing the point. They think AUM is a mantra and just by repeating it you will attain to God. That is sheer nonsense! You can repeat it your whole life, it is not going to help you.

It is just like a thirsty person goes on repeating, "H_2O, H_2O, H_2O. . . ." Of course what he is saying is right—H_2O means water—he is not wrong. But H_2O and its repetition is not going to quench his thirst. He misses the point. AUM is exactly the H_2O of mysticism!

And there are fools in this country . . . and now those fools are traveling all over the world and teaching people Transcendental Meditation. It is neither transcendental nor meditation. Just by repeating the sound AUM, nothing is going to be achieved. In fact, something totally different has to be done: you have to become so silent, so absolutely silent, that you can hear the sound within your innermost core. It has to be heard, not repeated. If *you* repeat it, it will be a head thing; it will only be your head playing a gramophone record. Let the head rest, let all noise from the head be gone, let the mind stop functioning, and then suddenly you will hear the sound. That is a totally different phenomenon; it has to be heard, not repeated.

But the scholars are the most unconscious people, full of unnecessary philosophies, very complicated systems of thought, and ready to argue, to prove, to comment, but absolutely unconcscious. They have not discovered the AUM within themselves.

It is called *anahat nad; anahat nad* means unstruck sound. There are two kinds of sounds. When you play on a sitar it is a struck sound; duality is involved, your hands and the strings, and you have to strike, then the sound is created. It is a little bit violent—you are being violent with the strings. You are not allowing them to rest, you are disturbing their sleep. And there is a conflict involved with your hands; there is a fight going on between the musician and his instrument.

AUM is the unstruck sound; there is no instrument. When you become absolutely silent, suddenly it is there.

Zen people have the right expression for it; they call it 'the sound of one hand clapping'. If two hands are there, of course, the clapping is easy, but one hand clapping and the sound of one hand clapping seems to be absurd —but they are truly expressing the reality. When you go inside and you are absolutely silent you hear for the first time the inner music.

The agitated barfly rushed from his car into the nearest pub and gulped down a double scotch. "Jack," he called out to the barman, "how big is a penguin?"

"Well," replied the barman, "about two feet, I suppose."

The barfly was visibly shaken. He persisted, "How about a really big penguin, Jack?"

"About two feet, six inches," came the reply.

"What about the biggest penguin in the world?" demanded the barfly.

After a moment's pause the barman answered, "About three feet—no more."

"Oh shit!" gasped the barfly, "then I've just run over a nun!"

The scholars, the pundits are drunk with knowledge, knowing nothing but full of words. And their words are almost intoxicating because those words are beautiful, and they know the art of how to go on splitting hairs.

Beware of the scholars if you want to understand the Upanishads. These are the words of the Masters, of the Buddhas, of the awakened ones; these are not the words of the pundits and the scholars and the priests.

> *The imperishable sound,*
> *is the seed of all that exists.*

AUM is the imperishable sound; it is the seed of all that exists.

The past, the present, the future
—all are but the unfolding of AUM.
And whatever transcends the three realms of time,
that indeed is the flowering of AUM.

This whole creation is ultimately Brahman.
And the Self,
this also is Brahman.

Simple words, direct, but you can make much dust around them, you can create many clouds around them. Thousands of commentaries exist on the Upanishads; in fact, no commentary is needed. I am not giving you a commentary on the Upanishad, I am simply expressing my own experience *through* the Upanishad. It is not a commentary on the Upanishad, I am just a witness to the Upanishad. I am saying that what the Upanishad is saying is true, because I have also seen it the same way. It is the eternal truth.

Whenever anybody comes to realize his own being suddenly he becomes a witness—a witness to all that is true. Yes, the sound *is* heard, but you have to learn silence and that is the paradox. The sound is heard only in silence; if you are full of sound you will not hear it. You have to drop all sound and then suddenly it is heard.

You are so full of sound. If you just close your eyes and watch your mind for a few moments you will become aware: "What kind of mind is this? Am I insane or something?" Thousands of things are going on, and it is working twenty-four hours, day in, day out; from the cradle to the grave it goes on and on. It is a very tiring process, exhausting, but you don't know how to put it off.

Meditation simply means the art of putting it off, and it is *very* simple. It is as simple as putting the light on and off.

When for the first time electricity was discovered, a friend of Sigmund Freud came to visit him. He was a farmer, came from a faraway village. He had heard about electricity but he had not seen it.

In the night when Sigmund Freud left him in his room and asked him if he needed anything, he said, "No, everything is perfectly okay and I don't need anything, thank you. You can go to sleep."

Freud went to sleep and the man was at a loss as to what to do with the electricity, because he had no idea that there are some buttons; all that he knew about was lamps. So he tried in every possible way to blow it out. It was so far away on the ceiling that he stood on the bed; still it was far away, so he dragged a table onto the bed and stood on the table and tried hard, looked from every side: "There seems to be not even a single hole! And what to do with this electricity? And how can one go to sleep in such blaring light?"

The whole night he turned and tossed, again and again tried this way and that, but nothing helped. And he was feeling bad about waking up Sigmund Freud and asking him, and it also looked humiliating: you don't know such a simple thing!

In the morning when Freud asked, "You look very tired. What is the matter?" he said, "I have never been so tired in my life and I have to ask—I cannot contain it any more—what is the secret of this light? How to put it off?"

And Freud said, "Why didn't you knock on my door? It is so simple! Come and I will show you." And he showed him the button.

And the man said, "This is strange! I could never have imagined that just behind the door there is a button. I have never seen anything like this!"

Meditation is a very simple process: all that you need to know is the right button. The Upanishads call it 'witnessing'—the right button. Just witness your mind process, don't do anything at all. Nothing needs to be done, just be a witness, an observer, a watcher, looking at the traffic of the mind—thoughts passing by, desires, memories, dreams, fantasies. Simply stand aloof, cool —watching it, seeing it, with no judgment, with no condemnation, neither saying, "This is good," nor saying, "This is bad." Don't bring your moral concepts in, otherwise you will never be able to meditate.

That's why I am against the so-called morality: it is anti-meditation, because a so-called moral person is so full of his moral ideas, shoulds and should-nots, that he cannot watch, he cannot simply watch. He jumps to conclusions: "This is not right and this is right." And whatsoever he feels is right, he wants to cling to it; and whatsoever he thinks is wrong, he wants to throw it out. He jumps among the thoughts, starts fighting, grabbing, and that's where he loses all witnessing.

Witnessing simply means a detached observation, unprejudiced; that's the whole secret of meditation. It is simple! Once you have known the knack of it it is the most simple thing in the world, because each child is born in that innocence. You have known it in your mother's womb, you have known it when you were a small child, so it is only a rediscovery. Meditation is not something *new*; you had come with it into the world. *Mind* is something new; meditation is your nature, it is your very being. How can it be difficult? You just have to know the knack: watch.

Sit by the side of a river and watch the river flowing. Yes, sometimes driftwood passes by and sometimes a boat comes and sometimes a dead body and sometimes a beautiful woman may be swimming in the river—you simply watch, you don't get bothered, you remain cool, you don't get excited. You are not supposed to do anything, you have nothing to do. It is the river and it is the river's business. You simply sit silently. Sitting silently, slowly slowly the art is learnt . . . and one day, the moment your watchfulness is total, the mind evaporates.

If you are fifty percent watchful, fifty percent of the traffic disappears; if you are ninety percent watchful, ninety percent of the traffic disappears; if you are one hundred percent watchful, totally watchful, the mind totally disappears, the river is no more there. And in that moment when the mind is no more there, the sound is heard:

> *AUM*
> *Purnamadah*
> *Purnamidam*
> *Purnat purnamudachyate*
> *Purnasya purnamadaya*
> *Purnameva vashisyate—*

And in that very moment you know *this* and *that*. This is whole, that is whole, the whole comes from the whole. Although the whole comes from the whole, still the whole remains behind.

It is because of this that I am not against anything: not against sex, not against love, not against money, not against matter, not against at all. I would like my people to live life in its totality. If you don't live it in totality you become a hypocrite, and the hypocrite is incapable of knowing the truth.

Little Peter and little Johnny asked their grandma, "How are children born, granny?"

"The stork brings them in his beak, my children," said the grandmother.

Little Peter and little Johnny looked at each other and then little Johnny said, "What do you think, Peter? Shall we tell her?"

"No! No!" said Peter. "Leave her in her innocence!"

The husband and wife decided never to fight in front of their children, so all their fights were wreathed in smiles and full of endearments such as 'dear' and 'darling'.

It was only when one day they heard their two sons fighting viciously that they then realized what the effect of their charades had been. When asked who had started the fight, one of the little boys exclaimed, "He called me 'darling' first, mommy, honest, he did!"

Did you hear about the Polack priest? Everybody calls him Father, except his sons—they call him Uncle!

The hypocrite's mind becomes very upside-down; he cannot see things as they are. He wants to see one thing, but he tries to show that he is seeing something else. He says one thing, he means another. He wants to do one thing, but he goes on doing something else. His life becomes unnecessarily complicated, unnecessarily he creates conflict within himself. He becomes divided and there is a constant civil war.

Three criminals are standing in front of a cross-eyed judge in the courtroom. The judge says to the first, "Where were you yesterday at eleven o'clock?"

The second criminal answers, "At home sleeping, sir."

"I didn't ask you," says the judge to the second.

"I didn't say anything," replies the third criminal.

The hypocrite becomes cross-eyed—avoid being a hypocrite! But our society all over the world, the so-called civilization and culture only create hypocrites. The earth is full of hypocrites, pretenders, deceivers. That is not the way to hear the primordial sound; one has to be simple and innocent.

And why this hypocrisy? Why in the first place does it start? It starts because of our condemnation. If you condemn something, of course that has to be denied, ignored, overlooked. You have to forget all about it as if it does not exist.

If some being from some other planet comes to earth he will be very much puzzled and surprised as to how children are produced, because he will never see what is happening, he will never see the truth. And all kinds of nonsense will be told to him which will be as far away from reality as possible.

The Upanishads are life-affirmative—life in its totality. The Upanishadic seers lived as ordinarily as you live. They were not mahatmas, they were not saints. They were seers but not saints, they were sages but not saints. They lived a very ordinary life, of course with a very extraordinary intensity and passion.

It is afternoon tea in a country mansion. The lady of the house and the vicar have been discussing arrangements for the yearly fete to be held in the mansion's vast gardens.

The vicar, a country bumpkin, manages to be polite despite getting a bit hot under the collar at the way the nose-in-the-air wife of an aristocrat beats down his every suggestion of something new. At last, the arrangements are over and the lady of the house, having got her way as usual, lifts the teapot and says, "More tea, vicar?"

"No!"

"No what, vicar?" asks the lady as her eyebrows arch, shocked at his lack of manners and determined to hear him say thank you properly, as a gentleman of the frock should do. She prompts him again, "No what?"

To which the vicar replies, "No more fucking tea!"

People should be simple, people should be ordinary and live the ordinary life with extraordinary intensity.

The Upanishads are not knowledgeable; they don't give you much knowledge. They simply tell the experience of the seers:

AUM,
The imperishable sound,
is the seed of all that exists.
The past, the present, the future,
—all are but the unfolding of AUM.

The unfolding of the music. The existence is music, like Heraclitus says: the hidden harmony. It is an orchestra.

And whatever transcends the three realms of time,
that indeed is the flowering of AUM.

And the ultimate flowering comes when you have gone beyond time, and the moment you go beyond mind you have gone beyond time. It is mind which lives in the past, it is mind which projects the future, and because of the past and the future the present is created. When the mind is no more there, there is no time at all.

Jesus was asked, "What will be the special thing in the kingdom of God, the *most* special?"

And he said, "There shall be time no longer."

Patanjali defines meditation as transcendence of time, because it is the same. Time and mind are two apsects of the same coin. The ultimate flowering happens when you have gone beyond mind, beyond time.

> *This whole creation then is nothing but Brahman.*
> *And the Self,*
> *this also is Brahman.*

The consciousness within you and the existence without you are not separate—it is all one. The Upanishads are not knowledgeable, the Upanishads are not statements of wise guys, not like the great Murphy. Look at his sutras:

The great Murphy, the wise guy, says: The secret of success is sincerity—once you can fake that, you have got it made.

To err is human—to blame it on someone else is even more human.

If you have a difficult task, give it to a lazy man—he will find an easier way to do it.

The one who snores will fall asleep first.

Most people deserve each other.

Assumption is the mother of all screw-ups.

Anything good in life is either illegal, immoral, fattening or married.

If you don't care where you are, you ain't lost.

How long a minute is depends on which side of the bathroom door you are on.

Now this great Murphy has reminded me of the bathroom, so excuse me, please. . . . !

Discourse 2

December 12, 1980

MAN IS BORN AS FREEDOM

The first question

*Bhagwan: I heard you say once
that the misuse of freedom is harmful.
How can freedom be misused?*
Prem Tara

THE PHILOSOPHERS HAVE ALWAYS believed that essence precedes existence, that man is born with what he is going to be already determined. Just like a seed he contains the whole program; now the question is only of unfoldment. There is no freedom.

That has been the attitude of all the philosophers of the past: that man has a certain fate, a destiny. One is going to become a certain entity; that is fixed, the script is already written. You are not aware of it—that's another matter—but whatsoever you are doing, you are not doing it, it is being done through you by natural, unconscious forces, or by God.

This is the attitude of the determinist, the fatalist. The whole of humanity has suffered from it immensely, because this kind of approach means there is no possibility of any radical change. Nothing can be done at all about man's transformation; everything is going to happen the way it is going to happen.

It is because of this attitude that the East has suffered most. When nothing can be done, then one starts accepting everything—slavery, poverty, ugliness; one has to accept. It is not understanding, it is not awareness; it is not what Gautam the Buddha calls suchness, *tathata*. It is just despair, hopelessness hiding itself in beautiful words. But the consequence is going to be disastrous.

You can see it in India in its most developed form: the poverty, the beggars, the illness, the crippled people, the blind people. And nobody takes any note of it because this is how life is, this is how life has always been this is how life is always going to be. A kind of lethargy seeps into the very soul.

But the whole approach is basically false. It is a consolation, not a discovery. It is somehow to hide one's wounds—it is a rationalization. And whenever rationalizations start hiding your reality you are bound to fall into darker and darker realms.

I would like to say to you that essence does not precede existence; on the contrary, existence precedes essence. Man is the only being on the earth who has freedom. A dog is born a dog, will live like a dog, will die like a dog; there is no freedom. A rose will remain a rose; there is no possibility of any transformation—it cannot become a lotus. There is no question of choice, there is no freedom at all. This is where man is totally different. This is the dignity of man, his specialness in existence, his uniqueness.

That's why I say Charles Darwin is not right, because he starts categorizing man with other animals; the basic difference he has not even taken note of. The basic difference is: all animals are born with a program, only man is born without a program. Man is born as a *tabula rasa*, a clean slate; nothing is written on it. You have to write everything that you want to write on it; it is going to be your creation.

Man is not only free—I would like to say man is freedom. That is his essential core, that's his very soul. The moment you deny freedom to man you have denied him his most precious treasure, his very kingdom. Then he is a beggar and in a far more ugly situation than other animals, because at least they have a certain program. Then man is simply lost.

Once this is understood, that man is born *as* freedom, then all the dimensions to grow open up. Then it is up to you what to become, what not to become. It is going to be your own creation. Then life becomes an adventure —not an unfoldment but an adventure, an exploration, a discovery. The truth is not already given to you, you have to create it. In a way, each moment you are creating yourself.

If you accept the theory of fate, that is also an act of deciding about your life. By accepting fatalism you have chosen the life of a slave—it is your choice! You have chosen to enter into a prison, you have chosen to be chained, but it is still your choice. You can come out of the prison.

That's what sannyas is all about: accepting your freedom. Of course people are afraid to be free, because freedom is risky. One never knows what one is doing, where one is going, what the ultimate result of it all is going to be. If you are not ready-made then the whole responsibility is yours. You cannot throw the responsibility on somebody else's shoulders. Ultimately you will be standing before existence totally responsible for yourself, whatsoever you are, whosoever you are. You cannot shirk it, you cannot escape from it. This is the fear. Out of this fear people have chosen all kinds of determinist attitudes.

And it is a strange thing: the religious and the irreligious are agreed only on one point, that there is no freedom. On every other point they disagree, but on one point their agreement is strange. The communists say they are atheists, irreligious, but they say that man is determined by the social, economic, political situations. Man is not free; man's consciousness is determined by outside forces. It is the same logic! You can call the outside force the economic structure; Hegel calls it History—with a capital H, remember—and the religious people call it God; again the word is with a capital G. God, history, economics, politics, society—all outside forces. But they are all agreed upon one thing: that you are not free.

This is where a really authentically religious person differs.

Prem Tara, I say to you, you are absolutely free, unconditionally free. Don't avoid the responsibility; avoiding is not going to help. The sooner you accept it, the better, because immediately you can start creating yourself. And the moment you create yourself great joy arises, and when you have completed yourself, the way *you* wanted it, there is immense contentment—just as when a painter finishes his painting, the last touch, and a great contentment arises in his heart. A job well done brings great peace. One feels that one has participated with God.

God is the creator and the only prayer is to be creative, because it is only through creativity that you participate in God; there is no other way to participate. God has not to be thought about, you have to participate in some way. You cannot be an observer, you can only be a participant; only then will you taste the mystery of it. Creating a painting is nothing, creating a poem is nothing, creating music is nothing compared to creating yourself, creating your consciousness, creating your very being.

But people have been afraid, and there are reasons to be afraid. The first is: it is risky, because only you are responsible. Secondly: the freedom can be misused, because you can choose the wrong thing to be. Freedom means you can choose the right or the wrong; if you are only free to choose the right, it is not freedom.

Then it will be like when Ford made his first cars—they were all black. And he would take his customers into the showroom and tell them, "You can choose any color, provided it is black!"

But what kind of freedom is this?—*provided* it is right, *provided* it follows the ten commandments, *provided* it is according to the Gita or the Koran, *provided* it is according to Buddha, Mahavira, Zarathustra. Then it is not freedom at all! Freedom basically means, intrinsically means that you are capable of both: either choosing the right or the wrong.

And the danger is—and hence the fear—that the wrong is always easier to do. The wrong is a downhill task and the right is an uphill task. Going uphill is difficult, arduous; and the higher you go, the more arduous it becomes. But going downhill is very easy; you need not do anything, gravitation does everything for you. You can just roll like a rock from the hilltop and the rock will reach to the very bottom; nothing has to be done. But if you want to rise in consciousness, if you want to rise in the world of beauty, truth, bliss, then you are longing for the highest peaks possible and that certainly is difficult.

Secondly, the higher you reach, the more there is a danger of falling, because the path becomes narrow and you are surrounded on all sides by dark valleys. A single wrong step and you will simply be gone into the abyss, you will disappear. It is more comfortable, convenient to walk on the plain ground, not to bother about the heights.

Freedom gives you the opportunity either to fall below the animals or to rise above the angels. Freedom is a ladder: one side of the ladder reaches hell, the other side touches heaven. It is the *same* ladder; the choice is yours, the direction has to be chosen by you.

To me, if you are not free you cannot misuse your unfreedom; unfreedom cannot be misused. The prisoner cannot misuse his situation—he is chained, he is not free to do anything. And that is the situation of all other animals except man: they are *not* free. They are born to be certain kinds of animal—and they will fulfill it. In fact, nature fulfills it; they are *not* required to do anything. There is no challenge in their life. It is only man who has to face the challenge, the great challenge. And very few people have chosen to risk, to go to the heights, to discover their ultimate peaks. Only a few—the Buddha, the Christ—only very few; they can be counted on the fingers.

Why hasn't the whole of humanity chosen to reach the same state of bliss as Buddha, the same state of love as Christ, the same state of celebration as Krishna? Why?—for the simple reason that it is dangerous even to aspire to those heights; it is better not to think about it. And the best way not to think about it is to accept that there is no freedom—you are already determined beforehand; there is a certain script handed over to you before your birth and you have just to fulfill it.

Prem Tara, you ask:

How can freedom be misused?

Only freedom can be misused, slavery cannot be misused. That's why you see so much chaos in the world today. It has never been there before for the simple reason that man was not so free. You see more chaos in America than in Russia for the simple reason that in Russia people are not free to choose. In America they are enjoying the greatest freedom that has ever been enjoyed anywhere in the world at any time in history. Whenever there is freedom chaos erupts, but that chaos is worth it because only out of that chaos are stars born.

My sannyasins will be hated all over the world, will be condemned all over the world, for the simple reason that they have chosen to live a life of freedom. And I am not giving you any discipline, because every discipline is a subtle kind of slavery. I am not giving you any commandments, because any commandments given by anybody else coming from the outside are going to imprison you, to enslave you.

I am only teaching you how to be free and then leaving you to yourself to do what you want to do with your freedom. If you want to fall below the animals that is your decision and you are perfectly allowed to do it, because it is your life. If you decide it that way then it is your prerogative. But if you understand freedom and its value you will not start falling; you will not go below the animals, you will start rising above the angels.

Man is not an entity, he is a bridge—a bridge between two eternities: the animal and the God, the unconscious and the conscious. Grow in consciousness, grow in freedom, take each step out of your own choice: create yourself. A sannyasin is one who creates himself and takes the whole responsibility for it.

The second question

Bhagwan: What is spirituality?
And what is enlightenment?
Mind is a monkey.
The more someone wants to erase the impressions
carried by him,
the more he goes on gathering new ones.
Bhagwan, could you please show me a way?
G.D. Murthi

Y OU HAVE ASKED many questions in one. The first thing to be understood is: your questions are not authentic, they are not yours; they come from your Indian conditioning.

You ask:

What is spirituality?

First one should ask, "Who am I?" First one should ask, "What is this consciousness in me?" But we make a philosophical question out of an existential one. And the existential is forgotten, and the philosophical becomes very significant: "What is spirituality?"

Spirituality is not something that can be defined, is not something that can be answered. It is something that you have to explore. And the right beginning will be, don't ask such stupid questions; start with something sensible. Ask, "Who am I?"

And I cannot answer that question; you have to ask within yourself, "Who am I?" Go on using that question as a digging instrument within your being. Just as a person digs a well one has to dig a well in oneself, because there are layers and layers of conditioning, layers and layers of knowledge. Unless you have thrown all those layers out you will not know your own being, your own center.

And the Indian mind is the most rotten in the world because it is the most ancient in the world. For at least ten thousand years it has existed—it has forgotten how to die. It does not know how to live, it has forgotten to die. It is in a kind of limbo, it is in a kind of coma—breathing, not dead, not alive either. And it asks great questions, but those questions arise out of borrowed knowledge.

What is spirituality? What is enlightenment?

All bullshit! There is no spirituality, there is no enlightenment. To know this is to be enlightened! To be just ordinary, to live—to enjoy, to love, to dance, to sing, to create—the very ordinary existence with an extraordinary intensity, with passion, that is enlightenment.

But you must be looking for some esoteric answer. I am against all esoteric things.

One of my sannyasins, Almasta, has asked: *Bhagwan, will you please answer a few very esoteric questions for me?* But her questions are beautiful, far more beautiful than asking, G.D. Murthi: *What is spirituality? And what is enlightenment?* And then your knowledge immediately comes in:

Mind is a monkey.

As if you know what mind is! If you know what mind is you will not ask these questions, because the moment one knows one's mind one has discovered one's soul too—immediately, instantly; it happens together. If one knows what one's mind is one knows what enlightenment is, because enlightenment is a state of no-mind. If you know, "This is the mind," you are *immediately* no more it, you are out of it. You are just awareness and that awareness is enlightenment.

So, G.D. Murthi, your questions are really esoteric. Almasta's questions are far more beautiful—small questions but significant. She asks first:

How many politicians does it take to screw in a lightbulb?

Now this is spirituality! Almasta, only one—they don't like to share the spotlight.

Her second question is:

How many Indians does it take to screw in a lightbulb?

Almasta, seven hundred millions, not a single person less—the whole of India to pray to God for the old bulb to go back on.

Her third question is:

How many Catholics does it take to screw in a lightbulb?

Almasta, two—one to screw in the lightbulb and one to repent.

Her fourth question is:
How many nuclear physicists does it take to screw in a lightbulb?
Almasta, at least fifty—one to screw in the lightbulb and forty-nine to figure out what to do with the old one.

Her fifth question is:
How many Italians does it take to screw in a lightbulb?
Almasta, only one—but don't expect results.

Her sixth question is:
How many mice does it take to screw in a lightbulb?
Almasta, two—just two, and you can always expect results too.

Her seventh question is:
What is the difference between a pregnant woman and a lightbulb?
Almasta, you can unscrew the lightbulb.

Her eighth question is:
How many Rajneesh sannyasins does it take to screw a lightbulb in?
Almasta, five thousand plus one: one to screw the lightbulb in—whose name is Haridas—and the other five thousand to celebrate the great occasion.

And her ninth and the last question is:
How many Bhagwans does it take to screw in a lightbulb?
Almasta, none . . . sitting silently doing nothing, the spring comes and the lightbulb screws by itself.

G.D. Murthi, this is far more beautiful than your stupid question which appears to be spiritual. You are thinking you are asking something great:

What is spirituality?

Never heard of it!

And what is enlightenment?

How am I supposed to know? You seem to know everything!

Mind is a monkey.
The more someone wants to erase impressions
carried by him,
the more he goes on gathering new ones.

Then stop erasing! Then why do you go on erasing? If you know this much, that *the more someone wants to erase the impressions carried by him, the more he goes on gathering new ones*, then don't erase the old ones. Just stop erasing and they will stop gathering, and you will be enlightened. It is so simple! Enlightenment is such a simple thing that I sometimes wonder how people manage *not* to be enlightened. It is really arduous to manage, because enlightenment is a natural phenomenon. You are *born* enlightened! You are *born* Buddhas!

But the moment you start asking, "What is enlightenment and how to become enlightened?" you will be in a mess. It is like a man asking, "What is it to be a man? *How* to become a man?" Now he will be in a mess! All that he needs is to stand before a mirror and see that he is a man already.

Meditation is only a mirror. You stand naked before yourself and suddenly you start laughing. You look so ridiculous standing naked before a mirror! That is the greatest joke of all. Once you see yourself naked, totally naked, you are enlightened. Just uncover yourself . . . and you are wearing many clothes, clothes upon clothes. If you drop one dress another dress is there; drop that, another dress is there.

You are like an onion, and meditation is nothing but the process of peeling the onion. Of course a few tears will come to your eyes! Go on peeling the onion, layer upon layer, and ultimately nothing is left in your hands. And Gautam Buddha has said that is the moment when you know who you are—when nothing is left in your hands, just nothing, when your hands are full of nothing, the whole onion has disappeared and with it all the tears have disappeared—just pure nothingness.

But it will be difficult for you. Your knowledge, your knowlegeability will create problems for you.

You are asking:

Bhagwan, could you please show me a way?

I can show you a way, but where do you want to go? I don't know where you want to go!

You are asking me . . .

please show me a way?

To where? Do you want to go to Timbuktu or to Tokyo? Where do you want to go? The way can be shown to you, but the real problem is that enlightenment happens when you stop going anywhere, neither to Timbuktu nor to Tokyo—when you stop going, when you are simply resting in your own being, not going anywhere, not even a ripple, no desire to reach, no desire to achieve.

You are full of desires: you want to achieve spirituality, you want to achieve enlightenment. Your name is G.D. Murthi; you simply want an O to be put between G and D. That's what your whole desire is: how to become God Murthi. Just O is missing; you can write it yourself! There is no problem in it. Who can prevent you? Make it G-O-D.

But that O also represents zero, and if you can manage to be a zero, just a nothingness, you have arrived, you have found. There is no way leading to it; all ways are *mis*leading. A way as such is going to mislead, because a way means you are going farther away from yourself—a way always takes you away. There is no way to come to yourself—you are already there! There is no need to come. Simply stop these fantasies of going somewhere, of becoming spiritual, of becoming religious, of attaining enlightenment, *nirvana, samadhi* —simply stop all this nonsense. Just rest within your being, at home, at ease, relaxed . . . and *this* very moment, now and here, you are enlightened!

You become enlightened every morning here, and again you forget. And I am not joking—this is so! I make you enlightened every day, but you again get into the mess, you again start raising dust around yourself. You become afraid: "What is happening? Have I become enlightened?" And that is the beginning of raising the dust and the cloud and the smoke: "Have I become enlightened? Now what to do? Where to go? And if my wife comes to know then she will create trouble. It is better before I reach home to forget all about it!" By the time you reach home you are again unenlightened. You enter the same way again, your tail between your legs, afraid, because if you are really enlightened you will reach home and roar like a lion! Today try it, and the whole neighborhood will know that you have become enlightened! Your wife of course will shout, "Shut up! Don't become enlightened so quickly! Wait! Let your children grow, let them get married. And enlightenment is for old age when you become retired; this is not the time. Put a stop to it right now—enough is enough!"

Enlightenment is a simple phenomenon: just breathing, resting, doing nothing, and you *are* silent and there is no mind. Just right now . . . is there any mind? . . . All the minds have disappeared. Where are the monkeys?

But these so-called Indian mahatmas go on telling people, "Mind is a monkey." And you listen and you start repeating like gramophone records, "Mind is a monkey." And you go on worshiping the monkey god Hanuman to prove that of course the mahatmas are right. "If mind is not a monkey, why am I worshiping this monkey? I must be a monkey!" And then comes Charles Darwin who says that you are born of the monkeys, so not only is the mind a monkey, your body is a monkey too. And you don't know what spirituality is, so all that is left . . . body is a monkey, mind is a monkey, so two monkeys and that's enough to bring results!

Forget all about this spirituality and enlightenment. Relax in your ordinary life. Eat when you are hungry, drink when you are thirsty, go to sleep when you are feeling sleepy, and wake up in the early morning when you are feeling that you have rested enough. Just live the ordinary life joyously, live moment-to-moment. Don't hanker for something great, ultimate, far away. Don't bother about the other world, the beyond—this world is more than one needs. This world is so beautiful, who cares about the other world?

People ask me, "What happens after death?" And I ask them, "First try to find out what is happening *before* death!" And they look at me as if I am joking. I am never joking, I am simply telling you the truth! But because you are not finished yet with your desires and longings, you don't listen to the truth.

Two salesmen were standing together at a bar, a little distance away from a drunk who was having trouble propping himself up and balancing his drink. The men were chatting about their job when one of them noticed a very unpleasant smell.

"Hey, Joe," he interrupted, "do you smell shit?"

The other salesman sniffed and nodded, fingers closing his nostrils. "I think it is coming from that old drunk over there," he said.

The first salesman walked over to the drunk. "Excuse me," he said, "there is a foul smell around here. Did you shit in your pants?"

The drunk looked up at him over his glass, bleary-eyed. "Yeth," he slobbered, "whath abouth ith?"

Shocked, the young salesman replied, "Well, why don't you go to the men's room and wash yourself?"

The drunk looked up again, thought for a moment, and then said decisively, "Because I haven't finished yet!"

That's the trouble—you are not finished yet! Otherwise go to the men's bathroom and wash yourself and be enlightened! Who is preventing you? Just a little washing is needed and the whole foul smell will disappear. You are born fragrant, you become foul. It is your great work—you can undo it!

The last question

Bhagwan: Has anyone ever become enlightened
while listening to a joke?
Maybe there is hope for me yet!
Anand Jean

THE FIRST THING IS: nobody ever becomes enlightened. People become unenlightened, that is true, but nobody ever becomes enlightened. Just when one gets tired of becoming unenlightened again and again, day in, day out, year in, year out, life in, life out, then one day one says, "It is enough. I should stop becoming unenlightened." And that is the moment one is enlightened.

Enlightenment is natural, unenlightenment is something that you are doing. So nobody really ever becomes enlightened. One only discovers that "I need not do a few things which I have always been doing and which have been preventing me from seeing who I am." And this can happen in any situation. It has happened in strange situations.

Mahavira became enlightened in a very strange posture. Jainas have given it a name . . . they must have been hiding the truth, because their name says that he was sitting in a *godohasan*. *Godohasan* means the posture in which you milk the cow. Now, what was he doing? He was not milking a cow, certainly. He had no cow, so what was he doing in that posture? Strange fellow this Mahavira! You can understand what he was doing—I will not tell you, because if I say it all the Jainas will say I am destroying their culture. But the question is worth asking: What was he doing? One thing is certain, they cannot agree that he was milking a cow because he had dispossessed everything. Sitting naked in a *godohasan*, what was he doing? And he became enlightened!

People have become enlightened in all kinds of situations, because it is only a question of understanding. It can happen any moment. Yes, sitting on your toilet seat. . . Mahavira was a little old-fashioned. And in fact when you are sitting on the toilet seat, *great* thoughts arise. So what is wrong in becoming enlightened while listening to a joke?

When you are really in laughter your ego disappears; both together are not possible. That's why the egoist becomes incapable of laughing. Even if he tries, that is just an exercise of his lips, nothing more than that. How can he do such a worldly thing? so mundane, so ordinary? Laughing?—impossible.

Christians say Jesus never laughed. They cannot believe Jesus laughing, because to laugh means to be human, too human. They can believe Jesus walking on water—that's perfectly okay; Jesus raising the dead —that is really great; Jesus coming alive after crucifixion—all these stupidities can be believed in . . . but Jesus never laughed! If it is true, then I will say that is the only miracle he did.

But it is *not* true. I can say from my own experience: it is *not* true. It *cannot* be true! Even if Jesus says he never laughed, I'm not going to listen to him. Jesus and not laughing? Then who else will be able to laugh? this beautifully ridiculous existence, this whole absurd, but so beautiful life, and Jesus not laughing? I cannot believe that.

Jesus must have laughed, loved, shared jokes. They may not have been compiled—that shows the mind of the compilers—but Jesus was a very earthly man, loved eating, drinking, gossiping, because what was he doing? Every night his disciples and friends would gather and eat and drink for hours, till the late hours; only in the morning would they go to sleep. What was he doing all this time? You cannot just go on eating and drinking. You can see that this man has not eaten so much; you can look at pictures of him. If he was just eating and drinking he would look like an elephant! But he looks so proportionate; he must have been gossiping, sharing jokes, laughing. In fact, only an enlightened person can have a real sense of humor.

So there is no problem, Anand Jean, you can become enlightened listening to a joke. And I am giving you, every day, opportunities to become enlightened.

Listen to these jokes and give it a try. Who knows? Enlightenment is always unpredictable—it may happen today. But don't expect it. These are the problems with enlightenment: if you expect, you miss. Such strange conditions are attached to enlightenment: if you expect you miss, if you desire you miss. So don't expect that it is going to happen; just sit relaxed and listen to the joke. It may happen, it may not.

The marriage between the elderly farmer and his young wife was not working out too well, so the farmer consulted his doctor for advice. "The next time you are down in the field plowing and feel a yearning for your wife," said the doctor, "don't wait until lunchtime or the end of the day, but quit what you are doing and go to the house!"

"I tried that," said the farmer, "but by the time I get to the house, I am so tuckered out it is no use."

The doctor thought for a minute. "Take your shotgun with you when you leave the house in the morning, and if you feel the urge, shoot the gun and she will come down there where you are."

A few weeks later the two men met on the street.

"How did it work?" asked the doctor.

"Fine . . . the first three days," said the farmer, "then the hunting season opened and I haven't seen her since."

Giuseppe, an immigrant to the United States, works very hard his whole life and finally makes it to his sixty-fifth birthday when he can apply for benefits. He goes down to the Social Security office to apply, but when he gets there the girl behind the desk tells him that he must bring his birth certificate to prove his age.

He does not have a birth certificate so, dejected, he goes home. Suddenly, he gets an idea and rushes back to the office. He sees the girl, runs over to her and pulls open his shirt to display his grey hair.

"You *must* be sixty-five," she says, "with all that grey hair on your chest!"

Giuseppe is very pleased and rushes home to tell his wife that he will receive the benefits.

"How-a did-a you get-ta it?" asks Maria.

"I opened my shirt-a like this-a and showed her all-a my grey hair!"

"You idiot-a! You blew-a it!" screams Maria. "You should-a have opened your trousers and-a applied-a for the disability pension!"

A man was attending a banquet held in his honor at the local Rotary Club. At the end of the supper he had to give a short speech. He was really nervous because he was not good at public speaking, so he asked his wife to pinch him every time he started bungling his speech.

Immediately after he had finished his ice cream, he got up from his chair and began, "Ladies and gentlement, I am overwhelmed, I shudder with emotion from top to bottom. . . .ouch!" his wife pinched him. He stopped talking and thought for a moment, then began again, "Sincerely, gentlemen, I feel emotional chills invading my soul. . . .ouch!" another pinch and a moment's consideration, then, "Seriously, gentlemen, this is the most thrilling time of my life. . . ." There was another pinch from his wife, but this time he turned to her and asked, "What's wrong, honey? I'm telling the truth . . . I'm not saying something stupid, am I?"

"The problem is," said his wife, "that your fly is open!" He turned white and she continued, "and your balls are sitting inside your ice cream dish!"

Discourse 3

December 13, 1980

I TEACH THE COMMUNE

The first question

Bhagwan: The Pope is on about sex again!
At a recent national convention
of Christian family advisors in Italy
he condemned pre-marital and extra-marital relations,
as well as contraception and abortion.
The future of the world and of the church
lies in the family, he said.
What do you say?

Krishna Prem

THE MOST OUTDATED THING is the family. It has done its work, it is no more needed. In fact, now it is the most hindering phenomenon for human progress. The family is the unit of the nations, of the state, of the church—of all that is ugly.

The Pope is right in a way—that there is no future for the church if the family disappears—because without the family and its conditioning, from where are you going to get Christians, Hindus, Mohammedans?

That's why I say the family *has* to disappear. Without the disappearance of the family all these ugly monsters will continue. The family is the root cause of all our neurosis. We have to understand the psychological structure of the family, what it does to human consciousness.

The first thing is: it conditions the child to a certain religious ideology, political dogma, some philosophy, some theology. And the child is so innocent and so accepting, so vulnerable that he can be exploited. He cannot yet say no, he has no idea of saying no, and even if he could say no he would not say it because he is utterly dependent on the family, absolutely dependent. He is so helpless that he has to agree with the family, with whatever nonsense the family wants him to agree.

The family does not help the child to inquire; it gives beliefs and beliefs are poisons. Once the child becomes burdened with beliefs his inquiry is crippled, paralyzed, his wings are cut. By the time he is able to inquire he will be so conditioned that he will move into every investigation with a certain prejudice—and with a prejudice your inquiry is not authentic. You are already carrying an *a priori* conclusion; you are simply looking for proofs to support your unconscious conclusion. You become incapable of discovering the truth.

That's why there are so few Buddhas in the world: the root cause is the family. Otherwise every child is born Buddha, comes with the potential to reach the ultimate consciousness, to discover the truth, to live a life of bliss. But the family destroys all these dimensions; it makes him utterly flat.

Each child comes with a tremendous intelligence but the family makes him mediocre, because to live with an intelligent child is troublesome. He doubts, he is skeptical, he inquires, he is disobedient, he is rebellious—and the family wants somebody who is obedient, ready to follow, imitate. Hence from the very beginning the seed of intelligence has to be destroyed, almost completely burnt, so there is no possibility of any sprouts coming out of it.

It is a miracle that a few people like Zarathustra, Jesus, Lao Tzu, Buddha, escaped from the social structure, from the family conditioning. They seem to be great peaks of consciousness, but in fact every child is born with the same quality, with the same potential.

Ninety-nine point nine percent of people can become Buddhas—just the family has to disappear. Otherwise there will be Christians and Mohammedans and Hindus and Jainas and Buddhists, but not Buddhas, not

Mahaviras, not Mohammeds; that will not be possible. Mohammed rebelled against *his* background, Buddha rebelled against *his* background, Jesus rebelled against *his* background. These are all rebels—and the family is absolutely against the rebellious spirit.

The Pope is right, in a sense, that the future of the church depends on the family, but he is wrong to say that the future of the world and the future of the church lies in the family. The future of the church certainly lies in the family, but not the future of the world. They are not synonymous, in fact they are opposites.

If we want to save the future of humanity then all these churches have to be destroyed, only then can humanity be one. All these religions have to go, only then can man create a universal brotherhood. Mohammedans, Hindus and Christians have been talking about brotherhood, love, humanity, but that is mere talk, phony talk; what they have done is just the opposite. Their hands are full of blood. They have been the cause of more violence on the earth than anybody else. They have killed, murdered, raped; they have committed all kinds of crimes in the name of religion. And these murderers have been promised that they will have a special privilege in paradise because they are killing or being killed in the name of religion. These are the people who have been creating *jihads*—religious wars, crusades. On the one hand they talk about love, brotherhood, humanity, God, but that is only talk. That gives a beautiful cover to all the cruelty, to all the destructiveness that they are carrying within themselves.

I am not in favor of teaching Hindus to be brothers to the Mohammedans, because that is not possible. Five thousand years of experience is enough proof that that is not possible. Unless a Hindu gets out of his conditioning and the Mohammedan gets out of his conditioning there is no posibility of brotherhood. I am not in favor of synthesizing all these religions. That will be synthesizing all kinds of diseases—cancer and tuberculosis. . . .That will not help, that will be far more dangerous.

Humanity is passing through a very critical phase. It has to be decided whether we want to live according to the past or we want to live a new style of life. It is enough! We have tried the past and its patterns and they have all failed. It is time, ripe time, to get out of the grip of the past and to create a new style of life on the earth.

That's what is happening here with my sannyasins. Here are Christians, Mohammedans, Hindus, Buddhists who are no more Hindus, no more Christians, no more Buddhists, no more Mohammedans, who have again become innocent like children. Great courage is needed for that—to get rid of the family conditioning—because one feels guilty, as if one is betraying one's parents. But if the parents are mad then it is perfectly right to get out of their possessiveness. And they *are* mad, they *are* neurotic! In fact, to condition a child with any ideology is inhuman, but inhumanity is practised with such beautiful labels that unless you dig very deep you will not find the reality.

Mother Teresa of Calcutta has been serving poor orphans and she has been respected for that all over the world, but just a few days ago a Protestant family from America came to Mother Teresa's place; they wanted to adopt a child. And that's what she has been doing: she raises the orphans and then those orphans are given to families where they can be adopted and they can live in a better way. But the Protestant family was refused for the simple reason that they were not Catholics. So the whole purpose of serving the orphans is not the orphans; the purpose is to increase the number of Catholics. That is the true purpose, and the Nobel prize is given for something else: serving poor children. The real purpose is political.

Giving the Nobel prize to Mother Teresa has degraded the whole value of the Nobel prize; it is no more of any worth. Now deceivers, charlatans, hypocrites will be getting the Nobel prize.

The future of the world and the future of the church are two different things—not only different but diametrically opposite.

I teach the commune, not the family. The commune is the alternative to the family. The family conditions the child in the first place. Secondly, it is the cause of all kinds of insanities.

A child is brought up by one woman, the mother, by one man, the father. If the child is a boy he becomes obsessed with the mother; if the child is a girl she becomes obsessed with the father. Now these are proven psychological facts. The boy's consciousness becomes imprinted with the mother's figure, qualities. . . .Now his whole life he will be searching for a woman who is an exact replica of his mother. And the same is true about the girl: she will be trying to find a lover who exactly represents her father. Now this is not possible —they will never succeed.

That's why all love affairs fail, they are *bound* to fail. From the very beginning we have managed everything in such a way that love cannot succeed. Where can you find your mother or your father? It is impossible, because there are no two persons who are exactly alike, but this remains the unconscious search. Every time you fall in love with a man or a woman you are again hoping that this woman is going to prove to be your mother. This is not conscious, of course, it is a deep, unconscious imprint. But soon you will discover that she does not fit with your unconscious imprint—and the conflict starts, and you start falling apart. No man can be your father, no woman can be your mother.

Now if *this* so-called family continues, then love cannot succeed in the world. And without love there can be no bliss, without love misery is our fate. We have chosen misery if we choose the family.

A commune is a totally different phenomenon. In a commune there will be no obsessions with particular people. Here there are at least three hundred little sannyasins, boys and girls. Many small boys and girls never turn up in the night to stay with the father and the mother—they have so many uncles and aunts. The whole commune is theirs! And small children in this commune start having an individuality of their own, they start moving on their own. They are not attached to the mother, to the father, to the family; they go on moving with different people. And their fathers and mothers are not obsessed with each other either.

Just the other day Teertha's daughter, Soma, wrote to me: "Bhagwan, I am going to England for one month to be with my mother, Poonam. Of course I will miss you, I will miss Teertha, and I will miss my stepmother, Krishna. . . ." This is beautiful, to miss the stepmother!

Parents are changing, they are in a flux. The child will come across many stepmothers, many stepfathers. He will never become obsessed with one person. That will give him scope, freedom, multi-dimensionality. He will never be tethered. He will be able to experience many women as mothers, many men as fathers, and he will live in a flux, in a moving riverlike phenomenon. He will not live in a pond, he will float in a river where scenes go on changing. That will help him to have the capacity to love many people, and he will have a more composite view of what kind of a woman or man he would like to have in his life. All his mothers will give him a synthetic vision. There will be no single woman in it but many women, many qualities all mingled into one, all merged into one. He will be able to succeed in finding love in his life because there is no obsession with any person, with any personality. He will be more concerned with qualities and less concerned with personalities. And he will know that there is no need to be possessive because he has known the parents were not possessive; everything was shifting and changing, lifelike.

Marriage is dead. It is a fixed entity, it is a commodity, it is like a thing—it is furniture. It is not like a rosebush growing: today it is full of flowers, tomorrow all the flowers are gone; today it is so green, and tomorrow the leaves start getting yellow and they start falling. He will see all the seasons, all the moods, all the conflicts, all the agonies, all the ecstasies, and he will become more centered, grounded. He will know that life is not a fixed phenomenon. He will not expect anything because life is not fixed. He will be available to all kinds of changes. He will be able to change with life, he will never fall out of step. He will be always in tune with life.

And that's what is needed to make humanity more wholesome, more healthy, more loveful, more blissful. Of course the church will disappear, nations will disappear, races will disappear, but they *need* to disappear—they have already lived too long. They are living a posthumous kind of existence; they need to be burnt and buried. We are carrying corpses, and those corpses are stinking. You can go on sprinkling perfume on them and somehow trying to manage to live with the corpses in the house. And I know that they *did* have some purpose in the past; of course, when your father was alive it was one thing, but now the father is dead. So cry and weep a little, but get rid of him! And if you are my sannyasins, then there is no need even to cry and weep—celebrate a little and get rid of him! But there is no need to carry the corpse on your shoulders your whole life. And there is not only one corpse but many corpses; there are so many dead people in your house that there is no space for the living ones to live. The living ones are living outside the house and the dead are keeping the whole place full. We need space!

The family is a dead thing, but we somehow go on patching it up. What is a divorce? It is a patching-up.

People go on living in misery thinking that "Next life I will find another woman—or another husband—but this life nothing can be done. It is better to accept." So people remain somehow satisfied, whatsoever the situation is, and they call it contentment—it is only consolation. And they have rationalized all these ugly things in many ways.

The Pope must be be afraid—once the family is dead, the church is dead. The word 'pope' means the father; it is the same as 'papa' . And the Christians even call God 'the Father'; it is just an extension of the family. The whole idea of religion is rooted in the concept of the family: God the father, Jesus the son . . . and who is this stupid guy, the holy ghost? They could not even put a woman there, a mother, which would have been more logical; but God living with a woman looks unsaintly! And then who knows?—he may fall in love, something may go wrong . . . and you cannot trust women: she may seduce the old fellow. So to protect him, a holy ghost! But see the stupidity: the father is there, the son is there, without the mother. Then who got pregnant?— the holy ghost? This seems to be a more dangerous thing—God making love to the holy ghost! But the whole idea is a projection of the same structure, and because the extension and the projection was done by male chauvinist pigs, the woman has been discarded.

The Pope must be afraid—he is against pre-marital relationships. Now this is so illogical. Unless a man or a woman has lived in many pre-marital relationships there is no possibility of choosing a right partner. This is such a simple phenomenon! Unless you have experienced many women and men in your life, how can you choose who is going to be the right person to live with? But they don't allow any pre-marital relationships, so people start falling in love at first sight—which is nonsense. Then, of course, the same people say love is blind. First they throw acid in your eyes and then they say love is blind! You see the strategy? Don't allow boys and girls to meet and mingle with each other so that they can experience many people before they decide—don't allow them. Suffocate their sexual energy!

Boys and girls become sexually mature at thirteen and fourteen, but they will get married after their twenty-fifth year, near about thirty. For these fifteen, sixteen years, when they have been sexually the *most* potent . . . because the boy is the most sexually powerful at the age of seventeen and eighteen. Never again will he have the same power, never again will he have the same youthful vigor. By the time he gets married he is already old; then you start calling him a dirty old man. Strange logic! When he is young you don't allow him; because you don't allow him his whole sexuality starts getting into his head, it becomes cerebral. Then he is dirty—because the head is the only little space where the sexuality can go, otherwise where does it have to go? You don't allow any outlet so it starts accumulating in the head. That is the only place—the basement, where you go on throwing anything which is not allowed. It is in the unconscious part of the mind that it accumulates.

By the time you allow, he is so obsessed with sex that he falls in love at first sight. Just keep anybody hungry for fifteen years, and then do you think he will think, "What food to chose?" Any food, any rotten banana . . . and love at first sight! And then you call love blind: "Look at this fool—he has fallen in love with a rotten banana!" And you are the cause of it—just keeping him hungry for so many days. . . .

Just try one week's fast and then see what happens. Your whole mind will be full of food—spaghetti, spaghetti, spaghetti. . . ! And the brain looks almost like spaghetti! And then you fall in love—you see spaghetti and you fall in love immediately! There is no time. Who bothers about what it is? "First eat and then we will see!"

Pre-marital relationship is a very scientific pheno-menon. It has to be allowed, it has to become part of human rights. It should be one of the basic rights of every human being to have love relationships before one decides for some intimacy, to live with somebody for a longer period. I will not say for your whole life, because who knows?—life is a big thing!—but for a longer period. Tomorrow you may find a far more beautiful woman, a far more beautiful man; then your intelligence will say that it is better to choose. Then why go on being tortured by your past? Remain free for the future, open to the future. So I say only for a longer period, when you decide.

When you have enjoyed many relationships you will be able to choose, you will be able to judge what kind of woman or man suits you, what kind of woman or man is a nourishment.

I am all for pre-marital relationships. Without them man will remain insane.

And he says he is also against extra-marital rela-tionships. That is a little more complicated, but it has to be understood. That too is one of the latest psycholog-ical findings, that extra-marital relationships help mar-riage, they don't destroy it. It is always good to have a little change, just at the weekend. It does not harm at all. That idea—that if a man starts having a little love affair with some woman other than his wife it will destroy the marriage—is absolutely wrong. It will help, it will renew the relationship, because one gets tired. Man is, after all, human. Don't ask impossible things! One gets tired—the same woman, the same man. One loses all taste.

If you have to eat the same food every day, like I do, you will get fed up. Even my kitchen people who prepare the food, they are utterly fed up with it. Except me, everybody is fed up. My gardeners are fed up because they have to grow the *same* vegetables. Vivek, Astha, Nirgun, Pragya—they are *all* fed up—they have to prepare exactly the same every morning, every evening. There is no difference between my lunch and supper. And there is no dinner ever. Dinners don't exist in my life at all—just supper and lunch, the same, exactly the same. And I can understand they get fed up preparing, preparing the same thing every day.

Unless you are enlightened you are bound to get fed up. I, of course, enjoy it every time—because I go on forgetting about the morning, so I am again tremendously excited. When Vivek brings the food I immediately look: "What have you prepared?" And she looks very embarrassed. And I don't miss a single moment, I start eating. Because who cares what I had eaten yesterday and the day before yesterday? I don't carry all these psychological memories, so each time it is new.

Unless you are enlightened, extra-marital relationships *are* good. So please have as many as you can have before you become enlightened, because once you are enlightened I cannot help! Then you are finished.

Once in a while just a little taste of a new woman, a new man revives your interest in the old woman and the old man. You start thinking, "After all, she is not so bad." A little change is always good.

I am not against extra-marital relationships. The people who are against them are really teaching you possessiveness in an indirect way. When I say I am not against extra-marital relationships I am teaching you non-possessiveness. Just see the point: if I talk about non-possessiveness people think, "That's spiritual, that's religious—that's great!" But if I talk about extra-marital relationships, the spiritual and the religious are immediately offended.

But I am saying the *same* thing. Talking about non-possessiveness is abstract, talking about extra-marital relationship is concrete. And you cannot live with abstractions, you have to live with concerete life. And what wrong can it do? If a man is tired of the same woman—the same contours, the same geography, the same topography—once in a while a little bit different geography, a little bit different landscape . . . and he comes home again interested in exploring the old map. It gives a break—a coffee break. And after each coffee break you can again get involved in the same work, the same files, and you open them and you start working . . . .The coffee break helps you.

I don't want people to be interested in impossible ideals. I am not an idealist at all. I am down-to-earth, a pragmatist, a realist.

If people want to live together in a deep intimacy, they should not be possessive. They should allow freedom. And that's what extra-marital relationship is—freedom. But people are very strange.

Just a few days ago, Divya said she wants to give Hamid absolute freedom, she wants to work it out, she does not want to be possessive. Just to see whether she really meant it I inquired, "Then let Hamid be removed to another room." She said, "No!" What kind of absolute freedom is this if Hamid cannot be allowed to go to another room, to live separately—what *kind* of freedom is this? And she was calling it absolute freedom! And Hamid *wants* to go! Even in front of Divya he goes on saying, "I want to live separately." And she says, "You keep quiet, you don't understand." And of course he keeps quiet because he is an Iranian and he can't understand much. Who has ever heard about Iranians understanding? So he keeps quiet. But how long can he keep quiet? Again and again he says, "But I want to live separately." And Divya says, "Don't get emotional. Keep cool and let me try to give you total freedom."

Now this total freedom, absolute freedom, what does it mean?

Nobody wants to give freedom to anybody else. People say beautiful words, sweet nothings. This sounds so good: total freedom, unconditional love, non-possessive intimacy. Just the sound is good, just like AUM. . . . It sounds good, but what else can you do with it?

Extra-marital relationships are very significant, immensely helpful to psychological growth and maturity, because when you start moving with another woman or man for a day or two, or a few days, a distance is created between you and your old lover. And that distance is very helpful. When you are exactly at the same distance as you were before you fell in love with each other, again a honeymoon is possible. That space will allow a new honeymoon. Again you will become interested, again you will start reconsidering, rethinking the whole matter.

And being with the new man and the new woman, you will see that after all they are not so different. So what is the point of destroying a certain intimacy that has developed? What is the point of destroying it? And intimacy is far more fulfilling than any sexual relationship can ever be.

If two persons are really intimate they will allow absolute freedom, because they know that intimacy is far *more* beautiful, far *more* significant—they have experienced it. So any sexual relationship is just a little diversion, nothing can go wrong just because of it.

But the old idea of marriage is of possessiveness, and the whole church has depended upon possessiveness in everything—possess! They talk about non-possession, but that too is out of greed: greed for the other world. If they talk about renouncing the world, it is to gain the pleasures of paradise. It is greed, pure greed, simple greed, and nothing else.

And he is against contraception. He is bound to be because *all* religions are against contraceptive methods—for the simple reason that their numbers will be reduced. It is a political game: who has got more numbers—Catholics or Protestants, Hindus or Jainas or Mohammedans? Hindus are against contraceptives for the simple reason that Mohammedans will go on increasing, and sooner or later again India will have to be divided into two parts. The Mohammedans will make demands if they start growing in numbers, and they can grow more in numbers because Mohammedans are allowed by their religion to marry four women. Now that is also a strategy. If you have four women. . . .One man is capable of making four or forty women pregnant. But vice versa is not true: if four men are married to one woman, only one child will come out of it. But if four women are married to one man, then four children will come out of it.

Mohammed himself married nine women. So, of course, when the prophet himself married nine, the followers should be allowed at least four. That seems logical, rational. So Mohammedans are allowed four women. And if you stop it you are interfering with their religion, and nobody should interfere with anybody's religion.

Now I am interfering with their religion. Soon there will be protests that I am interfering with their religion, and I am talking against Mohammed, that I am talking against their religion and the idea of marrying four women. That is allowed by their religion, nobody can stop it.

Hindus are afraid that if this goes on, naturally they will grow in number, and if Hindus are forced to use contraceptive methods they will be reduced in number. The whole politics is of numbers, particularly because of democracy. Each single person brings a vote; the more children you have the more votes you have. And whosoever has more votes will rule the country, will rule the world. So all religious heads, all religious institutions, all religious propagandists are against contraception.

But, in fact, contraception is one of the greatest blessings that has happened to humanity in the whole of human history. It is the greatest revolution. No revolution is so great compared to the invention of contraceptives, because it is through contraceptives that women can become equal to men. It is only through contraceptives that the woman can have all the rights that man has always claimed for himself. Otherwise she was almost always pregnant.

She cannot work in the factory, she cannot work in the office, she cannot be a doctor, she cannot be a professor. At the most she can only be a housewife, and that simply means a house-servant. And her whole life is wasted in giving birth to children. She cannot do anytying else—she cannot paint, she cannot compose poetry, she cannot play music, she cannot dance. How can you dance if you are continuously pregnant? It is so sickening, so nauseating.

But her whole work in the past was just like that of a factory—to go on giving birth to children. It started nearabout the age of fourteen and it continued as long as the man was potent enough to go on procreating. Two dozen children was not an exception, one dozen was a very normal thing. Now a woman giving one dozen children to the world or two dozen children to the world will not have time for anything else.

That was the root cause of woman's slavery. And when she was continuously pregnant and ill and sick because of pregnancy, she had to depend on man—economically depend on man. And if you depend on man economically you cannot be free. Economics is one of

the most fundamental factors. If the money comes from-
the man, then the money comes with conditions.

If we need a humanity where man and woman are
equal, then contraceptives should be used as widely as
possible; they should become normal. And only then
will extra-marital relationships, pre-marital relationships become very simple. The whole problem was that
if you were moving in a pre-marital relationship and the
woman got pregnant, there would be great trouble. The
contraceptive has eradicated that trouble completely.

The Pope is afraid that if contraceptives are used then
pre-marital relationships cannot be prevented. That was
a tragedy to prevent them: the woman was so afraid
that she would lose all honor, all respect if she got pregnant; the man was so afraid thaf if he made a woman
pregnant then he would have to get married to the
woman. He may not be ready for that; it may have been
just a momentary affair. It may have been just fun! But
it has become now a great responsibility, a whole life's
responsibility.

Contraceptives have transformed the very quality of
sex: sex becomes fun. Sex is no more such a serious
thing as it used to be. It becomes just a playfulness—two
bodies playing with each other, that's all. There is
nothing wrong in it. You play football—what is wrong
in that? You play volleyball—what is wrong in that?
Two body energies are involved.

Sex is also a game; but it was not a game before.
Before contraceptives it was a serious thing. Contraceptives have eradicated that whole seriousness about it.
Now the religions are bound to be afraid, because their
whole edifice can collapse because of contraceptives.
What the atheists could not do in centuries, contraceptives can do within decades. They have already done it:
contraceptives have made man free of the priest.

Contraceptives are a blessing, but the Pope cannot be
in favor of them because his power is at stake—and not

only the Pope but all other religious heads, the shankaracharyas and the ayatollahs and the imams, they will all be against contraceptives. Their whole business is at risk.

And I am all for contraceptives. They should be widely used. Children should be taught by parents, by the schools, how to use contraceptives so sex becomes just fun, it loses all seriousness. And then only can woman be liberated. Without contraceptives the woman is bound to remain a slave, half humanity living in slavery is not a good scene to look at.

And he is against abortion. Why should these people be against abortion? On the one hand they go on talking about the immortality of the soul. Then why be afraid of abortion?—the soul is immortal so there is no sin in it. All that you have done by abortion is you have prevented the soul getting into this body. The soul will find another body, if not on this earth, then on some other earth, because scientists say there are least fifty thousand planets—at least. That is the minimum which have life on them. There may be more but fifty thousand is almost a certainty. So if not on this planet then on some other planet. . . .And it is good to shift people—what is wrong in it? If this planet is getting too crowded, just shifting a few people to some other planets. . . .That's what abortion is. The soul says, "May I come in, madam?" and you say, "No, the place is too crowded. Knock at some other door."

And there are other possibilities, so you are not destroying anything. These same people on the one hand say life is immortal, the soul is immortal, and on the other hand they make you afraid that you are killing a soul, that you are killing a life, they make you feel guilty.

Now Hindus worship Krishna and his Srimad Bhagavad Gita. And he says in the Srimad Bhagavad Gita that even if you cut the body the soul is not cut, if you burn the body the soul is not burnt. . . .*Na hanyate hanyamane shareere*: destroy the body nothing is destroyed—*nainam chhindanti shastrani*: neither you can cut it with the sword—*nainam dahait pavakah*: nor can you burn it in fire. And Hindus are against abortion. Why?—because you are killing a life. Nothing is killed, nothing can be killed. There are only two possibilities: either the soul is immortal, then nothing is killed; or the soul is mortal, then too nothing is killed. And these are the only two possiblities. Either you believe in the immortality of the soul, then nothing is killed because nothing *can* be killed—or you believe in the mortality of the soul, then there is nothing to kill; there is no soul really, there is only body.

And we have to decide how many people can joyously live on this planet. But there is also a hidden strategy behind it: the religious priests, the popes and others, would not like man to live joyously for the simple reason that if people started living joyfully, cheerfully, blissfully, who will bother about their paradise and their heaven? People have to live in utter misery, only then can they teach "Look, this life is miserable. Search for the other life, the life beyond. This life is hell, so don't waste your time in living it. Use your time in finding some other life, life divine."

It is to their advantage if the world remains in misery. And psychologically they have managed to keep you in misery, physiologically they are trying to keep you in misery, biologically—in every possible way they are making you so miserable that you have to go for their advice, that you have to look up to them as your saviours.

My whole vision is different.

You ask me, Krishna Prem:

What do you say?

I support the idea that this life, herenow, has the capacity of becoming heavenly. There is no need to hanker for any other heaven, for any other paradise. We can transform this life into such a beautiful phenomenon. And I know there is a beyond, but if you live herenow beautifully, only then will you be able to live the beyond also beautifully. This is a training place, this is really a school. Life is a discipline, a preparation, for the other life. If you live here miserably, even in heaven you will live miserably, you will not be able to drop your habits. It will be impossible for you.

Live now and here and create this planet in such a way that there is no misery left, that love is overflowing, that people are flowering, that people become lotuses. And then of course life is eternal. But when you move to another plane you will be able to carry some of the fragrance of this life with you. Then even if you go to hell you will be able to create a heaven out of it.

So don't ask God to send my people to heaven. I ask God every day . . . this is my only prayer: "Let me and my people go to hell"—because hell needs much help. It needs great transformation, and we can do it! Let the saints go to heaven, we are bound for hell, we are going to make hell orange. And I tell you that your saints will be jealous of hell!

The second question

Bhagwan: I don't know!
There is so much love showering on me.
Sitting silently, doing nothing,
and the grass grows by itself.

I am so happy having eyes that can see,
and even if they don't see, it never gets dark.
Yesterday while listening to Almasta's
esoteric questions
it was like taking a bath in the ocean of love.
I love her and like to sit at your feet looking at you,
hearing the music of love and being a child again.
Are there any more questions from Almasta?
There must be more—at least one more.
I know that she has at least ten questions.
Oh, Bhagwan, life is good to me!
Dhyan Almuth

Yes, ALMASTA HAS EXACTLY ten questions again! First:

How many gay men does it take to screw in a light bulb?

Almasta, two: one to buy an art deco bulb, and one to shriek, "Marvelous, darling!"

Second:
How many lesbians does it take to screw in a light bulb?

Almasta, five: one to screw in the light bulb, and four to discuss how it is more gratifying than a man!

Third:
How many Zen Masters does it take to screw in a light bulb?

Almasta, two: one to screw in the light bulb and one not to screw in the light bulb.

Fourth:
How many Chinese does it take to screw in a light bulb?

Almasta, ten thousand . . . to give the light bulb a cultural revolution.

Fifth:
How many anarchists does it take to screw in a light bulb?
Almasta, all of them!

Sixth:
How many negroes does it take to screw in a light bulb?
Almasta, none—there are not any—any more!

Seventh:
How many Polacks does it take to screw in a light bulb?
Almasta, one, but he needs a lot of light bulbs!

Eighth:
How many neurotics in therapy does it take to screw in a light bulb?
Almasta, one—three hours a week for five years!

Ninth:
How many psychotherapists does it take to screw in a light bulb?
Almasta, ask Teertha. Every possibility is that he will encounter you and ask, "When did you start this fantasy?"

Tenth:
How many philosophers does it take to screw in a light bulb?
Almasta, this is a question for J. Krishnamurti, not for me. Ask him and he will go into deep meditation and then ask you, "Do you mean, how does a light bulb screw you?"

Discourse 4

December 14, 1980

BE ASSERTIVE !

The first question

Bhagwan: Working at Amitabh,
your Amsterdam center,
for the last few years, I have become aware that
in our contacts with the media or government agencies
we have been on the defensive
and have been trying to be acceptable.
Now the pressure is building up,
specifically with the recent Dutch government inquiry
into what they call 'sects'.
It is coming to a point
where becoming still more defensive
would be a denial of our innermost experience.
It feels that the time has come
to be less accommodating,
less compromising and less defensive.
Could you give us your guidance, please?
Anand Niketana

THE MOST IMPORTANT THING to remember is truth cannot be defensive; it is against the nature of truth to be defensive. Just think: if Jesus had been defensive or Buddha had been defensive or Lao Tzu had been defensive, then humanity would have missed all that is valuable. Truth has to assert itself. There is no need to be aggressive, remember that too. Truth is neither defensive nor aggressive, but truth has to be assertive.

Jesus said to his disciples, "Go to the rooftops and shout the truth from there!"—because people are deaf. Unless you shout they are not going to hear.

Only lies are either agressive or defensive; truth is neither. Truth simply is as it is—available, open.

The great political philosopher, Machiavelli, said in his treatise, *The Prince*, that if you want to be accepted as true then even if you are not true be aggressive, don't be on the defensive. That is for the politicians, because to be on the defensive, according to Machiavelli, is to be fighting a losing battle. Your very desire to be defensive shows that you are weak, that you are afraid, that you are willing to compromise. Truth cannot do these things. Lies will either be aggressive, when they are winning, or, when they start losing they become defensive.

By the way, Machiavelli's great-granddaughter, Anado, is here; she is my sannyasin. If Machiavelli comes to know he will toss and turn in his grave, because I am against politics. Politics is basically rooted in lies.

So, Niketana, you have been doing something wrong from the very beginning. There is no need to be defensive, there is no need to compromise, there is no need to be accommodating. It is better to be destroyed than to compromise, because when truth is crucified that's its victory, when truth is crucified it is crowned.

So don't be afraid of crucifixion. It is beautiful to die on the path of truth, it is ugly to survive through compromising. Each compromise means you have fallen from the truth into the ditch of lies. What else can a compromise be?

I have come across the news that the Dutch Government has made a commission of inquiry to investigate 'impartially' about sects. Now, this is sheer stupidity! How can they inquire impartially? And the people, the majority of the people, who have been appointed to the commission are Christian Democrats. Now, how can Christians be impartial? And they call it 'an inquiry into sects'. The very word 'sect' is condemnatory. Christianity is a religion—and my sannyasins are a sect, a cult! That is the beginning of prejudice. Now, how do you define a cult or a sect?

When Jesus was alive, whatsoever he was teaching, and the people who were following him, were they a religion or a cult, a sect? Of course, in the eyes of the

Jews—the established religion—it was a cult, a sect; it was not a religion. If it was religion, then Jesus could not have been crucified. A cult is something that takes you away from religion, that distracts you from the true religion, from the main path.

Jesus was a cult when he was alive. Now, how can Christianity be a religion? If in the source it is a cult, if the seed is the cult, how can the tree be religion? And when Jesus was alive, *then* it was a cult, and now he has been dead for two thousand years and around his corpse a religion has grown. When Buddha was alive it was a cult, a sect; now Buddhism is a religion. So what is the definition?

When the Master is alive, when he is living, when the truth is breathing, then it is a cult—it has to be condemned. And when the Master is dead . . . and with the Master's death the truth disappears, because truth needs an embodiment. It is an experience; it has to exist in the person who has realized it. When the person is no more, the truth is no more.

If Jesus, Buddha, Lao Tzu, Zarathustra, Mohammed, while they are alive are only creating cults and sects, then the definition of religion is: the corpse of truth—rotten, stinking.

Jews were also very impartially inquiring about the phenomenon that Jesus was—*very* impartially. Hindus were inquiring into Buddha and his disciples *very* impartially. Now they are inquiring about me *very* impartially! And who are they to inquire? And why should they be worried? And not only are Christians worried—Hindus are worried, Mohammedans are worried, Jainas are worried, Buddhists are worried, Parsis, Sikhs. All the established religions are worried because I am taking away their sons and their daughters, and the fear is: "What is going to happen to our tradition?"

Tradition belongs to the past. Spirituality has no tradition, cannot have; it is against the fundamental law of existence. Tradition has no soul, how can it have spirituality? Science is a tradition because science depends on the past. If there had been no Newton, no Edison, no Rutherford, then there would have been no possibility for an Albert Einstein. Albert Einstein has to stand on the shoulders of the giants of the past. Take away Newton and Albert Einstein will fall flat on the ground! He cannot stand on his own. That's what a tradition means: a continuity; it is a chain. If one link is missing, the chain is broken.

But religion is not a tradition, spirituality is not a tradition. If there had been no Krishna, I could still be; it does not matter. I am not standing on the shoulders of Krishna or Buddha or Jesus. I am standing on my own feet just as *they* stood on their own feet.

Buddha denied the Vedas; that was the tradition—Hinduism. He denied it absolutely. He was utterly against the Hindu scriptures. Any man of understanding is bound to be against the scriptures, because truth cannot be contained in the scriptures, truth cannot be expressed through words. And what can scriptures have?—only words, theories, hypotheses, assumptions. Buddha said, "Get rid of all the scriptures if you want to know the truth." Naturally the Hindu priesthood was against him. Buddha was not standing on the shoulders of the past giants, in fact he was denying them. He was saying, "Get rid of them, only then can you be your own self." That's the beauty of religion.

Science is borrowed; it is information, and information has to come from others, That's why science can be taught in schools, colleges, universities, but religion cannot be taught. Religion can only be caught, it cannot be taught. It is like an infection: when you are with a Buddha you can get infected—if you are not too resistant, if you are not too much on guard.

If you remain vulnerable with Jesus, with Zarathustra, with Lao Tzu, something of their being can penetrate your being. The being of the Master can overlap the being of the disciple. A moment comes when the Master and disciple start merging into each other; that is the moment when something miraculous transpires. It is not information, it is transformation.

So religion is not a tradition: it is a heart-to-heart contact, it is a love affair. Christianity *died* with Christ; since then it has been only a cult.

The cultists in Holland are trying to inquire about religion! When I am dead it will be a cult, but while I am alive it is religion. That's my definition of a cult and of a religion: a religion means while the experience has still a heartbeat to it; a cult is a corpse, the heartbeat has stopped. It *looks* the same, but it is no more the same. It is only a concept, a philosophy; the life has departed. It is only a cage—maybe a golden cage, but the bird is dead, the bird is no more alive. It will not sing any more—or you can put gramophone records in it. That's what priests are: gramophone records. They go on repeating.

Friedrich Nietzsche is absolutely right when he says that the first and the last Christian died on the cross two thousand years ago—the first and the last Christian. Christ was the first and the last Christian. Buddha was the first and the last Buddhist. After that it is only footprints on the sands of time . . . you can go on worshipping.

So, Niketana, tell those fools there that "You are cults and we are a religion!" And make a commission of inquiry, because only *my* sannyasins can be impartial. Here are Christians and Hindus and Mohammedans and Parsis and Buddhists and Jainas; in my sannyasins all the rivers are meeting and merging. It is an ocean! Only my sannyasins can be impartial—how can these Christians be impartial? They have already shown their faces, that they are Christians. They are already prejudiced that Christ is right, that the Christian dogma is right, that anything that goes against it is wrong. How can they inquire? Inquiry needs no *a priori* assumptions, no conclusions.

So *you* can make, Niketana, a commission of inquiry to look into what Christianity has done in two thousand years. All kinds of crimes have been committed—murder, rape, arson—all kinds of crimes have been committed by these so-called religious people. In fact, they have proved the greatest calamity to humanity.

Be assertive! Drop all ideas of being defensive! But you are still talking in terms of defence.

You say:

> *It feels that the time has come*
> *to be less accommodating, less compromising*
> *and less defensive.*

Less defensive or *more* defensive, *less* accommodating or *more* accommodating, *less* compromising or *more* compromising, is only a question of quantity. It is not a change of your vision, of your perspective. Change the whole perspective! It is not a question of less or more—simply drop being defensive. And don't move to the other extreme: don't become aggressive—but be assertive. Open up your heart, say the way you feel, explain it to the people the way you feel.

You say:

> *It is coming to a point*
> *where becoming still more defensive*
> *would be a denial of our innermost experience.*

Never betray your own innermost experience. If you betray it you are committing suicide. A person who kills himself physically is not really committing suicide, because he will be born again; he will have a new body, that's all, a new model. But the person who goes against

his own inner experience is committing a far deeper
suicide— he is destroying his very soul. It is better to
suffer; it is *beautiful* to suffer on the path of truth. Even
death on the path of truth has a beauty of its own.

And these governments are going to do the same
thing everywhere, all over the world it is going to happen, because my sannyasins are now in almost all the
countries of the world. Sooner or later everywhere the
same problems are bound to arise. In Germany the government has appointed a commission, now it is
Holland, soon it will be Italy, and so on and so forth.
You are going to be tortured everywhere! That's how it
has always been.

Truth cannot be accepted because people are living in
such comfortable lies. Accepting truth means destroying
the whole edifice that they have created around themselves. It is cozy and comfortable, and they have put so
much energy into it. It has become their lifelong work,
and nobody wants it to be destroyed. Nobody wants to
be told that it is all dreamstuff: "You are just befooling
and deceiving yourselves. Come out of your decep-
tions!" And the masses, the crowd mind, the mob
psychology, has not that much guts; they cannot come
out of their comfortable lies. So the only way left for
them is to destroy truth.

That's why Jesus is crucified, Socrates is poisoned,
Mansoor is killed, Sarmad is beheaded. But I don't think
that that has destroyed anything. The crucifixion of
Jesus has made him one of the *most* significant expres-
sions of truth on the earth, so much so that now we
think of history being divided by *his* name: before
Christ and after Christ, as if history took a new route
with that crucifixion. That cross on which Jesus was
crucified has divided the whole of history. 'Before
Christ'—it means man was not yet aware, alert about
real religion; 'after Christ'—something happened,
something so tremendously significant that humanity

took a new step, rose higher than ever before. The same has happened with every enlightened person.

So, Niketana, change your attitude totally. You are not to be defensive at all. But let me remind you again—because mind moves to polar opposites—I am not telling you to be aggressive, I am not telling you to be violent. I am telling you to be simply *in* the middle, *exactly* in the middle, neither defensive nor aggressive but assertive—standing naked in the sun, in the rain, in the wind and telling the world what sannyas is all about.

The second question

Bhagwan: I have just realized that
some of my laughter at your jokes
comes because of my old-fashioned
Christian morality—
a 'saintly' man would never say 'fuck' or 'shit'.
Well, so much for saints.
I am loving this bursting laughter,
so share another joke with me.
Anand David

THAT'S THE ONLY THING that will be missed if all these churches, moralities, puritanic attitudes dis— appear from the world—the only thing that will be missed is the jokes, because jokes need a certain back- ground. Without the popes there will be no jokes, because the background is absolutely essential.

In the day you cannot see the stars—they are there. They don't simply evaporate in the morning; they are not like dewdrops evaporating in the sun. They are far bigger than your sun; suns millions of times bigger are there. Those stars look small because they are so far away; actually our sun is a very mediocre sun, bigger suns are there. They don't disappear, but in the light you cannot see them—the background disappears. The background is the darkness of the night; against the darkness of the night those stars shine forth.

So that much I also feel, that once all these fools disappear—the popes, the ayatullahs, the imams, the shankaracharyas—and this whole nonsense is no more there, one thing will certainly be missed: jokes will be missed. The best jokes arise around the priests, the rabbis, the popes. You are right, David, in saying:

I have just realized that
some of my laughter at your jokes
comes because of my old-fashioned
Christian morality.

Not some of it—all of it!

You say:

A saintly man would never say 'fuck' or 'shit'.

That is true, but I am not a saint! I don't want to be categorized as a saint. I don't want to stand with those long faces, with those stuffed tomatoes, with all kinds of rubbish. And they have only one idea in their heads: 'holier-than-thou'. That's why they cannot use these words—otherwise these words are there. They cannot use them, but the words are there.

At a southern Californian school for underprivileged Mexican children, the brightest boy in the class was named Jesus Christ Gonzalez. In preparation for the coming visit of Monsignor O'Brien, the teaching nun rehearsed with the boy, "My name is J.C. Gonzalez and I am going to spell 'rose'." The nun warned him against using his full name.

When the Monsignor arrived, the boy got up and said, "My names is J.C. Gonzalez and I am going to spell 'chrysanthemum'."

The bewildered nun remarked, "Jesus Christ, you can't spell 'chrysanthemum'!"

"Goddamit!" snapped the clergyman, "Let him spell 'chrysanthemum' if he wants to!"

They are human beings just as you are, they are just hiding behind masks.

I have heard:

A Pope—maybe this Polack Pope—was going for a morning walk with a rabbi. The rabbi stumbled on a stone, hurt his foot, and said, "Shit!"

The Pope said, "This is not right, because God is everywhere and he must have heard you."

They walked a little further and again the rabbi stumbled and again he said, "Shit!"

The Pope said, "Enough is enough! God will punish you."

And the third time it happened suddenly there was great thunder in the clouds, lightning struck the Pope dead, and then somebody in the clouds shouted, "Shit! I missed!"

There is nothing wrong—even God uses these words! I don't know about your saints, I know about God, and who cares about your saints?

David, are you English or something?

Judge: "You are accused of making love to a dead woman in the desert."

Drunkard: "Who me, Mr. Judge?"

Judge: "Yes, you!"

Drunkard: "But that woman . . . hic . . . that woman . . . hic . . . was she dead?"

Judge: "Are you trying to tell me that you didn't know?"

Drunkard: "I swear to God, Judge, Your Honor, Sir, I . . . hic . . . didn't know. I thought . . . hic . . . she was English!"

You say:

> *A saintly man would never say*
> *'fuck' or 'shit'.*

Then after me you will have to change the definition of the saintly man.

One Indian friend has written—his name is Iqbal Kureshi—he says:

> *Bhagwan, what you say between the jokes*
> *is beautiful, religious and spiritual,*
> *but the jokes destroy your image in the public eye.*
> *After all, what is the purpose of all these jokes?*

Iqbal Kureshi, that's exactly the purpose: to destroy the image! I don't want to be known as a saint—that's exactly the purpose. And I am not worried about what others think of me—I am not a politician. Only politicians are worried, continuously worried, about what others are thinking about them, because they have to depend on others—the others have the votes. I don't depend on anybody's votes, anybody's opinion. I am simply whatsoever I am. Why should I be bothered about my image?

The very worry about the image is egoistic, but your saints are worried, I know that. I have known all kinds of your saints—Hindu, Mohammedan, Christian, Sikh, Jainas, Buddhists—I have come across all kinds of your saints. They are far *more* political than your politicians, because this very idea is politics: what people are thinking, remain respectable. Respectability is nothing but nourishment for the ego.

I don't want to be respectable. Either you love me or you don't love me; respect is simply meaningless. Respect and the desire for it is egoistic. So those who love me, they will love me as I am. I am not going to compromise, I am not going to accommodate. And I could create that accommodation so easily: I could not use a few words—'fuck' and 'shit'—and I could become a saint. You see how cheap it is! But I am not interested in such cheap saintliness. If I am a saint then whatsoever I say is saintly; if I am not a saint then I may go on reciting the Gita and the Koran and the Vedas but I am not a saint, I am just a parrot.

I am not interested at all in mirrors. I know my original face—and the original face is not known through mirrors. Public opinion is only a mirror.

Iqbal Kureshi must be worried about my image. He says, "It puts your image upside-down." What is wrong with being upside-down? That's what they call in yoga *sirshasan*— the headstand. And as far as I am concerned, I know that *you* are upside-down, so when you see me upside-down that simply means I am standing on my legs and you are standing on your head!

There is a story:

Once a donkey went to see Pundit Jawaharlal Nehru when he was the Prime Minister. The guard was on duty and, as guards are supposed to, he was snoring. And when the donky went in he opened one eye and saw: "Only a donkey is there—there is no need to worry. A donkey cannot be a spy, a donkey cannot kill the prime minister, he cannot bring weapons with him. So there is no need to worry— a donkey is a donkey—let him go. What can he do? At the most he may eat a little bit of grass here and there." So he closed his eyes and started snoring again.

Pundit Jawaharlal Nehru was very much interested in *sirshasana*, the headstand, so early in the morning he was doing a headstand on the lawn. The donkey went close, looked at him and said, "Punditji, why are you standing upside-down?"

Jawaharlal said, "Am I standing upside-down or are *you* standing upside-down?" But he jumped onto his feet the moment he realized that the donkey had spoken. He said, "Am I hearing right? Have your really spoken?"

The donkey said, "Don't get so upset. I am only a donkey—I have just learnt the art of reading and speaking, In my spare time I have nothing else to do, so I go on reading newspapers. Don't get so upset."

Jawaharlal relaxed and he said, "I am not upset, because I have seen many speaking donkeys in my life. In fact, nobody else comes to see me except speaking donkeys!"

But the first idea in Jawaharlal's mind was that the donkey was standing upside-down. He had completely forgotten that he himself was doing a headstand.

The whole of humanity is standing upside-down, but because all are standing upside-down whosoever tries to stand on his feet will look upside-down—he will be a minority. The Buddha is always a minority.

Iqbal Kureshi has asked in a friendly way . . . he must be in love with me so he is worried. He says:

> *Whatsoever you say between the jokes*
> *is beautiful, religious and spiritual.*

I don't think so—that is really bullshit! Only the jokes are beautiful, religious and spiritual. But we cannot agree. I cannot agree with you because you are absolutely unconscious, and you cannot agree with me because I am absolutely conscious. We are living in totally different dimensions.

He asks:

What is the purpose of all these jokes?

I also ask, "What is the purpose of all these religious and spiritual things that I go on saying?" Just old habit, I think. Otherwise there is no point! And sooner or later you will see—I will only tell jokes.

His background is Indian, Mohammedan, and people think according to their background.

Mr. Bates first introduced his wife, Mrs. Bates, to President Lincoln. Then he introduced his son and said, "I would like you to meet my son, Master Bates."

President Lincoln said, "Oh? I'm so sorry to hear that!"

People hear according to their background! Now, Kureshi is hearing according to his Indian background. Otherwise what I am saying is very simple: I am using these jokes to bring a little sense of humor to religion. Religion has lacked a sense of humor so much so that H.G. Wells reported to have said that a religion had never been founded by a man who had any sense of humor. I want to prove him wrong so later on nobody can say that!

And a sense of humor has its own spirituality. If you cannot laugh you cannot understand life. If you cannot laugh you are not open. Laughter opens you towards existence. When you are not laughing, when you are sad and serious, you are closed; your doors, your windows are all closed. In laughter, heartfelt laughter, all your senses function at their optimum. You experience life entering you, touching you at the deepest core.

But Kureshi is worried because he thinks the jokes are sometimes dirty. I have never come across a dirty joke. The idea of the dirty comes from your interpretation, otherwise what is dirty? If you think sex is dirty, then any joke which implies some sexuality becomes dirty. It is your idea that makes it dirty. To me sex is as sacred as anything else—to me the whole of life is divine. And these so-called saints have always been telling you that the whole of life is divine, but it seems they don't mean it. I really mean it!

The annual contest for the best joke had been won for five consecutive years by the same person, Rabbi Abe Cohen from Brooklyn. Each year he sent in his entry and four weeks later he received the cheque and the winner's certificate from the sponsors, a world-famous glossy magazine. This year, however, two months had passed since the closing date for entries and he had heard nothing. Feeling a little worried lest the letter had been lost in the post, he phoned the editor and asked what had happened to his winnings.

"I'm terribly sorry, Abe," sympathized the editor, "but surprisingly enough, you only made second place this year."

"I don't believe it!" roared Cohen. "My jokes have always won. Who on earth could beat me?"

"Some new entry from India, a chap called Bhagwan Shree Rajneesh," the editor informed him.

"Look," said Cohen, "I find it hard to believe that anyone could tell a juicier joke than me. You must have made a mistake. But let me hear this joke so I can judge for myself."

The editor hesitated. "I'm sorry, Abe, but this joke is so juicy that I don't dare to tell it over the phone. It's really juicy!"

Cohen was indignant. "If you don't even let me hear the joke, I may have to take legal advice before I accept your decision!"

The editor thought for a few moments. "I tell you what," he offered, "let's compromise. I'll censor it a little to make it acceptable, and you use your imagination to fill in the gaps. Where the joke gets too juicy I'll say 'la-di-dah'."

Cohen agreed enthusiastically and the editor began, "Ready? Okay, here it goes: 'la-di-dah-di-dah-di-dah, la-di-dah-di-dah, da-di-dah-di-dah-di-dah . . . fuck!'"

Discourse 5

December 15, 1980

THAT STATE IS AWAKENING

सोऽयमात्मा चतुष्पात् ॥

जागरितस्थानो बहिष्प्रज्ञः
सप्ताङ्ग एकोनविंशतिमुखः
स्थूलभुग्वैश्वानरः प्रथमः पादः ॥

स्वप्नस्थानोऽन्तः प्रज्ञः सप्ताङ्ग
एकोनविंशतिमुखः प्रविविक्तभुक्
तैजसो द्वितीयः पादः ॥

यत्र सुप्तो न कञ्चन
कामं कामयते न कञ्चन
स्वप्नं पश्यति तत्सुषुप्तम् ।
सुषुप्तस्थान एकीभूतः
प्रज्ञानघन एवानन्दमयो
ह्यानन्दभुक्चेतोमुखः
प्राज्ञस्तृतीयः पादः ॥

एष सर्वेश्वर एष सर्वज्ञ
एषोऽन्तर्याम्येष योनिः
सर्वस्य प्रभवाप्ययौ
हि भूतानाम् ॥

So'yam ātmā catuṣ-pāt.

Jāgarita-sthāno bahiḥ-prajñaḥ
Saptāṅga, ekona-viṁśati-mukhaḥ
Sthūla-bhug vaiśvānaraḥ prathamaḥ pādaḥ.

Svapna-sthāno'ntaḥ-prajñaḥ, saptāṅga.
Ekona-viṁśati-mukhaḥ,
Pravivikta-bhuk,
Taijaso dvitīyaḥ pādaḥ.

Yatra supto na kañcana
Kāmaṁ kāmayate, na kañcana
Svapnaṁ paśyati, tat suṣuptam.
Suṣupta-sthāna ekī-bhūtaḥ
Prajñāna-ghana, evānandamayo,
Hyānanda-bhuk, ceto mukhaḥ
Prājñas tṛtīyaḥ pādaḥ.

Eṣa sarveśvara, eṣa sarvajña
Eṣontar-yāmyeṣa yoniḥ
Sarvasya, prabhavāpyayau
Hi bhūtānām.

This pure Self has four quarters:

The first is the waking state,
experience of the reality common to everyone.
The attention faces outwards,
enjoying the world in all its variety.

The second is experience of subjective worlds,
such as in dreaming.
Here the attention dwells within,
charmed by the mind's subtler creations.

The third is deep sleep,
the mind rests, with awareness suspended.
This state beyond duality,
—from which the waves of thinking emerge,
is enjoyed by the enlightened as an ocean of
silence and bliss.

The fourth, say the wise, is the pure Self alone.
Dwelling in the heart of all,
it is the lord of all,
the seer of all,
the source and goal of all.

CARL GUSTAV JUNG thinks that the Eastern approach to reality is introvert—he is utterly wrong. The Eastern approach is neither extrovert nor introvert; it is a transcendence of both. But to understand the transcendence one has to be a Buddha, one has to be really awakened.

The ordinary mind can think only of two things: the outside reality and the inside reality. There is no possibility of comprehending the beyond, and the beyond is the concern of all Eastern mysticism.

The Upanishads are the source of all that is beautiful, true, blissful, all that is significant as far as human evolution is concerned.

One of my friends, a great poet, Ramdhari Singh Dinkar went to China. He was talking to a great Chinese philosopher, Lin Yu-Tang. Ramdhari had heard much from me about Lao Tzu; he had become immensely interested in the Taoist approach to reality. He said to Lin Yu-Tang, "I love Lao Tzu." Lin Yu-Tang looked at the poet, puzzled, and said, "But the source of Lao Tzu is in the Upanishads!"

And Lin Yu-Tang is right, sincerely right: the whole mysticism of the East, wherever it has happened—in India, in China, in Japan—has its source in the Upanishads. And this Upanishad, the Mandukya Upanishad, is one of the most fundamental, because in a very essential way it describes the innermost core and also the ultimate reach of human consciousness.

The ordinary mind is dual; it thinks in terms of twoness: light and dark, day and night, summer and winter, life and death, good and bad, moral and immoral, extrovert and introvert, the real and the unreal, the momentary and the permanent. The duality is always there; it has entered into the very fabric of our languages.

But the moment you become really awakened . . . and remember the word 'really', because we think that every morning we are awake when we come out of sleep. That is only pseudo awakening, that is only so-called awakening. The real awakening is when one becomes a Jesus, a Buddha, a Mahavira, a Lao Tzu. When one has come to see the merger of the within and the without, when one has come to see the oneness of life and death, when there is no division left, that state is awakening. Before that everybody is a little bit schizophrenic, because the divided mind divides *you*. Then you are divided into the lower and the higher, then you are divided into the conscious and the unconscious, the body and the soul, and so on and so forth.

Carl Gustav Jung is not right at all in saying that Eastern mysticism is introvert. That is a condemnation, because in psychology the word 'introversion' is ugly. It means somebody is morbid, it means somebody is closed to the outside reality, it means that one is not open.

Jung had come to India while a great seer was alive, Sri Ramana Maharshi, and many people told him to go and see him—but he didn't go there. He traveled all over India, he went to see the Taj Mahal and Khajuraho, Ajanta and Ellora, but he didn't go to see Ramana Maharshi. Basically he was afraid. The fear was that a man like Ramana can become a mirror; he might see his own face, his own falseness.

But people rationalize everything. He rationalized that he didn't go to see Ramana because the Western mind is extrovert and the Eastern mind is introvert; their approaches are different and it is better not to get them mixed, otherwise one can lose one's path. As if he had some path! Whatsoever he was saying was a simple rationalization for not accepting the truth that he was afraid.

It is always a dangerous thing to encounter the awakened man, because immediately you can see where you are.

It is said in Arabian countries that the camel does not like to go near any mountain because he is afraid to be in the close proximity of a mountain—he will have to realize that he is nothing. Perhaps that's why he lives in the desert where he appears to be the most mountainous animal, incomparable.

Jung's fear of going to Ramana Maharshi is also associated with his fear of going to one other place. His whole life he was interested in going to Egypt to see the ancient mummies, the dead bodies which have been preserved for at least four thousand years. Many times he planned and many times he canceled the trip. He was just about to go so many times: his suitcases were ready, he just had to sit in the car and reach the airport, and suddenly he would feel sick, ill, some problem would arise, and he would cancel the trip. Once he even reached the airport and came back home.

Finally he had to look for the real cause why so many times he had been canceling it, and he had to take note of it: that he was afraid of seeing dead bodies, four thousand years old. Maybe he was still a little far away from the truth, but he had been looking in the right direction. He was afraid of death; those dead bodies would remind him of his own death.

These two things are in some way connected. Going to a man like Ramana is passing through the death of the ego, because the only way to go to the awakened is to go in deep surrender and trust. It is a death, far deeper than the physical death. He avoided Ramana, and still he went on saying things about the East which are not true, because he had never experienced the Eastern depth of mysticism.

You will see in the Mandukya Upanishad how penetrating has been the vision—psychology is lagging far behind. It has taken a very significant step, but only one step, and the journey is still incomplete; much further it has to go.

Before Sigmund Freud the Western mind accepted only one state, that is our so-called waking state; it had not even accepted the reality of dreams. Sigmund Freud's great contribution is: bringing the world of dreams into focus, allowing it to be analyzed, interpreted, observed—because before Sigmund Freud the West was living only with the first state, the so-called waking state. He at least took one step deeper, but there are still two more steps to be taken; only then will the psychological science be complete.

Hidden beneath the dreaming state is dreamless sleep, *sushupti*, and hidden even within and below and also beyond the third state is the real awakening, the fourth. The Upanishads simply call it 'the fourth', *turiya*. They don't give it a name, because to give it any name may give you some idea, and no idea can be given of it unless you have experienced it. So they simply call it 'the fourth'; that is significant. For the other three they have given names: *jagruti*, the so-called waking state; *swapna*, the dreaming state; *sushupti*, the dreamless sleep. But the fourth they have left only as 'the fourth', undefined; it has to be experienced to be known.

The Mandukya says:

This pure Self has four quarters . . .

The words 'pure Self' have to be understood—there is a possibility of misunderstanding because of the word 'Self'. But the condition of purity makes it clear that by 'the Self' ego is not meant at all. You can call it 'the egoless self', because the ego is the impurity. All that is arbitrary and artificial is impure; all that is natural and intrinsic is pure. You bring your original face with you, and then you start wearing masks; those masks are your impurity. And ego has many masks because you have to relate with many people; in different situations you need different faces. You have to change your face constantly.

It is said of George Gurdjieff that he was such a great actor that he would be talking to two persons, one sitting on the left and the other sitting on the right, and he would show different faces to both of them. When he turned to the left he would show one face, when he turned to the right he would show another face. And both the persons would argue later on about the man; they would both describe him in different ways. One would say, "How loving he was! How compassionate! How blissful!" And the other would say, "What are you saying? Have you gone mad? He was so arrogant, so egoistic, so cruel, so violent, almost murderous!"

Gurdjieff used to enjoy that very much; he would leave such different impressions. He was capable of changing his mask because he knew his original face. *You* don't know your original face. You change your masks, but that too is mechanical, almost autonomous—you don't change it, it changes by itself. When you are talking to your wife you have one face, when you are talking to your beloved you have another face.

Just watch a little and you will be able to see the truth of it. When you are talking to your boss you can't have the same face as when you are talking to your servant. When the boss enters your room you immediately stand up, wagging your tail—which does not exist but still you wag! And when the servant enters the room you don't take any note of him at all. If you are reading your newspaper you go on reading, if you are smoking you go on smoking. He is a nonentity; there is no need to take any note of him. He comes and goes as if he has not come and not gone; nothing has happened, he is not an event. If even a rat comes in the room you will take note of it—you many stand on your chair—but the servant does not exist.

Watch next time when your servant enters the room or your boss enters the room, your wife, your child, your friend, your enemy, and look how different you are.

The 'pure Self' means the original face, unadulterated, unpolluted, the pure mirror with no reflection, with nothing to reflect. It has four quarters—four dimensions you can call them, four stages you can call them, four quarters you can call them.

The first is the waking state . . .

The translation is not right. The translation should be: The first is the *so-called* waking state. The word 'so-called' is missing—because it is *not* really a waking state, it is only so-called. Do you think you are awake? Each morning you open your eyes, that is one thing, but to be awake is totally different. Just close your eyes any time in the day and you will find an undercurrent of dreams, fantasies going on.

Even modern psychology accepts that only a very small fragment of our totality is conscious, one-tenth, and that too is very fragile, just skin-deep, or not even that deep. Scratch it a little and immediately it disappears. Insult somebody, step on somebody's toes, and immediately he loses consciousness, he becomes mad. Just a word is enough to make him enraged. Anger is a temporary madness: that fragile part of his being which was just a little conscious—just a little candle—is all dark now.

That's why many times you say, "I did it in spite of myself." What do you mean, 'in spite of myself'? How can you do anything in spite of yourself? Is there somebody else within you too who can do something in spite of you? When you say it you simply mean, "I became so unconscious, so mad, that I did something which if I had been a little bit sane I would not have even thought about."

We are living in a so-called waking state; it is somnambulistic. There are people, and they are not few—one person out of every ten persons, ten percent of people who are somnambulists. You may have one in your family! If your family consists of ten persons, probably there is one person who is a somnambulist, who walks in his sleep. There are many people; they may not be aware, their families may not be aware, unless they are caught red-handed, and this rarely happens because everybody is asleep.

In the middle of the night they will wake up, not really awake—their eyes are open but very glassy. If you see their eyes—glassy. But they manage to get out of the door, to reach the kitchen, to open the fridge, to eat something, go to bed again. And in the morning they complain, "I don't have any appetite today. I don't know why I am getting fat!" And they may not be lying at all, they may be telling it sincerely—that they try to diet and they try to exercise, but somehow they go on gathering fat. They get up in their sleep.

People have been known to do strange things in their sleep—even murders have happened! People have murdered in their sleep, and they were absolutely true when in the court they said, "We don't know anything about this murder!" Of course every proof is there that they have murdered—their fingerprints are on the person's neck—still they are right, they are not wrong! A few husbands have killed their wives; they could not gather courage enough in their waking state, but while asleep they managed, gathered their guts. But in the morning they have forgotten all about it.

Papa Bear: "Somebody has eaten my porridge!"
Baby Bear: "Somebody has eaten my porridge too!"
Mama Bear: "Shut up, you idiots! I haven't served it yet!"

The plane transporting twenty-two inmates from one madhouse to another was flying at three thousand feet. The pilot and the steward were in the cockpit when all of a sudden the plane started tilting to the right, then to the left, then to the right again.

The frightened steward went to see what was happening. One minute later he was back in the cockpit and the plane was back to normal.

"What was the matter?" asked the pilot. "What were they doing?"

"They were playing football!"

"Well, how did you stop them?" asked the pilot.

The steward grinned. "I said, 'Hey, boys, it's such a nice day, why don't you go outside and play?' "

An insomniac who could not fall asleep until shortly before it was time to get up consulted his doctor who prescribed sleeping pills. He took a pill before retiring and sure enough he fell promptly asleep, but awoke before he heard the alarm clock.

For the first time in weeks he felt refreshed, and after bathing and breakfasting, leisurely strolled into the office. "I took a sleeping pill," he told the boss, "and didn't have any trouble getting up this morning."

"That's interesting," replied the boss, "but where were you yesterday?"

A woman had been killed, robbed of all her belongings and left naked on the footpath. The first person to find her, a rabbi, quickly took off his hat to cover her nakedness. The next man to pass by asked what was going on.

"Well," said the rabbi, "this woman is dead. I was going to find somebody to remove the body."

"Hold on a minute!" replied the other man. "Hadn't you better get that rabbi out of there first?"

People in the so-called waking state are not awake; they are still dreaming, just their eyes are open. They are behaving mechanically. Yes, they are efficient in doing the routine work, because they have become accustomed to doing it. There is something like a robot part of the mind: once you have learnt to do a certain thing it is transferred to the robot part of the mind; then it goes on doing it without your being aware of it. It is programmed.

And this is one of the things to be very deeply understood: we are all programmed. We have been programmed by the priests, by the politicians, by all kinds of ideologists. From the very childhood you have been programmed; a certain program has been put into your head and you are following that program.

When a Hindu sees a temple, suddenly he bows down—that is only a program. He is not doing it, he does not *mean* it; he may not even be aware why he is doing it or that he is doing it. He is simply bowing down because from the very childhood he has been forced to do it. Now he has learnt the trick—it is *only* a trick.

It almost always happens whenever you are repeating rituals; you need not be aware. Every Sunday suddenly you feel the urge to go to the church—for no reason at all. If you don't go you will feel as if you have missed something; if you go you don't gain anything at all.

It is just like smoking: if you smoke the cigarette you don't get anything, or perhaps you get something—cancer, et cetera—but if you don't smoke, the idea of smoking haunts you. You feel something is missing, you feel disturbed; the routine has not been fulfilled. You have to do it, otherwise your program inside goes on knocking, "Do it!" Unless you do it, it will not leave you alone. Whether it is smoking or prayer does not matter, it is all the same. If it is out of your programming there is no difference in it at all.

You don't feel like bowing down before a Mohammedan mosque if you are a Hindu or before a church if you are a Mohammedan or before a temple if you are a Christian. Why? Those are also places devoted to God, dedicated to God, but no desire arises because that is not *your* programming, that is not your conditioning.

Your so-called waking state is full of mechanical habits; you simply go on repeating them—and each generation goes on giving its mechanical habits to the new generation. That's why progress seems to be so impossible, because parents go on imprinting their children with *their* programming, and that programming has been coming for centuries, maybe thousands-of-years-old programming. Their parents programmed them and their parents and their parents, and it has been going on since Adam and Eve, perhaps even before that, because God programmed Adam and Eve. "Not to eat from this tree" is a program, is a conditioning. "You should do this, you should not do this. . . ." He behaved just like any other stupid father, *no* difference at all, and he punished like any father—he threw Adam and Eve out of the garden of Eden.

This waking state is not a real waking state. The real waking state happens only when you are completely deprogrammed, unconditioned.

Two drunks, Moe and Harry, meet. "How ya, Harry? Did we kill a bottle together last night?"

"No," replies Harry.

"Oh," says Moe, "must have been two other guys!"

Even the drunkard believes that he can reason!

The punch-drunk prize-fighter, having dropped to the mat from a crushing blow, was about to get up.

"Stay down until eight!" yelled his manager.

The fighter mumbled in a daze, "What time is it now?"

The honeymoon is over when she starts wondering what happened to the man she married, and he starts wondering what happened to the girl he didn't.

People just go on doing things, not knowing why they are doing them. People get married, then they become parents, then whatsoever has been done to them they start doing to their children. Perhaps they are taking revenge on their parents, paying the debts. They cannot do the same to their parents, but they can become parents and can do the same to their little children; and in their own turn the children will do the same thing. That's how diseases go on being transferred from one generation to another. Progress seems to be impossible.

It is really miraculous that a few people like Buddha, Lao Tzu, Mahavira, Krishna, escaped from this programming, conditioning process of the society. It is certainly a miracle! I don't call it a miracle when Jesus walks on water—even if he does, so what?—but I call it a miracle that he escaped from the Jewish conditioning. That is a miracle, a true miracle. I don't call it a miracle if he makes Lazarus come back from death—maybe he was just in a coma, perhaps he was not really dead. I don't call it a miracle that Jesus after crucifixion comes back alive, because in those days the method of crucifixion, the Jewish method, was so old-fashioned that it used to take at least twenty-four hours to forty-eight hours for a person to die—and he was taken down from the cross after six hours, and he was a young man, only thirty-three. Perhaps he was not dead. It was a very slow process of death—very torturous because it was very slow.

We are more human when we put a man in the electric chair: within seconds he is gone. He will not even be aware, he may be thinking of other things; while he is thinking, he is gone. Suddenly he finds he is gone—suddenly he looks at the chair and there is a dead body and he is hovering above! This is far more human. But forty-eight hours hanging on the cross, blood oozing out of your body, slowly slowly. . . .When all the blood has gone out of the body and nothing is left behind, then only will you die.

So I don't call resurrection a great miracle, but getting out of the Jewish tradition, getting out of the Jewish conditioning is certainly a miracle. Buddha getting out of the Hindu fold, the Hindu mob psychology, was doing a tremendous act, a great rebellion—effacing the whole mind. That's what he did for six years continously; people think he was meditating. . . .

Meditation, in fact, is a blanket word; it covers many processes, and the basic process is de-programming. For those six years he was simply de-programming himself, getting out of the clutches of Hinduism. The moment he was completely out he became enlightened.

Two hippies are walking along a road. One says, "Hey, man, I just had a great idea!"

"Wow! Far out! What is it?"

"Forgotten it, man!"

But that's how we are! We go on getting great ideas, but they are just like smoke: one moment they are there and then they are gone. It needs a dedicated effort, a continuous endeavor, to get rid of your programming, because it has been done over so many years. You have been chained within and without by such subtle conditions that unless you are very very watchful and intelligent you will not be able to escape from the prison.

But in fact we don't want to get out of the prison. All that we want is to make the prison a little more comfortable, a little more cozy. A beautiful painting on the prison wall, good furniture—maybe antique—wall-to-wall carpeting, and you are perfectly happy. That's what people are doing by earning money, power, prestige: making their prison cells a little bit better—maybe putting in an air-conditioner, installing electric lights, having a television set. . . .

People are not really interested in getting out of the prison. If they are interested then nobody can prevent them. Maybe it takes effort, constant effort, perserverance, but they can get out of it.

The bachelor prayer:
"I pray thee, O Lord, that I may not be married; but if I am to be married, that I may not be a cuckold; but if I am to be a cuckold, that I may not know it; but if I am to know it, that I may not mind it."

Our prayers, our desires are not really to be free, to be liberated. And this Mandukya Upanishad is basically for your total liberation. It is a key.

The first is the so-called *waking state,*
experience of the reality common to everyone.

What we call the objective reality. Science studies this objective reality of which we are aware in our so-called waking state. Hence the Upanishads call science *avidya,* ignorance—a very strange definition of science, but very true too. The Upanishads call science ignorance, *avidya,* and religion they call *vidya*—religion they call *true* science, *true* knowing, wisdom. And science they don't call science at all, because the word 'science' means knowing—it is not knowing. They call it *avidya*, ignorance. The English word 'ignorance' is beautiful; it means you are ignoring the essential and are getting too obsessed with the non-essential.

The Upanishads are right in calling science *avidya*, ignorance, because you are ignoring yourself and what you are trying to study is only a public reality of the so-called waking state. The waking state itself is pseudo, superficial, and the reality that it observes is bound to be superficial.

The attention faces outwards,
enjoying the world in all its variety.

The mind can function in two ways, either outwards or inwards. When it functions outwards it becomes extrovert and it creates science; when it functions inwards it becomes subjective, then it dreams.

Psychology studies dreaming and science studies your so-called waking, and this is our whole knowledge today: science plus psychology, Albert Einstein plus Sigmund Freud—two Jews! That's our whole contribution to human progress.

The second is experience of subjective worlds,
such as in dreaming.

Soren Kierkegaard has defined religion as subjectivity—he is wrong. Religion has nothing to do with subjectivity. Objectivity is science, subjectivity is psychology; religion is a transcendence of both.

What are you doing when you are dreaming? In fact, it is very strange, but true too, that you are far more real in your dreaming than your so-called waking state.

That's why psychoanalysis wants to know about your dreaming. Your waking state is so pseudo it is not reliable at all. Whatsoever you say is not trustworthy; your dreams are more reliable. It is strange: dreams, which are thought to be unreal, are more reliable and your so-called waking state is absolutely unreliable.

People say one thing and do another; everybody is a politician in his waking state. And the moment you are not a politician in your waking state, a miracle happens: your dreaming disappears, then you don't dream at all. Dreaming is a complementary process: whatsoever you are repressing in your waking state becomes your dreaming—and the repressed is truer.

This is the true story of how Andrew Young was fired from his post of ambassador to the United Nations by President Carter.

It all started at a party that they both attended. The President met Andy in the men's room. Stepping up to the urinal, the President looked over at Andy's machinery and exclaimed, "My God, Andy! Where did you get that big dick from?"

"Well, it's simple, Jimmy," Andy replied. "Each night before I go to bed I take it out and hit it up against the bedpost a couple of times. It springs right up, bigger than ever every time!"

The President looked amazed. He thanked Andy for the advice and left. When Jimmy got home he took his clothes off, stood by the bed and gave the bedpost an audible whacking with his machinery, and sure enough up it came!

Rosalind, awakened by the sound, sat up, rubbed her eyes and said, "Is that you, Andy?"

People are far truer when they are asleep! Dreams leak your reality. When you are in a so-called waking state you are cautious; you say only what has to be said, what is right to say.

Lokowicz and Koczela staggered out of a tavern, stumbled over to a lamp-post, unbuttoned, took things in hand and started to pee.

A policeman saw them, wagged his night-stick and barked, "Put those away and stop what you are doing!"

The drunks buttoned their flies in clumsy obedience, but one smiled. "What's so funny?" asked Koczela.

"I fooled that cop," said the other. "I put it away, but I didn't stop!"

When people are drunk they are truer, honest! When people are not drunk they are deceptive, cunning. Hence you will always find drunkards lovelier, nicer, better company to keep. Saints you will not find good company; you cannot live with a saint for twenty-four hours—if he is really a saint you cannot. Twenty-four hours will be enough for you to commit suicide!—either you will kill him or you will kill yourself. Criminals are more innocent because they have not been repressing. Saints are very ugly; their whole life is rooted in repression.

If you can make small windows in the heads of your saints you will be puzzled to see what goes on inside. Their dreams are all ugly. Criminals don't dream ugly dreams—I have lived with both. Criminals dream of becoming saints and saints dream of becoming criminals. It is a very upside-down world, a very strange world! Criminals are always thinking of how to become good, and saints are always dreaming of all that they have repressed: their sexuality, their desire for food, for money, for power. . . .They may be so deceptive that even their dreams are not direct, they are indirect. A psychoanalyst is needed to interpret them.

This is, according to the Mandukya Upanishad and according to all the Buddhas, the second state—closer to reality, remember. Sigmund Freud is not the discoverer of the fact. Waking, *your* waking, is the farthest from the real; dreaming is a little closer.

> *Here the attention dwells within,*
> *charmed by the mind's subtler creations.*

> *The third is deep sleep . . .*

which is even closer, the closest.

> *the mind rests, with awareness suspended.*

The first mind is focused outwards; it is the state of extroversion. In the second, the mind is focused inwards; it is the state of introversion. But in both cases the mind is functioning—in one with the objective reality, in the other with the subjective reality. In the third, the mind rests; it is non-functioning.

That's why Patanjali has said that dreamless sleep is closest to *samadhi*, with only one simple difference: if you can add awareness to your dreamless sleep you will become awakened, you will achieve *samadhi*.

> *The third is deep sleep,*
> *the mind rests, with awareness suspended.*

Only one thing is missing, otherwise the whole situation is ready. Just a little awakening, a little awareness, and your whole life will be transformed. Dreamless sleep is the sleep that nourishes your body, that gives you a taste of rest. If in the night you have been dreaming continuously, in the morning you will feel utterly exhausted and tired. If you had at least a few moments of dreamless sleep you will wake up totally refreshed, and in the morning you will say, "I had a beautiful sleep. It was so blissful!"—but in the morning, because at the very moment when deep sleep was happening you were not aware at all, you were totally unconscious.

So the third state, which is the closest, is a negative kind of *samadhi*. It is emptiness. Mind is no more functioning and the soul has not yet started functioning. It is called by the Upanishads 'the twilight zone': the evening or the morning when the one state is gone and the other has not come in, just the boundary line. You touch it every night; every healthy person touches it every night. If you don't touch it you go crazy, you go mad.

> *This state beyond duality,*
> *—from which the waves of thinking emerge,*
> *is enjoyed by the enlightened as an ocean of*
> *silence and bliss.*

Ordinarily you are not aware of it, but if you are enlightened then you will experience it as *an ocean of silence and bliss.*

The fourth—turiya—say the wise, is the pure Self alone.

The pure is simply awareness.

> *Dwelling in the heart of all,*
> *it is the lord of all,*
> *the seer of all,*
> *the source and goal of all.*

We have to reach the fourth. One who achieves the fourth has become fulfilled. His spring has come, his lotus has opened. He becomes a Buddha, a Christ.

Discourse 6

December 16, 1980

YOU TRANSCEND DUALITY

The first question

Bhagwan: Again you invite us
to shout the truth from the housetops.
Yes, since I am here,
creativity is becoming more intense and vast,
and my song is becoming more and more full
of colors and dance and grace.
But on the other side an empty space, a cool silence
is calling me more and more gently,
more and more seducing,
more and more scary, because
in this silence
all the colors of my creativity fade away.
The dance loses its passion. The song breaks.
The words fall from my hands,
and there I am sadly, empty-handed,
with no song to sing any more.
What am I going to shout from the housetops?
Sarjano

IT IS ONE OF THE MOST significant problems, almost perennial. In every time, in every country, in every mystery school, the meditators have faced it. If one becomes ecstatic, blissful, one loses silence, because ecstasy, after all, is a beautiful kind of excitement. It is a disturbance—lovely, but a disturbance all the same.

Blissfulness brings its own chaos, its own turmoil, its laughter, its tears, its creativity, its song. And one is bound to get tired of it—it is exhausting. You cannot be ecstatic all the time. Sooner or later you would like to move to the other polarity: silence.

Ecstasy is the logical end of all that is beautiful, passionate, intense, but because it is such a peak of passion and intensity you cannot remain on that peak for long. You have to go back into the deep, dark valleys of silence to rest, to sleep, to get nourished, to be rejuvenated.

Hence the desire for silence arises, a tremendous desire for silence, and of course it feels as if you are going to lose all your creativity, all your joy. And from the peak of ecstasy, silence naturally looks empty and the very idea of moving into silence seems to be suicidal —alluring, enchanting, seducing, but suicidal too, because you will lose your song, your dance, and a sadness arises. But even if the sadness arises one has to go to silence; one has to move to the dark valleys which *look* empty, which *look* like death. Hence the fear, the scary feeling.

Those who have tried to live on the peak of ecstasy have remained only poets; they have not been able to become mystics. A few people have tried, but then they have to find a certain kind of relaxation on the peak. Hence all the poets, all the creators—painters, dancers, singers—sooner or later become attracted towards intoxicating drugs, because the excitement is too much. One has to forget it all. Either you move to the silent valley, or you can remain on the peak but fall into deep oblivion.

It is not just an accident that since the very ancient days of the *Rig Veda* the poets have always been interested in some kind of psychedelic drugs. In the *Rig Veda* it was *soma*, now it is LSD or marijuana; all kinds of drugs have been used by creative people. The logical reason is that nobody can live continuously in excitement—it will kill you. If you don't want to move into silence, then the only way to avoid the constant, passionate, feverish state is through some intoxicant —alcohol, opium, or whatsoever it is.

The people who have moved to the silent valley, who have lived in silence, become afraid of going to the peak of ecstasy because they start feeling that once they move to the peak of ecstasy they will lose their silence. These are the monks; the monasteries were created for these people. These people moved into hidden caves in the Himalayas and other mountains, not to come back into the world, not to relate, not to love, not to live. They lived only at the minimum so that the silence they have achieved can be preserved, but then they become cold. In the beginning it looks very cool, but soon it starts getting colder and colder. They become almost dead.

The people who live in the monasteries are dead people. If you are not creative you cannot be alive. Life can have only one meaning and that is creativity.

God is ultimate life, hence he is the ultimate creator. If you want to live intensely, totally, fully, wholly, you have to create, you have to relate, you have to love, you have to be multi-dimensional. In a monastery people live a one-dimensional, flat kind of life. Of course there is no excitement, hence they are not tired, but because they are just sitting there without any songs arising in them, without any spring ever visiting them, they become deserts, empty deserts.

This has been one of the most significant problems for all the meditators: either you choose silence, but then you become dead, cold, unloving, hard, frozen, or if you choose creativity, you live an intense life, passionate, but very tiring.

My effort, Sarjano, is to bring these two polarities into your life together. If you ask me to define meditation, I would define it as the art, the alchemy of transforming the polar opposites into complementaries. There is no need to choose. One should be liquid, fluid, flexible, to move from one pole to the other, knowing that they are supportive to each other, they are not against each other; they are not enemies, they are friends. Just as electricity cannot exist without the positive and the negative poles, just as the day cannot exist without the night, just as life cannot exist without death, creativity cannot exist without silence. And vice versa is also true: silence cannot exist without creativity.

And my own experience and observation is this: that a life which has both is *really* a whole life, and I don't see any *real* problem except the old conditioning of centuries. Thousands of years of programming has made the division, otherwise there is no division.

Just as you come out of your house when it starts getting too cold inside, out into the sun, or when it becomes too hot outside you move inside into the cool shade . . . is there any opposition between the two? Do you need great effort to synthesize this coming out of the room and going back into the room? There is no question at all—you can simply walk in and out. It is your own house, it is your own garden! And the same feet and the same walk takes you out and in, only your direction is different. Sometimes you are facing inwards, sometimes you are facing outwards.

And one thing to be remembered: when you are capable of moving easily from the inner to the outer and from the outer to the inner you transcend duality, you are no more caught in duality.

That's the whole message of the Mandukya Upanishad: transcendence of duality. And the transcendence cannot happen by choosing one of the two; that is not transcendence, that will be clinging.

Sarjano, you say:

> *Again you invite us*
> *to shout the truth from the housetops.*

Again and again I will do it, because I would like your silence to be a singing silence. Remember, even the silence has a song of its own. It may not be *your* song—let me emphasize: it may not be *your* song, in fact it cannot be your song—the silence has its own song. You may lose *your* song; it *has* to be lost, only then can the silence sing.

What you are feeling as creativity, passionate and intense, is still adulterated with your ego. That's why silence looks empty, because in silence there will be no ego.

You say:

> *On the other side an empty space, a cool silence*
> *is calling me more and more gently,*
> *more and more seducing,*
> *more and more scary, because*
> *in this silence*
> *all the colors of my creativity fade away . . .*

Creativity will *not* fade away—*your* creativity *may* fade away, and they are totally different phenomena. In fact, *your* creativity is not of much value. When you are no more there *and* a creativity arises which you cannot claim as yours, then something real has started happening; then it is the song of the silence.

You say:

> *Since I am here,*
> *creativity is becoming more intense and vast,*
> *and my song is becoming more and more full*
> *of colors and dance and grace.*

It is still *my* song. Let it be just a song! Let it be just creativity, a dance without any dancer, a song without any singer, a creativity but without any creator. Then things are very simple. You can move from the peak of creativity easily, gracefully, into silence, and you will enjoy it and it will not be empty. It will be overflowing, it will be pregnant, not empty, because it will *nourish* you; it will nourish your sources of creativity.

Your songs will be born in your silence; they may not be *expressed* in your silence, but they will be born in your silence. And when the creative phase comes —which automatically comes, just as the day follows the night and the night is followed by the day . . . it will come. There is a balance: half the time you will be silent and half the time you will be creative. When the creativity comes you will know these songs were sown in your silence, your silence was pregnant with them.

For nine months the child is in the mother's womb; the womb is not empty. Of course you can't see the child, but the child is growing. In fact, it is better that nobody can see the child, because seeing the child may hinder its growth; it may be a deep interference.

Hence all things grow in darkness. Roots grow in darkness, seeds grow in darkness, children grow in darkness. In fact, everything grows in darkness, underground, hidden; nobody can see it, it is not visible, nobody even knows what is growing underneath the ground. And then one day suddenly the sprouts are there, but they were prepared by the silence. And the spring comes and there are flowers, but they were prepared by the phase that preceded it. One day the child is born—if the womb is empty, from where can the child come?

So don't call the silence empty. It looks empty to you, Sarjano, because of a lingering shadow of the ego. It is dying, but dying very slowly. That too is perfectly okay!—there is no hurry. And if you do it in a hurry it may come back. In a hurry it will be only patchwork. In a hurry you may hide it somewhere but sooner or later it will find its way back again—if not from the front door, then from the back door; in some subtle way it may come in. It is better to let it die slowly, with deep understanding, so nothing is left of it.

It is because of the ego that the silence seems to be empty. It is because of the ego that you feel that *all the* colors of my creativity fade away. Once the ego is gone, it will be the same scene but your interpretation will be different. Then you will not say *all the colors fade away.* You will say: all the colors mingle and merge into one color, and that is white. Then you will see the beauty of whiteness.

White is not a color, it is the synthesis of all the colors. It represents purity, innocence, egolessness. You will see it as tremendous whiteness, snow-white, and you will be able to decipher all the colors in it—of course now in a latent form, a silent form, sleeping, resting. When all the colors rest in the womb of existence they become white. They don't fade away, they only go to rest. It is seed-time.

Every tree comes out of a seed and one day disappears again into seeds. It will come back—those seeds are carrying the whole program. All the leaves—their structure, their pattern, their gestalt—all the branches, all the flowers, are hidden in the seeds, small seeds. But to see into the seed you need tremendous clarity, and the ego does not allow that clarity. Ego is contaminating, polluting your vision.

You say:

The dance loses its passion.

When the ego is gone you will not see it in that way. You will see the dance loses the *dancer*, not its passion. And when there is no dancer, the passion is not tiring, the passion is no longer exhausting. It has intensity, but now the fire no longer burns—it only gives light. It is the *same* fire, but now it gives light.

You say:

The song breaks.

It is not the song that is breaking, it is the ego. But because the ego is identified with the song, when the ego breaks you feel the song is breaking.

I can say to you from my own experience—and I have all the Buddhas of the past supporting me—the song has never broken. Buddha became enlightened and for forty-two years he was singing; for forty-two years his each gesture was a song, his silence was a song, his words were songs. Whether he said something or not, the song continued. The song is not breaking.

You say:

> *The words fall from my hands,*
> *and there I am sadly, empty-handed,*
> *with no song to sing anymore.*

No, your interpretation is wrong, Sarjano. You feel sad because the ego is disappearing and that has been your joy up to now. The only joy that people know is the joy of ego succeeding. Now the ego is by and by withering away and you feel sad, empty-handed, because your hands were full of the ego.

Once you have understood it you will not see your hands as empty, in fact you will see them having the whole space of the sky available—*sky* in your hands, not emptiness. You will see it as spaciousness, not emptiness.

I have always lived in empty rooms—no furniture, just the bare necessities, one chair, not even another chair for a visitor because nobody comes to visit. And I have always watched: whenever somebody came to see, either they said the room was empty or they said the room was spacious—but very rarely. Out of a hundred persons only one person would say, "The room is very spacious. I love it!"

The English word 'room' simply means spacious, roomy; it does not mean empty. So I have the biggest room in the world, the most roomy room—just space, nothing to hinder, the whole sky available. Only once in a while has somebody said, "It is spacious," and that man had a certain understanding; otherwise they say 'empty'. And both are right according to their vision.

But you have to understand, Sarjano, it is not empty, and it is not that you have no song to sing any more, it is only that your 'I' is disappearing. *You* are disappearing, not the song! And believe me, when you are completely gone, then only does the song arrive. Then it is divine.

We have called it in India, *Bhagavad Gita*—'the song celestial'. Then God sings through you, you are just a hollow bamboo flute.

The second question

*Bhagwan: I am coming across some conditioning
that often makes me feel tense and frustrated.
It is perfection, hurry, effort, et cetera.
Is this a special German conditioning? I am German!*
Dhyan Gyanam

CONDITIONING AS SUCH is always German, more or less, because conditioning means the desire of your parents, of your society, of your state, of the past, to make you perfect. And once the seed, the ambition to be perfect enters into you, you cannot remain sane.

Perfectionism is neurosis. Of course, Germans are far ahead of others—they are the epitome of perfectionism—but everybody has the same kind of desire. *All* parents have failed, and because of their failure they load their children with the desire to be perfect. They have not been able to be perfect; now they want to live a vicarious life through their children. They don't love the children—if they love them they will not condition them. That will be the only sign of their love. If you love somebody you cannot condition the person.

If your parents love you, the first thing that they will never do is to load you with their own ambitions. But they have been loaded by their parents and they have tried to live according to those desires—the desires of their dead parents—and they have failed. Now they think maybe there was not enough time, maybe circumstances did not allow: "Perhaps what has not been possible in my life may be possible in the life of my children." So they live through their children.

Conditioning means they know they have to die, but still they can live in a subtle way through the children. It is a desire for immortality. They know their bodies are going to die, that's why there is so much obsession for children. "And the child has to be *mine*, not anybody else's, so that a part of me, a cell of me, a seed of me, will be living. I will *not* be there, but at least something of me will go on living."

Hence all the societies have insisted on the virginity of women at least, to make certain that the child is yours, not somebody else's. Why this obsession? In a better world, in a more understanding and human world, if the father feels that he can find a better man and a better seed for his children, then certainly he will go for the best. If he is crippled and if he is carrying some disease, hereditary, it will be a sign of love not to give that disease to the child. It is better to find somebody who can give *his* child a better body, better health, longer life, more intelligence.

And that is possible, now it is very easily possible. Just as we donate blood, each genius dying can donate all his semen cells; they can be preserved. Albert Einstein can be preserved. He donated his head—that is stupid. He should have donated his semen cells, because then millions of children could have had the same capacity as Albert Einstein. People who love will find the best. And the same is true about the mother: there is no necessity for the mother to give birth to the child only through *her* womb; it can happen in a scientific lab.

We can create a totally different kind of humanity once these old, idiotic obsessions are dropped. These are all egoistic obsessions. But not only do we give our bodies to the children, we insist on giving our minds too. That's what conditioning is all about: trying to give your mind to your children.

Never give your mind to your children! You have lived it and you know its misery, still you insist on giving it to your children. You have been a Catholic, a Protestant, a Hindu, a Mohammedan—what have you achieved? Where are you? What is your meaning, significance? What poetry has arisen in your being? And still you are insisting on giving the same rotten pattern to your child? You are the enemy of the child, not a lover. You don't love! If you love, you cannot give your ideas to the child. You will insist, "Remember, avoid at least these ideas that I have lived. Do whatsoever else you want to do—just don't be a Christian, don't be a Hindu, don't be a communist. I have been, and this way of life at least is absolutely meaningless. So avoid this."

Each mother, each father should make the child aware that they have tried a certain pattern of life and it has failed. "So don't make the same mistake again. Try some other door, try some other way, explore on your own." But this has not happened yet, that's why humanity is living in such misery and hell.

Gyanam, perfection is bound to bring hurry because life is short, and perfectionism means you have to do thousands of things quickly, otherwise who knows? You may be incomplete before death comes. And particularly in the Western societies where religions have insisted on only one life, there is more hurry. In the East people are not in such a hurry for the simple reason that they believe that there are many lives, so what is the hurry for? There is no need, one can wait.

That's why the East is lazy: it has a psychological reasoning for its laziness. And the West is speedy: "Be quick, because there is only one life, and if you are not complete in this life then there is no other opportunity. No chances are given, no choices are given—only *this* life." Naturally hurry arises and effort. You have to make tremendous efforts to be perfect.

And in this whole rush for perfectionism you are not a gainer, you become a loser. There is no time to think, there is no time to be silent, there is no time to feel, there is no time to love. All is devoted to one goal: how to be a perfect man, a superman.

It is not an accident that Friedrich Nietzsche was born in Germany. He talked about the superman, and Adolf Hitler believed that he was the superman about whom Friedrich Nietzsche was talking. Adolf Hitler is not even human—he is sub-human, below humanity, but he thinks that he is super-human. And he was trying to create a race of super-human beings. He brought the whole German ideology of perfectionism to its logical end. And you *are* conditioned, whether you know it or not, by that fascist, Nazi idea.

With me you have to relax. With me you have to drop your being a German or being an Indian or being an Italian. Whatsoever you are you have to drop it. You have to be just silent, blissful. You have to be just human—there is no need to be super-human.

An Englishman thinks seated, a Frenchman standing, an American pacing, and a German afterwards.

There is no time, so it is always afterwards.

It was a tough spot and bullets flew from all sides. The tough German sergeant was not going to allow his men to retreat. "Stay here!" he shouted. "And keep firing, even if you run out of ammunition!"

Wolfgang, the blacksmith, came in with a badly damaged foot. The doctor was surprised, for Wolfgang was a careful man. "What happened to you, Wolfgang?" he asked.

"Well, thirty-three years ago I was a young apprentice to an old blacksmith."

"But what about your foot?"

"This is about my foot. The old man had a daughter and your eyes could gaze on her like the way a bullock would eat good grass. The first night I was there she came in when I was in bed and asked if I was comfortable and if I wanted anything, and I said I didn't. The next night when I was in bed she came in wearing her nightdress and she asked me if there was any single thing she could get me or do for me, and I told her I was as comfortable as a bug in a rug. The next night she came in and the girl had not a thing on her, and she asked me if she could do anything for me, and, not wanting to keep her standing in the cold, and she without a shift, I said there was nothing."

"What has that got to do with your foot, Wolfgang?" asked the doctor impatiently.

"Well, it was only this morning that I finally thought of what she meant, and I was so annoyed with myself that I threw my ten-pound hammer against the wall, and it rebounded and broke my ankle!"

Gyanam, now being a sannyasin, drop being German. Enough of it! You have suffered long, your parents suffered and their parents; it is time to stop this suffering. Relax a little bit—there is no need to be perfect. If God wanted you perfect he would have created you perfect! He has created you so beautifully imperfect. It is so clear—he never creates a perfect man, he always creates imperfect people, because only imperfect people can grow. The perfect man will be dead from his very birth, because there will be nothing to do; there will be no *possibility* of growing.

Growth is possible because of imperfection, and growth is the whole joy of life; it is the only ecstasy there is. And God goes on creating imperfect children, but we don't listen, we don't see that God loves imperfect people. And there is no end to growth, so in fact there is no perfection ever.

I don't call Buddha a perfect man or Jesus a perfect man or Krishna a perfect man. I call them *whole* men, but not perfect. They were total but not perfect—and remember the difference between these two words.

My sannyasins have to learn how to be total—total in each act, passionately in it, intensely in it, utterly involved, not holding back. That's what totality is. If you are dancing you are dancing; then the whole world disappears. Even *you* are not there, only the dance remains. That is totality. The dance may be perfect, may not be perfect, that is irrelevant. It can always be improved so it cannot be perfect. Everything can be improved so it cannot be perfect.

A Zen story is:

A king was learning gardening from a Zen Master. The Master was teaching him and telling him to go on creating a garden in his palace. After three years he would come to see the garden, and if it was total, then he would have passed the examination.

But the king misunderstood the word 'total'—and we all misunderstand it. He thought total meant perfect, so he made the garden perfect. He had thousands of gardeners to work upon it, and it was really the most perfect thing that had ever happened in Japan.

After three years the Master came, and the king was very happy and very satisfied with the garden. But the Master looked very serious and sad—and he was not a serious man at all. The king started feeling afraid—was he going to fail? Three years' effort, and the garden was so perfect you could not improve upon it. And the silence of the Master was getting heavier on him.

Finally he asked, "What is the matter? Why are you not saying a single word? Don't you like the garden?"

The Master said, "It is too perfect, hence it gives the feeling of artificialness. In nature nothing is so perfect. It is so perfect that it cannot be improved upon, that's why I am looking so sad. And I had told you, 'Let it be total,' but you misunderstood me. I don't see even a single dry, dead leaf in the whole garden! How is it possible?"

The king said, "We have removed all the dead leaves —there were many. Just to receive you we have removed them all!"

The Master said, "Give me a bucket!"

A bucket was given. He went out of the garden where the leaves had been thrown. He collected a bucketful of dry leaves, came in, and threw them on the path. And the wind started playing with the leaves . . . and the sound and the song of the leaves. He started smiling and he said, "Now it is perfectly okay! It is no longer perfect, hence it is perfectly okay! Now it looks more natural. Without these leaves there was no song, it was dead."

Be total, don't bother to be perfect. But this misunderstanding is one of the ancient ones.

The German missionary was preaching to the African tribe: "And I tell you that you must love your fellowmen."

"Moolagumbi!" shrieked the natives.

"White men and black men must learn to cooperate."
"Moolagumbi!" chanted the crowd.
The missionary was very pleased and he told the chief how pleased he was with the reception.
"I am glad, O man of Germany," said the chief, "but be careful as we pass my cattle that you do not step into the moolagumbi!"

All perfectionism is nothing but moolagumbi!

The last question

Bhagwan: What is enlightenment?
Prem Geetesh

SCREWING IN a lightbulb successfully!

Discourse 7

December 17, 1980

SPIRITUALITY IS
THE ULTIMATE IN LUXURY

The first question

*Bhagwan: In one of your lectures on socialism,
answering Sarjano's question,
you indicated that the proletariat were 'the lowest'.
Is this contradictory to Christ's
teachings on the poor as
being the children of God
and the rich as being 'the lowest'?
During years of rural development work
with poor peasants in Latin America, I found them
to be 'higher' spiritually than the rich landlords.*
Gerrit Huiser

THE OLD RELIGIONS ALL OVER THE WORLD have been consoling the poor in different ways. The same is being done by Jesus Christ too. Calling the poor the children of God is nothing but poison. Then Karl Marx is right—that religion is the opium of the people.

If it is true that the poor are the children of God, then we should not try to destroy poverty—otherwise we will be destroying the children of God. That will be very irreligious, unspiritual! In fact, we should destroy all richness in the world so everybody becomes a child of God. If spirituality is so simple, then why bother about improving the lot of the people, trying to make them richer, trying to make them more comfortable, giving them better technology, industry, food? This is all against religion! This is all against Jesus Christ!

Mahatma Gandhi used to call the poor *daridra narayan;* he went even one step further than Jesus Christ: the poor are not only the children of God, they are gods. This is a strategy: because your so-called religious people have not been able to find a way to solve the problem of poverty, they try to rationalize it.

And the best way to console people is to tell them, "The rich are lower than you—you are higher!" This satisfies the ego.

Jesus says: Blessed are the poor, for theirs is the kingdom of God. This is also one of the tricks of all the religions in the world: promise the poor a beautiful future—*after* death. Nobody ever returns, nobody ever tells what actually is the case after death, so it cannot be refuted at all. You will be received, welcomed in the kingdom of God, and the rich, they will suffer in hell.

It satisfies the poor tremendously, the very idea of the rich suffering in hellfire and the poor being welcomed by St. Peter at the pearly gates of heaven. So this life is not such a big problem, a question of only a few years. One can manage, one can tolerate, one can remain satisfied. One can hope that "Sooner or later, on the Judgement Day, everything will be settled. And because we are poor, ours is going to be the kingdom of God."

This is sheer nonsense. Who has said it makes no difference. Jesus may have said it, Mahatma Gandhi may have said it—I don't care a bit! My whole concern is with the truth, and this is untrue.

Poverty is not something to be praised; it is something to be condemned, totally condemned. It is like cancer: it has to be destroyed; no respect should be given to it, because that is nourishment. It should not be praised in any direct or indirect way, because that is how it has been prolonged in the past.

And you can't see the contradiction: on the one hand these people go on saying that poverty is something beautiful; on the other hand they are all trying to make people richer. The contradiction is in *them*. Why try to make these poor people more rich? Make them more poor so they will be closer to God. Take even what they have got! Deprive them of everything! Then their welcome will be far greater, they will be received more joyously.

And what is the implication of it all? It means God enjoys poverty, it means he wants people to be poor. It simply means that he is against riches, comforts, luxuries. Then why this paradise?—because paradise is nothing but comforts, riches, luxuries. A strange logic! On the earth people should suffer so that in heaven they can be rewarded. First make people ill so that they can be hospitalized and served; first wound them and then help to heal their wounds. This is ridiculous!

My arithmetic is very clear: poverty is ugly and it has to be destroyed totally. No trace of it should be left on the earth, and all these consolations should be withdrawn. I can understand why in the past the religious people could not say what I can say today. The simple reason was that scientific technology was not available; there was no way to destroy poverty. And when you cannot do anything, at least you can sympathize; it costs nothing to be sympathetic. At least you can console; it is better than nothing. And all these words of Jesus and Mahatma Gandhi and others are devices to console, to give opium to people.

In India it has been a long tradition; different ways have been discovered to rationalize poverty. The first was: the poor person is suffering because in the past he has committed some wrong actions. The past is made responsible—not the society, not the present, not the structure of the society, not the lack of technology, not the stupidity of the people, but the past. Nothing can be done about the past, you cannot undo it; it has to be accepted. And great hope is given with it: "If you accept it, if you are totally satisfied with it, you will be immensely rewarded in the future life."

Do you see the trick? The past and the future are made important. Nothing can be done about the past life and you don't know anything about the future life. The past is no more, the future is not yet, and people are being diverted from the present to the past which is no more and to the future which is not yet. These are very cunning tricks. And the problem is in the present—it has to be solved herenow.

You ask me, Gerrit Huiser:

*Is this contradictory to Christ's
teachings on the poor as
being the children of God
and the rich as being 'the lowest'?*

Yes, it is contradictory—it is absolutely contradictory. Jesus is wrong! And I don't consider the rich to be the lowest and I don't consider the poor to be the highest. If the poor are the highest then the problem is very simple: richness can be destroyed very easily. There is no problem at all.

You say to me:

During years of rural development . . .

What were you doing in rural development? Making people poor?—because if the poor are higher, then development means make them poorer! Gerrit Huiser, what were you doing there in Latin America? Aren't the people poor enough? not yet children of God? so you had gone there to make them absolutely poor?—because according to you, that will be development, progress, evolution!

You say:

*During years of rural development work
with poor peasants in Latin America, I found them
to be higher spiritually than the rich landlords.*

Do you know what spirituality is? Have you experienced anything of spirituality *yourself*? What criterion have you got to judge who is spiritually higher and who is spiritually lower? What do you mean by spirituality? According to you to be poor is to be spiritual because Jesus says the poor are the children of God, so naturally you found the poor to be higher spiritually—you must be a believer in Jesus Christ—than the rich landlords.

But my own understanding is totally different. Spirituality is the highest need—there is a hierarchy of needs. The first plane of needs is physical. The poor person remains tethered to the physical: he is hungry, he is ill, he does not have any shelter, not enough clothes. He cannot think of Beethoven, Mozart, Wagner; he cannot think of great poetry—Kalidas, Shakespeare, Dante; he cannot think of great novelists and novels—Dostoevsky, Tolstoy, Chekhov. There is no possibility—he is hungry. What is he going to do with *Brothers Karamazov*? He needs bread, butter, not *Brothers Karamazov*! He needs a shelter from the rain, from the hot sun; he does not need music. What will he do with music? Can you make a shelter out of music? Can you make clothes out of beautiful paintings? And he is so hungry he cannot be sensitive to any higher thing. He is tethered to the body, to the lowest part of his being.

When physical needs are fulfilled, then psychological needs arise—they are higher needs. Then there is a search for music, poetry, art, sculpture, architecture, gardening. These are higher needs, but with each higher need higher problems arise. Hence I welcome higher problems.

For example, in India nobody asks, "What is the meaning of life?" because that is a higher problem—the meaning of life. In the West you are concerned with the meaning of life, not in the East. It *cannot* arise—there is no background for it. People are so poor, how can they think of any meaning, any significance? The question is how to feed their children, the question is how to survive. *Survival* is the question! When you have survived and you are completely at ease in life, *then* you ask, "What is the meaning of life? Is survival enough?" But that question arises only when you have *managed* to survive.

Higher problems arise with higher needs. Then withhigher problems you have new kinds of troubles, buttheir plane is higher. Psychoanalysis is not needed in the East at all; Sigmund Freud or Carl Gustav Jung or Adler and others have no relevance. And the Indian religious mahatmas go on bragging about it: "Look, our country is so peaceful!" It is not peaceful, it is simply dead! It is the peace of the cemetery, it is *not* peacefulness. They say, "Look, our people are so contented!" They are *not* contented. The discontent has not arisen, because to be discontented with life first you have to manage to survive. They are struggling for survival, so there is no question of psychoanalysis.

But the so-called mahatmas who go on teaching in the West, saying to people in America and Europe, "India is a great spiritual country. People are so satisfied, so contented," are simply lying—maybe not knowingly, maybe they also believe that this is so. Certainly more people go mad in the West than in the East, because the West can afford it. Madness is a *higher* problem; hunger is a *lower* problem. A hungry person cannot go mad—it is impossible. When you are hungry, can you afford to be mad? Keep the madman hungry for three weeks and you will see that he has become sane! He will start talking sense. He will come down from the clouds to the earth.

The hungry person remains closer to the earth, rooted in the earth. When you are satisfied with the earthly plane you start having wings, and of course then there are new dangers. When you start flying then you will have to face new problems, new dangers, new crises. Madness belongs to the psychological realm, not to the physical.

More people commit suicide in the West than in the East, and I take it as a sign of growth—because when you are perfectly okay on the physiological plane, the question starts haunting you: "Why go on living? For what?" The hungry man has some goals, very immediate goals. He cannot see far away; it is an everyday question how to survive. In the morning he has to think about his lunch, in the evening he has to think about his supper.

Half of the Indians eat only once a day, and the whole country is undernourished. Millions of people go to sleep with a hungry stomach. Now, do you think these people can commit suicide? They have not even been able to be alive, how can they commit suicide? First you have to be alive! Even if you want to commit suicide, that much has to be fulfilled first.

When all your physical needs are fulfilled, then suddenly a question arises, a new challenge: "Why am I trying to survive?" It is philosophical, psychological: one searches for the meaning of life. Then one can go mad, one can commit suicide, one can start being creative. Then all the doors open, good and bad. One can be either lower than the animals or can rise higher than the angels.

When all psychological needs are fulfilled—when you have learnt the most beautiful music, enjoyed poetry, art, painting, when your psychological needs are fulfilled, you are psychologically healthy—then spiritual needs arise, never before it. Spiritual needs are the most luxurious needs; they come only in the end. They are like flowers.

If a tree is undernourished it *cannot* have flowers, remember it. It will be difficult for it even to have leaves. Flowers are possible only when there is an overflowing energy, too much to contain. Then the tree bursts forth into thousands of flowers, color and fragrance—but it is luxury! A tree in bloom is a picture of luxury, because flowers don't serve any purpose; they are just a luxury, sheer joy. The tree is enjoying its being, celebrating itself.

Walt Whitman says, "I celebrate myself." That is the ultimate in luxury, when one starts celebrating oneself. A sheer joy of being!

Then, after psychological needs are fulfilled, the question of meditation, prayer, spirituality, the search for the ultimate source and goal of life, the inquiry into consciousness and its ultimate peaks. . . .

I don't think, Gerrit Huiser, that you found in poor peasants in Latin America higher spirituality in *my* sense of the word; it is impossible. But I can understand what you really mean. You must have found them more simple than the rich landlords—that's what you are calling spirituality. You must have found them more innocent, childlike, than the rich landlords—that's what you are calling spirituality, higher spirituality.

Obviously, when there is so much poverty, only the cunning and the clever can be rich; the simple and the innocent cannot be rich. When there is so much competition, so much struggle, a certain cunningness is needed, otherwise you cannot be rich; then others will be rich who are more cunning than you.

You must have found . . . you can find it anywhere: poor people are always more simple, more innocent. But try to understand. It is not because of their poverty that they are simple and innocent: they are poor *because* they are simple and innocent; it is not the quality of poverty. They are simple and innocent—simple in the sense of simpletons, innocent because they are not intelligent. Their innocence, their simplicity is not a great achievement; it is just like every small child.

Every child is innocent, but that is not much to brag about; it is a natural phenomenon. And every child will have to lose it—unless he loses it he will remain a simpleton. If he loses it and goes into the ways of the world, goes astray, becomes cunning, becomes clever, cheats, does everything that is needed in this competitive life, and one day finds it all futile and drops it and again becomes simple—that is spirituality. That is a totally different phenomenon.

The sage is innocent because he has found that cunningness is futile, and the child is innocent because he has not yet found that cunningness is the way of the world. The child is simply *ignorant*—don't call his ignorance 'innocence'—and the sage *is* innocent, he is no more ignorant. He knows all the worldly ways, but he has found that they are not worth bothering about.

Two little girls were talking about religious knowledge. "I'm past Original Sin!" boasted the first one.

"That's nothing," answered the other. "I'm beyond Redemption!"

One day the teacher asked her pupils to write an essay covering three topics: religion, sex and royalty.

Two minutes later little Johnny handed his essay to the teacher. He had written, "And the queen said, 'Oh, my God, it is good!'"

The farmer showed the city laborer how to milk the cows, and sent him into the fields. "How many did you milk?" he asked when the laborer came back.

"Twenty, but there's one thing. . . ."

"What is that?"

"I think you should have given me a bucket!"

Angus decided to keep a few hives on his farm, and the first year Owen was curious to know how he got on. "Had you any luck with the bees, Angus?" he asked.

"The best, the best!" Angus chuckled.

"You got a lot of honey?"

"Not a drop, but they stung the mother-in-law seven times!"

The motorist was honest and when he hit the cock wandering on the road he stopped and went back to the cottage. "I'm afraid I killed your cock, madam, but I would very much like to replace him."

"Whatever you want," said the old woman. "Go around the side there and you'll find the hens in the back."

Yes, the poor people *are* simple, but that does not mean they are spiritual! Don't misunderstand their simplicity. And you are right that the rich landlords are *not* simple—they cannot be, otherwise they would have been poor themselves, they would have been children of God themselves. If they are not clever they cannot remain rich. Their parents must have been clever and their parents' parents must have been clever, *and* they must have been clever to choose clever parents. From the very beginning you have to be very alert to avoid the children of God! If you choose children of God you are lost!

For example, Gerrit Huiser: he is a professor of third world studies, Catholic University, Holland. I don't think you have chosen for your parents children of God, otherwise you would have been milking cows —without a bucket!

A rich and aged Jew woke up in the middle of the night. He turned over and touched his wife lying beside him. He was surprised to find she was cold, much colder than usual. Puzzled, he switched on the light and found that she was dead. He sighed, turned off the light, and said to himself, "Oh, dear me! I'm going to be a very sad man, tomorrow morning!"

A rich but very miserly Jew from New York was driving on the road in his rusty old Volkswagen. He was dreaming about better lifestyles when suddenly a beautiful new car passed him. The car was going very fast, and just after passing him it lost control and crashed into a tree.

The Jew in the old car slammed on his brakes, pushing his feet through the floor in his exuberance. The beautiful car was completely destroyed; the driver was scratched and bruised but alive.

The Jew helped him out of the wreck and asked, "Are you in pain?"

"A little," replied the victim.

"Do you think you can wait for help?"

"Yes, I think so," groaned the man.

"Do you have accident insurance?"

"Yes, I do."

"Is it with a good company?"

"Of course!" snapped the wounded man.

"Do they pay the full amount in the correct time?" asked the Jew excitedly.

"Always."

"Well," concluded the Jew, "can I just lie by your side?"

A young Jew, dressed in a suit and carrying a briefcase, walked up to the front door of a little house in a quiet neighborhood. He knocked loudly on the door and called out, "Burglar!"

After some time an old lady appeared at the door. "Who is it?" she croaked.

"Burglar, madam," came the reply.

"You're not selling anything, young man?"

"I'm here to steal everything you've got," replied the young man politely. "May I come in?"

"Hm, well, are ya sure you're no encyclopaedia salesman?"

"Madam, please accept my card. I am indeed a burglar!"

The Jew entered the house with the old lady and proceeded to collect anything of value he could find. He cleared out the living room of all its artwork and trinkets, found cash in the bedroom drawers, took crystal glasses, candlesticks, jewelry. . . .Finally, when there was nothing else of value left to take, he turned to the old lady and said, "Er . . . by the way, madam, while I'm here, can I interest you in our new range of children's encyclopaedias?"

The cunning and the clever are bound to become rich, but that is the only way to reach real simplicity. Unless you have been cunning, unless you have been clever, you cannot reach the status of a sage.

It is not an accident that in India all the twenty-four *teerthankaras* of the Jainas, the twenty-four great Masters, were princes, and all the *avataras* of the Hindus were kings, and Buddha's twenty-three previous incarnations were all in royal families. That's why there is a tremendous difference between Jesus' teaching and Buddha's teaching. Buddha's teaching soars really high like an Everest. The Upanishadic seers were rich people; that's why the Upanishadic statements have a beauty and a deep aesthetic sense about them.

Jesus was the son of a poor man, a carpenter. His words don't have *that* flavor which the words of Mahavira, Yagnavalka, Patanjali, Buddha and Lao Tzu have. These people have a totally different height and a multi-dimensionality. Jesus' words are simple, as simple as a poor man's can be. Of course they have a certain straightforwardness, but they are not like Everest; compared to Buddha's words they are just molehills.

And you can see that—that only poor people of the world are becoming interested in Jesus' words. In India the people who are converted to Christianity are the poorest people. Christian missionaries have not been able to convert a single rich Indian to Christianity—all the poor people are converted.

And the other extreme is also happening: the West is turning Buddhist. The intelligentsia of the West, of the rich countries, is becoming more interested in Zen, in Tao, in Yoga, and the poor people of the East are becoming more interested in Jesus. It is not just an accident; there is some hidden reason behind it. The poor people in the East are now finding a consolation in Jesus' words, and the rich people of the West are finding insights in the words of Buddha and Lao Tzu, Chuang Tzu, Bokuju, Rinzai. The height is appealing. Jesus seems to be plain—beautiful words but with no sophistication.

Why is the East turning closer to Jesus and the West turning closer to Buddha? And one should also take note of the fact that socialism is a by-product of Christianity; it has not happened in Hinduism, it has not happened in Buddhism, it has not happened in Jainism, it has not happened in Taoism. Christianity has given birth to the idea of socialism, because basically Christianity has been a consolation for the poor. Socialism is now the ultimate consolation for the poor. Socialism does not make them rich, it simply destroys the rich people, but then the poor feel happy because there is no comparison left.

The poor of America are in a far better situation than the people of the so-called communist countries, but the poor of America are not happy. Even the poor people of

America have cars and television sets, and in Russia even the big communist bosses do not have such beautiful cars and television sets and radios. But Russians seem to be more contented than the Americans—for the simple reason that the comparison is no more there—the rich have disappeared. Poverty has been distributed. That's what socialism is all about: distribution of poverty, *equal* distribution of poverty.

When all are equally poor you don't feel discontented. Discontent arises only when you see a few people becoming richer. You may also be becoming richer-with those few people, but that is not the point: the distance between you and the rich hurts.

Socialism is the ultimate consolation for the poor. If religions have provided opium for the poor, then socialism provides LSD for the poor!

Gerrit Huiser, my own approach is this: let people become rich. And the way to make them rich is not socialism; the way to make them rich is to introduce more technology, more industry, more science. And capitalism is the only form of society which knows how to create wealth.

Sixty years of socialism in Russia have not done much—people are still poor. And once a person from Russia goes to America he does not want to come back. People go to participate in the Olympics and they don't want to return, they escape. And Russians are not allowed to go outside the country, simply so they can remain in ignorance about what is happening in the world. Russia is now the dark continent; nobody knows what is happening in the world. It is better to keep them ignorant. If they become alert about what is happening in the world, then they will suddenly become aware of their poverty. They have to be stopped from knowing about other countries.

Capitalism is a form of society which knows how to produce wealth. We have to use capitalism more; we have to introduce the same wealth-creating procedures everywhere. Make the people rich! One day, when there is so much wealth in the world—just as there is free air—when there is too much wealth in the world, nobody will want to possess it. People want to possess things only when they are in scarcity; when the scarcity disappears, possessiveness disappears.

The world has to become as rich as possible, only then will the explosion happen—the explosion I call spirituality. I don't mean the peasant-like simplicity; that's why I called the proletariat the lowest. They *are* the lowest because they are living undernourished lives, they are living very deeply rooted in the body; even their bodies are not satisfied. And to talk about spirituality to those people who are hungry is absurd. Even if these hungry people go to the temples and the mosques and the synagogues and the churches they are not going for spiritual reasons, they are going to ask for something from God.

I have been receiving hundreds of letters from South Africa, and they all think they are inquiring about something very spiritual. And all those letters are basically the same. They are asking me: can I help them to be healthier, to be richer, to be more successful? Can I give them a mantra, a talisman, or something magical? They think they are asking for some spiritual guidance —they are asking for worldly things. And it is not only so in South Africa—the same is the situation in India.

When I receive letters from Indian so-called seekers it is *never* about meditation, it is *never* about the inner inquiry; it is always about poverty, unemployment. Their daughters and sons are unemployed, unmarried; they need my blessings. And they think this is something spiritual! They ask because their wives are ill and they can't afford any other treatment—"So please bless us." They write to me about retarded children, paralyzed children; they have to be blessed.

It is very rare that any Indian asks about real, authentic spirituality, but I can understand—they cannot ask. What they are asking is inevitable; that's what they go on asking in their prayers. They go to the temples, they go to the priests, in order that they can survive somehow. They are not capable of surviving on their own; they want help, some magical help from the priests, because they think the priests are directly connected to God and everything is possible through God.

These are the people who have invented all kinds of miracles; those miracles have never happened. For example, the miracle told about Jesus: that out of a single loaf of bread he fed thousands of people, that he turned the whole sea into wine, that he turned stones into bread, that he helped the ill people and cured them, that the blind came to him and he gave them eyes, and the crippled came to him and he healed them. These miracles show much about the people who have written these stories; they don't show anything about Jesus. These are their desires.

People ask me again and again, "Why are so many Westerners here and not so many Indians?" If you want to see Indians you can go to Satya Sai Baba—there you will see thousands of Indians. Here you will not see them for the simple reason that to me spirituality is the ultimate in luxury. Only those who have done everything, who have lived life in all its possibilities, can inquire about the ultimate life. Those who are still worried about their bodies and employment and money and business, they cannot come to me—I am not for them. Only the spiritual seekers will be here. And to me, the capitalist system is the only system that can transform humanity towards spirituality.

It is not illogical on the part of Karl Marx to deny religion, to say that there is no need for religion. In fact, communism will never allow people to be religious;

they will always remain so poor that they will never be fed up with life, they will remain always hoping.

The poor person always lives in hopes and desires and fantasies. It is only the rich person who starts getting tired of food, of sex, of money, of power, of prestige; he has seen it all and he has found that it is not worth wasting any more time and energy on. Suddenly he becomes aware that "What I have been doing is absolutely non-essential"—and then begins the search for the essential.

Gerrit Huiser, I don't agree with Jesus Christ. I have tried my best to agree with Jesus, with Buddha, with Patanjali, with Mahavira, with Lao Tzu. Now my new phase of work starts. I am fed up with agreeing, tired of it! So now I will simply say the truth. Enough is enough!

The second question

Bhagwan: I am a drunkard,
and today is my birthday.
Can you tell some jokes to me?
Gandharvo

A WOMAN CALLED UP her husband at the office. "Charles," she said sternly, "when you came in last night you told me that you had been to the club with Mr. Brown, but I just met Mr. Brown and he said you had been at the Trocadero Tropical Paradise. Why did you lie, Charles?"

"I didn't lie, dear," explained the husband. "I was in no condition last night to pronounce Trocadero Tropical Paradise!"

Shawn was a noted drinker in the village. At intervals he became a teetotaller and took what is known in Ireland as 'the pledge'.

"Well, Shawn," asked the curate, who was new to the place, "how long do you want to take it for?"

"It's easy to see you are new, Father. Sure, everyone knows I never take it for anything less than life."

You missed it!

Poteen is an Irish illegal brew that can burn holes in steel plates. O'Sean Flaherty, after a pint of it, saw so many animals in his room that he put a sign on his house: "Flaherty's Zoo."

The local Garda sergeant went to reason with him and was no sooner in than he was offered a glass of the Mountain Dew, as it is called. When he staggered out thirty minutes later he raised his hand for silence. "Ish all right, men, the worst is over. He shold me half the elephants!"

The Roman Catholic parish priest of a Belfast church was amazed to find two bigoted and drunken Orange Protestants outside his window at two o'clock in the morning. "What do you want?" he called.

"Well, we wanted ye to tell us if it was tha Pope that called the Ecumenical Council?"

"Look, come back in the morning and I'll discuss it when you're sober."

"Sure, when we're sober we don't give a damn about the Pope!"

The Garda watched Mulligan desperately trying to open his front door as he swayed from side to side. "Here, Mulligan," he said, "can I help you with that key?"

"Nosh at all, guard, I can manage the key if you—hic—could hold the house steady!"

They drove towards the city in a zigzag pattern. Shamus, ish we near Dublin yet?"

"Yesh, we're knocking down more people so we mush be!"

"Drive slower then!"

"Whaddaya mean, drive slower? *You* are driving!"

Discourse 8

December 18, 1980

SIMPLY GET OUT
BY THE DOOR

The first question

*Bhagwan: I am another 'development worker'
whose questions you answered
most beautifully yesterday.
For me, though, one question remains:
working to help brothers out of the molasses
seems also to keep me from flying.
Should we fly and leave them be,
and stay here in this magic place, for example?
Or should we stay on land to help?
How is a synthesis possible?*
Oscar Mann

I DON'T BELIEVE IN ANY KIND OF SYNTHESIS. Synthesis is always hotchpotch; synthesis is basically confusion. Synthesis means you are schizophrenic and somehow managing to keep yourself together. I don't trust synthesis, because then we have accepted the division and are somehow trying to bridge the division.

I believe in a single vision, not in synthesis. The single vision is liberating; it takes you beyond confusion and chaos, it creates integrity, it gives you a centering, a grounding.

Moreover, a synthesis remains intellectual, it never becomes existential. It is like trying to synthesize darkness and light: intellectually you can do it, but existentially it is impossible. If there is light there cannot be any darkness; if you want darkness then the idea of light has to be dropped.

This is the first thing to understand clearly: I am not trying to create any synthesis here; I am simply communicating, communing my single vision. It is comprehensive and multi-dimensional. It includes all, but it is not a synthesis.

For me the question is not whether to go on helping people or whether to make an effort to be blissful, to be meditative, to make your life a celebration. The question does not arise because you are starting from a wrong assumption. The assumption is that a man who is not blissful himself can be of some service to others —that is impossible. You can give to others only that which you have already got; you cannot give that which you have not got yourself. Of what help can you be to others?

A miserable person is bound to infect people with his misery; he cannot do otherwise. He can *intend* to do otherwise but he cannot really do it. That is not in the very nature of things; it is impossible. It is against the law of existence.

If you are stinking, how can you give fragrance to others? Whenever you are giving something to others you are giving yourself in some way or other; you are imparting your being, your existence, you are sharing. You are sharing your innermost space.

The so-called public servants have been the most mischievous people on the earth; they have created more misery than anybody else. If we can get rid of all public servants, humanity will be in a far better situation—but these do-gooders won't leave humanity alone. And what are *they* gaining out of it? They are gaining only one thing: they are miserable and they want to forget all about it, and the best way is to start thinking of others' miseries; that is an escape from your own miserable space. When you become too much concerned about others' problems, naturally your own problems recede into darkness.

It is a well-known fact that the people who become interested in psychoanalysis, the people who become psychotherapists, are basically trying to avoid their own psychological problems. They are afraid to face them, and the easiest course is to become focused on others' problems. And when you are surrounded by others' problems—and they are so many and bigger than yours—naturally you start forgetting about your own problems. There is no time to think about yourself.

These so-called public servants, social reformers, are simply escapists. They are full of misery, tension, anguish, anxiety. I know these people—I know their innermost lives. They are carrying a thousand and one wounds, and still they are trying to help others. They can only contaminate others, they can only infect others.

The first thing is to create a blissful state in your own interiority. Your subjectivity should be full of fragrance. You should be a dance, a song, a festival of lights. Then out of that joy, compassion arises. I don't call it 'service', I don't call it 'duty'—I call it love. And then you are not obliging anybody, you are simply overflowing with joy. Then you are just like a cloud full of rain-water: it has to shower. Then you are just like a lotus full of fragrance: it *has* to give its fragrance to the winds. It is not obliging the winds, neither is the cloud obliging the earth. In fact, the cloud feels obliged to the earth, because it allowed it to unburden. The lotus feels obliged to the wind, grateful, thankful, because the wind allowed it to release its splendor. It is infinitely grateful. There is no question of service and there is no question of helping others; it is a natural consequence of blissfulness.

Oscar Mann, you have to consider only one thing deeply: Are you blissful? Are you in a state of celebration? Are you a cloud full of rain-water? If you are not, then forget this great idea of helping others, of 'helping brothers out of the molasses'. You will drag them more into the molasses! You will become a burden. You will sit on their heads—they will have to carry you. And, of course, being a public servant, being a great social worker, it is your birthright to sit on people's heads! They have to worship you: you are great, your work is great. They have to feel your greatness, your superiority, your compassion. And all that is bullshit! Unless you are blissful it is not possible for you to help others.

A candle that is unlit cannot help other unlit candles; only a lit candle can help other candles to become lit. And the miracle is: when the flame goes from the lit candle to the unlit candle, the lit candle loses nothing, and from one lit candle millions of candles can be lit—still it loses nothing. Others gain, but you are not losing anything. In fact, just the opposite happens: the more you give, the more you have. And when you are ready to give all, you have all the joys of the world available to you. When you are ready to give totally, you become open to all God's grace, you become a vehicle. But then there is no idea of service, duty; the question does not arise.

Hence there is no need to think about a synthesis. One is blissful—and out of bliss, just as the shadow follows you, compassion follows you. You are not even aware of your shadow following you; it does not make any noise, not even the footsteps can be heard. It simply comes following you, without any noise, not even a whisper. In the same way compassion comes: it follows the meditator.

Gautam the Buddha defines meditation as the source of compassion. He says unless you are a meditator you cannot have compassion. 'Compassion' is a beautiful word: it is passion transformed, it is passion gone through the alchemy of meditation. It is the same energy that was involved in your passions now passing through the alchemical process of meditation, silence, awareness. It is freed from all pollution, from all that is foreign to it; it becomes purer and purer. When your meditation reaches its ultimate height, your whole energy becomes overflowing love—it is compassion.

So the question of synthesis does not arise—either you are blissful or you are not. If you are blissful, compassion follows; if you are not blissful, whatsoever you are doing is just an escape from your own misery.

You say:

I am another 'development worker'
whose questions you answered
most beautifully yesterday.
For me, though, one question remains . . .

The mind goes on creating questions. When I have answered *this* question, Oscar Mann, you will find that a few more questions have arisen. The mind is very fertile about questions; about answers it is impotent. The mind has no answers, it has only questions. Meditation has only answers and no questions, and meditation is a state of no-mind.

I can answer your question, but don't think that you will *get* the answer—you will simply get a few more questions.

In New York a bus was standing at the bus-stop. The driver informed the passengers that he would leave the stop only if the blacks moved to the back of the bus and the whites came to the front.

"Hey, man!" said one of the blacks. "Stop this discrimination. We're under the Carter administration, you know!"

Exactly at this moment, the President drove past the side of the bus in his car. One of the blacks called out to him and told him the story.

"I'll have none of this!" replied Carter with vehemence. "In my government there are neither blacks nor whites. In the USA we are all greens!" (the color he used in his election campaign).

Everybody applauded the President, and he drove away.

"Okay," said the bus driver after he had gone, "let's get this organized. All the light greens come to the front and all the dark greens go to the back!"

Only questions go on changing, but basically the mind remains the same. So if you are trying to get answers *through* the mind you are not going to get them at all. Listen to me in silence, listen to me without the mind. Put the mind aside.

You have been conditioned by Christianity for service, and the conditioning of Christianity has gone so deep that not only has it conditioned the Christians, it has conditioned even the Buddhists, the Jainas, the Hindus, the Mohammedans. It has a logical appeal in it.

For example, in India we always respected the man of meditation. We never asked Buddha to go and serve the poor.

I receive every day hundreds of letters saying "If you are really a *Bhagwan* then you should open hospitals, schools, houses for the poor, for orphans, for widows." But nobody asked Buddha, nobody asked Krishna, nobody asked Mahavira, how many hospitals they had opened and how many schools they had opened. All that we asked them was whether they have achieved blissfulness. If they have achieved that, then all is achieved. Then their very presence is a healing force, then their very presence is educative, then their very presence is nectar. Then their very presence gives eyes to the blind and ears to the deaf and tongues to the dumb and hearts to the dead—their very presence!

But Christianity has contaminated the whole world. Now even Hindus think that Mother Teresa is a *real* saint. Jainas think, Buddhists think, that unless you serve the poor, unless you serve the old, you are not a really religious person.

The East has defined the religious person in a totally different way and I *insist* that the East is right, Christianity is wrong. First one has to become blissful oneself, then only can one share.

Con had returned to his native town after many years abroad. "I hope," said his parish priest, "that you have been loyal to your faith while you have been away."
"Indeed, Father, I have. I lied, I fought, I cursed, I robbed and I had women, but not for one moment did I forget the religion I was brought up in!"

People are only paying lip service, but nothing else can be done because Christianity has put everything upside-down.

It was a typical shop selling Roman Catholic religious goods and there were many statues of the saints. With savage energy a Protestant Orangeman shattered them with his stick. In court he explained why.
"Milord, I couldn't pass the place by and not *do* something. If there's one thing I hate it's bigotry!"
Oscar Mann, you are asking me:

> *. . . working to help brothers out of the molasses*
> *seems also to keep me from flying.*

If you cannot fly, you cannot be rooted in the earth either. The question of synthesis does not arise. A tree is rooted in the earth: the deeper its roots go, the higher its branches rise. The tree can whisper with the clouds only if its roots go very deep into the earth; the proportion is the same: the higher the tree, the deeper the roots. There is a balance. The tree can touch the stars, but then the roots have to go to the very rock-bottom.
I don't see that there is any question of synthesis between flying and remaining on the earth. In fact, a tree

which is only roots is not a tree. Roots are ugly, that's why nature keeps them hidden underneath the earth. And a tree which has no roots cannot survive, not even for a single moment; it cannot grow, it will be dead immediately. It is possible to flower, but it is possible only because of the roots.

You are asking me as if there is a question of choosing whether to fly or whether to remain on the earth, and I say to you: both are possible only in togetherness; you cannot do one alone.

If you feel the magic of this place then be immersed in that magic, be drunk with it! Then one day perhaps you may be of some help to humanity.

The sales manager had a busy week in the country, and on Saturday evening he was exhausted when he dropped into the local bar to have a quick one before going home.

"Give me something to pick me up," he asked.

"Brandy? Vodka? Tullamore Dew? Bushmills?"

"No, no. I need something different."

"Well," said the barman with hesitation, "the only thing that might do it would be our Bhagwan's special."

"I'll try it!" said the sales manager—and he had to admit that the first made him feel a new man, while the second and the third sent him home floating on air.

He was telling a friend about it. "It was terrific!" he said. "And the next morning I jumped out of bed and gave all the family their breakfast, packed them into the car and took them to Shree Rajneesh Ashram's Buddha Hall. There we listened to a strange sermon *against* Jesus and saw thousands of strange people in orange robes. I could not believe my own eyes! Everything was so strange, it looked as if I was dreaming. And then it was when we came out that the trouble started."

"In what way?" asked his friend.

"Sure, we're not Rajneeshees, we're Christians!"

Try to get it—don't be Germans!

The second question

Bhagwan:
In your early years you were alone on your path
and revolting against belonging to any family,
group, community, religion, society or country.
Now you have found, and you relax in your being.
Around you a community is created,
and with it the seeds of establishment.
Now, I want to be close to you and to the source,
but I am revolting against being part of these intense
masses, groups (sleeping)
and group-leaders (half-sleeping).
I hear your voice saying,
"This is a community of individuals but . . . "
Here I am again, sitting near the river,
hearing the birds' songs,
seeing them flying and playing,
and meditation happens to me.
Now, the part in me which is revolting
is asking if I know
deeply in my heart that nature is the right space
for my growth, for my therapy
and for my meditation.
Why should I again fall into the groups?
If I know the bullshit that is running in my mind,
why should I look for meditation in intense places?
And there is no urge in me
to listen to the 'half-mirror'.
Veet Adam

T HE FIRST THING: I never asked anybody *any* question. The moment you ask a question you are getting into a community—you are getting into communion! I never asked anybody.

And you are wrong when you say:

You were revolting against belonging to any family . . .

If you want to revolt against a family, group, community, religion, establishment, first you have to *belong* to it. I never belonged! I never became a part of any group, of any society, of any establishment, so the question of revolting does not arise.

One woman was asking another, "Do you believe in the liberation of women?"
She said, "Yes, I do."
The other looked puzzled and said, "Then why are you getting married?"
She said, "But before I can be liberated I have to be trapped! Otherwise how can I be liberated?"

Liberation needs imprisonment. I never revolted because there was nobody to revolt against. I simply never belonged.
You are revolting . . . that means that you belong. Don't belong! Why are you creating unnecessary trouble?—first getting married and then making efforts to be liberated! Simply be liberated.
Just the other day I was reading the definition of a bachelor: A bachelor is a person who has not commited the same mistake even once. So be a bachelor! Who is preventing you? We prevent people from coming in, but we never prevent people from going out.

If somebody wants to go out we help him in every possible way! We have created barriers for people to come in—we give them every opportunity to escape —but if they want to get trapped, what can be done? They are free, and we cannot hinder them forever. And if *we* hinder them they will get trapped somewhere else. If they are *determined* to become prisoners they will become prisoners somewhere or other. Then this is the best place to become a prisoner, because the gates are open and you are always pushed and helped to get away as quickly as possible! In other places they don't hinder you from getting in, but they hinder you from getting out.

Who is telling you to be here? But you are understanding in your own way.

You say:

In your early years you were alone on your path . . .

Not only in early years: I have always been alone on my path. Even today I am absolutely alone. Your being here does not make any difference—my aloneness remains untouched—because aloneness is so intrinsic. Nobody can enter into your aloneness. You can be in the crowd and absolutely alone, but you may be alone and not alone at all. You can sit in a cave in the Himalayas and still think of the crowd, of the girlfriend and the boyfriend and the marketplace and what is going on there. . . .

I was traveling in the Himalayas and I visited many people who lived in caves for years—thirty years, forty years. When I visited them the first thing they asked was, "Any news about the world? What is going on there?" Still waiting for news! Then what is wrong with reading a newspaper? If that is the first question—"Tell us something about the world, what is going on there?"—then their minds are there in the world.

You *can* be alone, but that aloneness may not be true aloneness. It may be only loneliness, and you may be thinking and fantasizing about all kinds of things.

Aloneness comes out of awareness; it has nothing to do with where you are in the outside world but where you are in the *inside* world. You have been misunderstanding me.

You say:

. . . and you revolted against belonging to any family, group, community, religion, society or country.

I don't take that much trouble. I see the point and simply get out of it—there is no question of revolting! Have you seen a snake slipping out of the old skin? Do you think it revolts against it? It simply slips out! When I saw the stupidity of *anything*, I immediately slipped out of it; there was no question of revolting.

Revolt means fighting and fighting means remaining there. And with whomsoever you fight you become very intimate, or vice versa: if you are very intimate you will start fighting. So now they say about couples that they are intimate enemies. Either become intimate and you will fight, or fight and you will become intimate.

You see something is wrong—you see this is the wall and not the door: do you revolt against the wall? Do you shout, do you protest, do you do something against the wall? You simply get out by the door! Whenever I saw any wall I never in the whole of my life fought against it. It is stupid! The wall will not be harmed, *you* will be harmed.

But you are understanding according to yourself . . .

A gay guy was passing a church when he had an overwhelming impulse to go inside and listen to the sermon. He was deeply moved by it and enjoyed it so much that, when the time came for the collection plate to be passed around, he pulled out a five-hundred-dollar bill and placed it on the plate.

The preacher was ecstatic when he saw the money, and launched into a heartfelt talk about the virtues of generosity. "Such a fine example of Christian charity!" he declared with great emotion. "The man who offered this money may choose any hymn he wants."

The gay guy stood up excitedly and started to gesticulate wildly. "I'll take him!"—pointing to a handsome young man in the pew. "And him . . . and him!"

You are not listening to me! I am saying something else! You are hearing something totally different, diametrically opposite to it.

I am a simple man. I am not in any way interested in fighting any stupid fight. I simply see the point and I get out of it. Only understanding is needed and all that is wrong falls away from you; it is not a question of revolt.

And you say:

Now you have found, and you relax in your being.

It is not that I have *found* and that's why I relax in my being—I relaxed in my being, that's why I have found! You are just putting things upside-down!

> *Around you a community is created*
> *and with it the seeds of establishment.*

That's true! Whenever there is communion there will be a community. It cannot be avoided—and there is no need to avoid it. I invite it! I have invited you all, I have called you all to be with me, to share the joy that I have found, to share the truth. But there is no establishment.

Establishment happens only when the Master is dead. Establishment is when the community no longer has any center, only a circumference. A *dead* community is what an establishment is. I know that whenever a community is born, sooner or later there will be an establishment, but that does not mean that the community has to be prevented from being born. That will be like killing a child because if the child survives then sooner or later he will have to die—so better kill him now. Why let him live just to die? Everybody knows that everybody is going to die; that does not mean that every child has to be killed. When death comes it is perfectly okay.

The only thing to be remembered is that when the Master is dead, the community should start dispersing; it should start seeking and searching for new Masters. Either the Master will leave many Masters behind him, alive, enlightened . . . then the community can still remain a community, it will not become an establishment. If one enlightened person is there then the community is still a community; it does not matter who the enlightened person is.

And I can assure you that I am going to leave many more enlightened people in my commune than has ever been done before. Jesus could not leave a single enlightened person . . .

The scene is the Last Supper. In a humble room lit by just one candle sits Jesus, surrounded by his twelve disciples. A soft golden glow fills the room . . .
Words are unnecessary in the warm silence.
Jesus gently speaks to Peter on his right hand, "Would you like the last egg, Peter?"
"No, my Lord, you have it!" murmured Peter.

Jesus then asks Luke, "Would you like the last egg, Luke?"

"No, my Lord, you have it!" Luke replies.

Jesus asks Steven, "Would you like the last egg, Steven?"

Steven replies, "No, my Lord, you have it!"

And so Jesus asks every one of his closest disciples. They all refuse, leaving the last egg for him.

As he reaches to pierce the egg with his fork, a gust of wind blows out the candle. There is a muffled shriek. When the candle is relit, Jesus is looking at his hand—with twelve forks sticking from it.

These twelve fools became twelve apostles! Hence, the moment Jesus died the religion disappeared—it became a cult! It became an establishment. And now the ultimate fall has happened: the Polack Pope. Now it cannot fall any more. One thing is good about it—it cannot fall any more. This is the last! Now Christianity has reached the seventh hell, there is no lower to go than that.

I know that whenever there is a commune there is danger of an establishment. Krishnamurti is trying to avoid that danger by killing the baby—so that there is no death later on. But what is the point? Death will be right now; later on . . . the baby can live for at least a few years, maybe a hundred years or maybe more.

Buddha said, "My commune will live for five hundred years." Before he used to say, "My commune will live for five thousand years," but the day he allowed women into his commune he said, "Now I cannot say five thousand years, only five hundred years!" And he was right—right in the sense that, according to him, the way he founded his discipline, there was no place for women. And he was getting old; now it was impossible to change the whole structure.

My commune can live five thousand years or more, because I have started it with women! Now, who can destroy it? I have my own ways! Nobody can destroy it—I have taken every care. I have handed over the commune to women . . . there *is* a danger, but five thousand years is a long time. Veet Adam, by that time you can become enlightened! Don't be afraid of the seeds —seeds are there, but they will not sprout for at least five thousand years. And I am going to leave many enlightened people behind me—they are getting ready.

A woman visited the psychiatrist for the first time. He invited her into his office and asked her to make herself comfortable on the couch. Seeing that she was hesitating and seemed to be bashful, he said, "Go ahead and lie back and get comfortable. This is the way I have all my patients talk to me. This is an important part of your treatment."

The women did as she was told. She carefully smoothed her dress around her knees and then reclined and began to relax.

"Now," the doctor said, "let's begin at the beginning. How did your troubles begin?"

"Exactly like this!" she said.

I know, exactly like this trouble begins, but it will take at least five thousand years to come into power. By that time only stupid people will not be enlightened —very stupid people! And, Adam, I don't think you are *that* stupid!

And you say:

Now, I want to be close to you and to the source . . .

But that is the seed of the commune! All these people want to be close to the source, that's why the commune is needed. Everybody wants to be close, but then some discipline has to be managed, otherwise there will simply be chaos.

And you say:

> *. . . but I am revolting against being part*
> *of these intense*
> *masses, groups (sleeping)*
> *and groupleaders (half-sleeping).*

Don't participate in them! Who is telling you? It is up to you.

And you say:

> *I hear your voice saying,*
> *"This is a community of individuals, but . . ."*

I never use buts and ifs! It must be your own voice—beware of it!

A man was playing roulette and was down to his last chip. As he stood undecided about what to do with it, he heard a wee voice whisper in his ear, "Play 32!"

So, figuring he probably would lose it anyway, he played 32—and won.

The little voice then whispered, "Put it all on 8!"

He did, and he won again.

"Now let it all ride on 19," the little voice said.

The player followed the advice of the little voice and won a third time.

"Here we go for the last time," the little voice said, "and your fortune! Put all of it on 3."

The man did as he was told. As the little white ball snuggled down in the 15 slot, the man heard the little voice say, "Aw, shucks! that's the way it goes."

It is your *own* voice you are hearing! One thing is absolutely certain: I have not been speaking to you. That much I can say with absolute certainty, that I have no direct line with you yet—because you are half-hearted. I can speak directly only to those who are *totally* here. You are not yet totally here, hence this question has arisen.

You say:

> *Here I am again, sitting near the river,*
> *hearing the birds' songs,*
> *seeing them flying and playing,*
> *and meditation happens to me.*

So far so good! Let it happen more and more!

> *Now, the part in me which is revolting . . .*

Now still something is there which is revolting—and meditation is happening by the river? What kind of meditation is this? Suddenly the birds are no more flying and playing, and again the revolt?

> *Now, the part in me which is revolting*
> *is asking if I know*
> *deeply in my heart that nature is the right space*
> *for my growth, for my therapy*
> *and for my meditation.*

It is all your mind—that meditation too, those birds flying and playing. That is just mind and nothing else!

> *Why should I again fall into the groups?*

But who is telling you?—aw, shucks!—who is telling you? *You* are telling me:

> *. . . If I know the bullshit that is running in my mind,*
> *why should I look for meditation in intense places?*

You have come to know that bullshit only because of these groups, and that little bit of thought about meditation is happening only because of this community. Otherwise there are many fools sitting by the river, and no birds are flying and no birds are playing and nothing is happening.

> *And there is no urge in me*
> *to listen to the 'half-mirror'.*

If there is no urge, perfectly good! But there seems to be some urge in you. And it is better to have a half-mirror than to have nothing—at least some vague idea of your original face, some reflection, even in the half-mirror. It is better to have a dim old half-mirror than just a wall. Unless you have found your own mirror it is better to use others' mirrors—there is nothing wrong in it.

But you are unnecessarily getting into troubles. You seem to be, Adam, very new here . . .

A white Brazilian arrived in South Africa and wanted to go to the theater. The price was five dollars for the stalls and ten dollars for the balcony. It was strange —never had he seen stalls cheaper than the balcony.

The ticket-man said, "I can see that you are new here. In this place the whites go to the balcony and the blacks go to the stalls."

"Okay," said the Brazilian, "give me a ticket for the balcony."

Half an hour after the performance had begun he needed to piss, so he asked the guy next to him where the toilet was.

"I can see that you are not from these parts," stated the man, "because there is no toilet. We just piss over the railing onto the blacks' heads!"

When he was almost finished pissing, a black guy from the stalls shouted up to him, "Hey, man, I can see that you are not from here. In this place the whites don't aim at only one person, they piss all over the stalls!"

Adam, you are just new here! Be here a little bit more, and all these nonsense thoughts will disappear. Use the half-mirror till you have found the mirror of your own meditation. It can be found—every device is available here to help you to find it. Don't miss this opportunity—it can be missed. . . .

The last question

Bhagwan:
I have no claim to gifts or fame,
but I have never heard you say my name.
Oh, Bhagwan, please set me free,
and tell a little joke for me.
Deva Kalimba

THIS IS THE JOKE FOR YOU:

The family of the recently deceased Abe Cohen gathered together as the executor prepared to read the last will and testament.

"To my wife, Ida," began the executor, "who has been a loving wife to me for over twenty-five years, who has borne me two beautiful children, who has been faithful, kind and generous, I leave my house, my car, and one-third of the profits of my business."

"Aaah!" responded all the relatives. "What a generous, wonderful man!"

"To my daughter, Alice," continued the executor, "who has given me nothing but joy and happiness since the day she was born, I leave another one-third of the profits of my business, my yacht, and two hundred and fifty thousand dollars."

"Aaah!" responded the relatives. "What a generous and wonderful man!"

"To my son, David," went on the executor, "who has made me so proud by becoming a brain surgeon, who has been top of his class right through school and college, I leave the remaining one-third of my business, my motor boat and two hundred and fifty thousand dollars."

"Aaah!" responded the relatives again. "What a wonderful man!"

"Finally," said the executor, "to my brother-in-law, Louis, who has lived with us in our house for most of his adult life, who has never done a single day's work in his entire life, who smokes only the finest cigars—my cigars—who for years has been going around saying to everyone I will never mention him in my will . . . hello, Louis!"

Hello, Kalimba!

Discourse 9

December 19, 1980

SILENTLY BLISSFUL, BLISSFULLY SILENT

नान्तः प्रज्ञं न बहिष्प्रज्ञं

नोभयतः प्रज्ञं

न प्रज्ञानघनं

न प्रज्ञं नाप्रज्ञम् ।

अदृष्टमव्यवहार्यमग्राह्यम्-

लक्षणमचिन्त्यमव्यपदेश्यमेकात्म-

प्रत्ययसारं प्रपंचोपशमं शान्तं

शिवमद्वैतं चतुर्थं मन्यन्ते

स आत्मा स विज्ञेयः ॥

Nāntaḥ-prajñaṁ, na bahiḥ-prajñaṁ
Nobhayataḥ-prajñaṁ
Na prajñaṇa-ghanaṁ
Na prajñaṁ, nāprajñaṁ
Adṛṣṭam, avyavahāryam, agrāhyam
Alakṣaṇam, acintyam, avyapadeśyam, ekatma-
Pratyaya-sāraṁ, prapañcopaśamaṁ, śāntaṁ
Śivam, advaitaṁ caturthaṁ manyante
Sa ātmā, sa vijñeyaḥ.

It is not outer awareness,
It is not inner awareness,
Nor is it a suspension of awareness.
It is not knowing,
It is not unknowing,
Nor is it knowingness itself.
It can neither be seen nor understood,
It cannot be given boundaries.
It is ineffable and beyond thought.
It is indefinable.
It is known only through becoming it.
It is the end of all activity,
silent and unchanging,
the supreme good,
one without a second.
It is the real Self.
It, above all, should be known.

AUM
Pūrnamadaḥ
Pūrnamidaṃ
Pūrnāt pūrnamudachyatē
Pūrnasya pūrnamādāya
Pūrnamēva vashisyatē.

AUM
This is the cold.
That is the cold.
From coldness emerges coldness.
Coldness coming from coldness,
coldness still remains!

THIS MORNING IS REALLY COLD, hence the change of the meaning. I don't stick to the words, I stick to the reality! Therefore, before we enter into the cold waters of the Mandukya Upanishad, a few jokes to warm you up.

Two fleas were sitting on their deck chairs on the beach in Miami, Florida. It was January, the weather was warm, and the fleas were lazing around with a cool drink, suntan lotion smeared over their bodies.

Their quiet was interrupted by a third flea who came in and sat down on a deck chair next to them. He was rugged up in heavy boots, an overcoat, hat and gloves, and still he was shivering.

"Why are you dressed for the Antarctic in the middle of the summer?" one of the fleas asked him.

"Oh," moaned the third flea, "I found myself in the beard of a hippie when he mounted his motorcycle back in the bitter cold and snow of Detroit, Michigan. He drove non-stop for two whole days to get here. I'm chilled to the bone!"

"Next winter," said one of the fleas, "go to the penthouse of an expensive apartment building during a cocktail party. There you are bound to find someone wealthy who is going south for the winter, and you can go in style!"

A year later the same fleas were sitting on the beach in Miami when the other flea approached them, still wearing a heavy overcoat and shivering violently.

"What happened to you? Why didn't you take my advice?" asked the flea.

"I did take your advice," grumbled the freezing insect. "I got to a penthouse and found a cocktail party going on. I located a beautiful lady, wearing furs and expensive jewelry. I knew she would be going south in high style, so I climbed onto her toe, up her ankle, up her calf, up her thigh, and then I came to a lovely warm spot, and I knew I would be going south in style.

'The next thing I knew, I was inside the beard of a hippie who drove straight through non-stop in the bitter cold!"

This reminds me of Almasto and her questions—she is back again to her questions.

Bhagwan, why do they sell so many lightbulbs in Iran?

Because they always try to fit them in with a hammer. This is called the Islamic revolution!

How many Tibetans does it take to fit in a lightbulb?
None. They have not heard of lightbulbs yet in Tibet.

How many Chinese does it take to screw in a lightbulb?
None. You are not allowed to screw in China these days.

Why does it take a Russian so long to screw in a lightbulb?
Because first he has to have a five-year plan.

Why was the Polack Pope horrified when taking up his office in the Vatican for the first time?
Almasto, he saw a lightbulb lying in a wastepaper basket next to his desk and he was horrified—he thought it was a contraceptive.

And the last . . . and then you take the dive in the cold waters of the Mandukya Upanishad. It is cold for you, not for me. As a proof you can see—my fan is still on!

A Brahmin priest was cycling down a country lane. He rounded a bend and was surprised to find a little boy screwing a rabbit. The priest, without hesitation, jumped off his bicycle, grabbed the boy by the hair and gave him a good talking to. He was really furious and asked the boy, 'What are you doing?"

The boy said:

> *"AUM*
> *Purnamadah*
> *Purnamidam*
> *Purnat purnamudachyate*
> *Purnasya purnamadaya*
> *Purnameva vashisyate."*

This was really too much! The priest gave the boy a good beating, got back on his bicycle and went on. A few miles further up the road he spied an old man atop a grassy verge screwing a goat. The priest was utterly shocked and he stormed over to the old man.

"Not two miles back down the road," he yelled, "I found a little boy doing exactly the same thing with a rabbit! You should know better at your age!"

The old man looked up at the priest with a grin and said, "Do you expect me to catch a rabbit at my age?"

The priest looked at the sky and said:

> *"AUM*
> *Purnamadah*
> *Purnamidam*
> *Purnat purnamudachyate*
> *Purnasya purnamadaya*
> *Purnameva vashisyate."*

Now it is up to you how deep you can dive in the cold waters. Before the jump one has to go a few steps back, so I will start from the sutras of the last sutra session:

> *The third is deep sleep,*
> *the mind rests, with awareness suspended.*

> *This state beyond duality,*
> *—from which the waves of thinking emerge,*
> *is enjoyed by the enlightened as an ocean of*
> *silence and bliss.*

The only difference between deep, dreamless sleep and the awakened state, the enlightened state, is that of awareness. If you can be aware in your deep sleep you are a Buddha. You are not aware even while you are awake, and the Buddha is one who is aware even while he is deep asleep. He may be snoring: just as *you* will hear his snoring he also hears his snoring. The snoring is a physiological phenomenon. You are watching from the outside, he is watching from the inside. In fact, he is more aware of it than you are, because you may be having other thoughts, a thousand and one, but he has no thought at all.

The awakened person is called enlightened because this small flame of awareness continues to burn twenty-four hours a day, whether he is awake, whether he is asleep, whether he is doing something or not doing anything. Nothing matters; everything remains on the circumference. At the center there is only the flame of awareness, and this flame of awareness is experienced as silence and bliss.

This is one of the most significant things to understand: it is easy to be silent, it is also easy to be blissful, but to be silent *and* blissful is impossible for the mind to comprehend. It can only be experienced at the ultimate peak, at the ultimate culmination, where all dualities merge and become one.

This is a duality: silence and bliss are poles apart. Hence it is easy to be on one polarity; if you are ready to renounce the other you can easily have one, but to have one is to remain partial. And unless you are whole you are never fulfilled. Only wholeness is holiness; only wholeness is flowering, blossoming, is fulfillment, is contentment.

The person who has only a part of his being actualized is in a constant conflict with the other part which is not actualized. He cannot dance—he is paralyzed, *half* of him is paralyzed. How can he dance? He cannot even walk! He needs a thousand and one supports, he needs all kinds of crutches. He is not able to stand on his own feet, he cannot live out of his own being. He needs this and he needs that, and those needs are infinite. So he goes on desiring and desiring, and his mind remains a beggar; he cannot be an emperor. To be whole is to be an emperor.

Silence is easy if you are ready to renounce bliss. That's what has been done for centuries by the so-called religious saints: they have decided to be silent and for that they have dropped the idea of being cheerful, blissful, joyous. But then their silence is dead, then their silence is no longer breathing, then their silence has no music, then their silence is like a graveyard. You can whitewash the graves, you can keep them clean, you can even grow roses, but a graveyard is a graveyard. You can try to hide the facts, but they are there. And how long can you deceive? Maybe you can deceive others, but you cannot deceive youself. You know that something in you has died; the moment you dropped cheerfulness, something in you stopped singing.

It is because of these escapist, so-called religious people that religion has become a graveyard. You can see the vibe of this death in the churches, in the synagogues, in the temples, in the mosques. Wherever your so-called religious people gather together they are always deadly serious. They cannot laugh—they have become incapable of laughter. They are absolutely cold, they cannot be warm, because they are afraid of warmth. Warmth means love, warmth means joy, warmth means bliss, warmth means laughter. Just to be silent they went on cutting everything that could have disturbed their silence. Their silence is very arbitrary; a silence that can be disturbed is not much of a silence. Only a silence which can*not* be disturbed is true silence—but there is no need to escape from the world.

What is the fear of the world? Why have these people been running away from the world? The fear is within them, it is not in the world. They are afraid that if they are in the world they may fall in love, they may start enjoying something, they may start living. Where so many people are alive they may start forgetting their commitment to silence. They may start singing! Afraid of the possibility, of their inner potential, they escape from the opportunity where it can be realized. They imprison themselves in caves, in monasteries. Of course they become silent, but their silence is worthless; it has no value at all. It is not sacred—it is not even alive, how can it be sacred? Nothing grows out of it; it is a desert. It is absolutely impotent. It is uncreative, insensitive.

That's why I am against the old, routine religious attitude, its escapist tendencies. I am against renunciation, I am all for rejoicing. I would like the temples to be full of laughter, the churches to be full of joy, the mosques full of music and dancing.

Do you know that the mosque avoids music so much that you cannot even play on any instrument before a mosque—it may create a riot. In India it happens almost every day in some part or other. Even if you start playing on a flute in front of a mosque you are against the Mohammedans—you are doing something wrong. Playing on the flute! You may be playing the tunes of the Koran, but music cannot be allowed in the mosque, not even in the close proximity of it. Such fear of music? Such fear of joy? Such fear of life?

It is good that these so-called religious people were not able to convince the majority of humanity—they could not convince because their whole approach was life-negative; they could not convince because not so many people are as suicidal as they were. They could not convince the major part of humanity for the simple reason that people are not so sado-masochistic. But they could get hold of a few sado-masochistic people, psychologically ill people, suicidal people. They could get hold of a few negative minds, and these negative minds have dominated the past.

I want to introduce affirmation, and that's the beauty of the Upanishads: they are affirmative. The Upanishadic vision is the only affirmative vision that has happend in the past, but it is strange that even Hindus who go on reading the Upanishads can't see its life-affirmative approach. They remain life-negative, they remain escapists. They go on interpreting the Upanishads in such a way that they lose all meaning—in fact, they go on imposing just the opposite meaning on the Upanishads. They turn and twist the words in such a way that affirmation becomes negation, that yes becomes no. They are very skillful.

Scholars *are* skillful people. They know how to play with words, they are hair-splitters. They create much dust, so much dust that you can't see what is happening. They create so much smoke of logic that you start forgetting what the real question was.

But the Upanishads are life-affirmative, totally life-affirmative.

It is easy to have silence if you are ready to renounce bliss, but renouncing bliss means renouncing life, renouncing life means renouncing God. Then that silence is of no worth at all—you have committed suicide. Of course, the man who has committed suicide *is* silent . . .

One man had murdered his wife. The judge asked him, "Are you aware of what you have done?"
The man said, "I am a very peace-loving person."

The judge said, "What do you mean by 'peace-loving'? You killed your wife, and you think you are a peace-loving person?"

He said, "Since I have killed her there has been so much peace in the house!"

Of course, when you kill your wife there is peace! You escape from the wife and there is peace and there is silence. You escape from your children and of course, in a cave somewhere in the Himalayas, there *is* peace and there is silence. But is it worth having it at such a cost? It is stupid!

And the other extreme is: people can choose bliss *and* renounce silence. That's what the majority has been doing down the ages. They have chosen cheerfulness, pleasure, joy, all the shades of bliss, all the colors of bliss. Bliss is a rainbow: it has many colors, from pleasure to bliss; it has the whole spectrum from the physical to the psychological to the spiritual *and* the beyond.

The people who have chosen pleasure, joy, happiness, bliss, cheerfulness, have renounced silence. Then their blissfulness is feverish, it is almost insane. It is alive, but in a very insane way. They are dancing, but their dance has no rhythm. It is chaos, it is anarchy. They are singing, but they don't know what they are singing. Their song is meaningless, it has no significance, because it does not contain silence.

A song without silence is empty; it is only a container without any content in it, it is a flower without fragrance. It is a false flower—maybe a paper flower or a plastic flower, but not a real flower. It has no roots. It has not grown, it has been manufactured.

People are manufacturing all kinds of pleasures, but they don't satisfy, they don't bring contentment; they only drive people more and more insane. So the so-called religious have become dead and the so-called worldly have become insane. This is the situation of the whole of humanity—this is where we are standing. A few people have forgotten how to laugh and a few people are laughing in a neurotic way. Their laughter is neurotic, hysterical. They are not the masters of it, they are slaves of it. Both the extremes are wrong.

The Upanishads follow the golden mean, the middle way. One has to have both, nothing has to be sacrificed. Only then—when your silence is pregnant with bliss and your bliss is full of silence—is there wholeness, totality. Then all duality and all schizophrenia disappear.

That's what I would like my sannyasins to be: silently blissful, blissfully silent. This state of silent bliss or blissful silence:

> . . . is not outer awareness,
> It is not inner awareness,
> Nor is it a suspension of awareness.
> It is not knowing,
> It is not unknowing,
> Nor is it knowingness itself.
> It can neither be seen nor understood,
> It cannot be given boundaries.
> It is ineffable and beyond thought.
> It is indefinable.
> It is known only through becoming it.
> It is the end of all activity,
> silent and unchanging,
> the supreme good,
> one without a second.
> It is the real Self.
> It, above all, should be known.

Now, go into each statement very carefully. This state the Upanishads call 'the fourth', *turiya*; now the

Mandukya is trying to help you by giving some hints of what it is. First:

It is not outer awareness . . .

It is not extroversion; that is what you call your ordinary waking state. You are aware of the outside world, but you are not aware of the inside. You are aware of objects, but you are not aware of your interiority. You are aware of everything except your subjectivity. You know the trees, the mountains, the rivers, the stars, but you are absolutely oblivious of who this knower is—who am I?

The outer awareness, extroversion, gives you science; that is the world of science. It is because science is based on outer awareness that it cannot conceive of any interiority in you, it cannot find any self in you, it cannot discover any soul—for the simple reason that its very method prohibits it, its very method gives it a limitation.

You cannot see with your ears and you cannot hear with your eyes; that does not mean that if you cannot listen with your eyes there are no sounds in the world. If you cannot see with your ears that does not mean there is no light, there are no colors in the world; it only means that you are trying to find something through a wrong method. Eyes can see, ears can hear; that is their limitation. If you try to hear with the eyes, then there is no music, of course—but it does not prove the non-existence of music; it only proves your obsession with a certain limited methodology.

Science is obsessed with the outer awareness, and of course, when you are limited to the outer awareness you cannot know the inner. You have rejected it already, you have bracketed it out already, by your very choice of method. Science will never discover consciousness. If it remains fixated on the outer method, then of course there is no possibility of discovering God; then for science God is non-existential.

The same is true from the opposite pole. There have been people like Shankaracharya who say that the outer world is illusory, *maya*. In a way he is doing the same as the so-called scientists have been doing: now he has become obsessed with the inner. Because he has chosen the inner awareness as the *only* awareness, the world becomes illusory; he has to reject the world.

The scientist has to reject consciousness, and Shankaracharya and the Vedantins have to reject the outer world; they say that it is illusory. But neither the scientist behaves according to his science nor do Shankaracharya and his followers behave according to their philosophy—they cannot. The scientist is continuously using his consciousness; even when he denies it, in that very denial he is using his consciousness. You cannot deny consciousness; that is the only thing which is indubitable, undeniable.

It happened:

Mulla Nasruddin invited a few of his friends home. He had been talking so much of his generosity and one of the friends said, "If you are really so generous, why don't you give some proof of it? You have never even invited us to your house, not even for a tea party!"

He forgot all about his wife—in that moment of excitement—he said, "Come on, this very moment! You all come to my house for dinner!"

But as the house came closer he became aware of what he had done. Now there would be trouble! In fact he remembered that in the morning when he had left the house his wife had asked him to bring vegetables—he had been playing chess with these friends and he had completely forgotten about the vegetables. The wife must have been furious by this time—it was evening, the sun was setting.

He told the friends, "You know, you are all married people, so you can understand my difficulty—just wait outside. Let me first go in and persuade my wife that I have invited a few of my friends. . . ."

They understood it—every husband will understand it—so they remained outside. Mulla went in. He told the wife that he had fallen into a trap: "It was sheer stupidity to invite these people, but now only you can help me out of this mess. You can just go out and tell them that I am not in the house."

The wife went out and asked, "What are you doing here?"

And they said, "We are waiting for Mulla Nasruddin!"

She said, "But he is not in the house—I have not seen him since the morning. He went to the market to fetch a few vegetables and he has not returned."

They said, "What are you saying? He came with us, we saw him go in, we have even heard him talking to you. We actually heard that it is *his* idea! And whom are you trying to befool? We came with him! We know he is inside the house!"

The wife was of course puzzled. What to do now? She had not expected that there was going to be such an argument about it.

Seeing the situation—Nasruddin was hearing it from a top-floor window, the whole thing—he became so excited because "My wife is not able to convince these fools!" He opened the window and said, "You may be right that he came with you, but he may have gone out by the back door! And are you not ashamed of arguing with a poor woman? Get lost! He is not in the house!"

You cannot say, "I am not in the house," because that very statement will prove that you *are* in the house!

The scientist says, "I am not in the house." He says, "There is nobody inside." Then who is saying this? Then why this whole effort to prove that there is nobody inside, that there is utter emptiness inside? Then who is this person who is trying to prove this?

Karl Marx says that consciousness is only a by-product of matter—the by-product itself is saying that consciousness does not exist! And he is ready to argue, and he has written big books with great arguments to prove that there is no consciousness.

And Shankaracharya said there is no world—and every day he went to beg. Where did he go to beg? He traveled all over the country to convince people that there is no world, it is all *maya*. And I am sometimes surprised that nobody ever asked him, "If all is *maya*, then with whom are you arguing?" If he meets me, this will be the first thing to decide: "Then whom are you talking to?" I will simply slap his face and see what happens! If the world is illusory, *I* am illusory, my slap is illusory, so if he gets angry or anything, why? for what? There is nobody! Unnecessarily getting into a quarrel, argument. . . .

And the followers of Shankaracharya have written a book, *Shankar Digvjay*—'The Conquest of the World by Shankara'—conquest of the world! because he conquered all the philosophers of India. He went from one corner to another, challenging everybody, and he was a good arguer, a good logician. But with whom was he talking?—to the illusory people? And conquering illusion, fighting with dreams which do not exist at all?

If you deny something real, this is going to happen: your behavior will prove that you are wrong, because reality cannot be denied. You can argue against it, but your very life will prove . . . because when Shankara is thirsty he asks for water, and water is illusory. Now, how can illusory water quench a real thirst?

And why did you renounce the world in the first place if it is illusory? You don't renounce anything that does not exist at all, otherwise anybody can renounce anything. You can say, "I have renounced the whole kingdom." And if somebody asks, "Where is your kingdom?" and you say, "It is all illusory! It does not exist really, but I have renounced it anyway". . . . He renounced the world; that proves the world is real.

There are people who have become focussed on the outer consciousness—these are the so-called scientists; then there are people who have become focused on the inner awareness—these are the so-called Vedantins. In the East Shankaracharya represents them, in the West Berkeley represents them. They say the world is nothing, it is made of the same stuff as dreams.

The Mandukya says:

It is not outer awareness . . .

The fourth state, the enlightened state, is not outer awareness; it is not extroversion.

It is not inner awareness either.

It is not introversion—because the division between the outer and the inner is arbitrary. What do you call the outer and what do you call the inner?

You are breathing. The breath goes in, then it becomes inner; just a moment before it was outer, and just a moment afterwards it is again outer. The breath going in becomes inner, coming out becomes outer. The same breath going in again is inner, coming out is again outer. What is the breath?—outer or inner? Outer and inner is the whole circle: half is inner, half is outer, and both together make the whole circle.

It is not *a suspension of awareness* either.

But then two possibilities still remain: if it is not outer awareness, not inner awareness, then it may be that it is suspension of awareness. Many have been befooled by suspension of awarenesss. They have thought of a deep, dreamless state as the fourth—even people like Ramakrishna.

Ramakrishna, his whole life, just leaving out the few days in the end, believed that suspension of awareness, *sushupti*, is *samadhi*, is the fourth, *turiya*. Those who know, they say it is *jad samadhi*, it is unconscious *samadhi*, it is not true *samadhi*. It is a state of deep silence, but because there is no awareness there can be no bliss, because there is no awareness there can be no joy, no dance, no celebration.

Ramakrishna used to go into *jad samadhi* for days together. Once he remained unconscious for six days, but it was almost like a coma. The doctors who supervised him thought that it was a coma—according to *their* approach it was a coma and nothing else, suspension of consciousness. He was utterly unconscious—breathing, but unconscious.

I have seen one woman who was in a coma for nine months, breathing and alive, but what kind of life?—just vegetating. And the doctors were convinced: "Now she will not be able to come back, because the coma has remained so long that it must have destroyed her brain cells, and without those brain cells she may not be ever able to come to consciousness again"—and she *never* came back to consciousness. Three years more she lived and then died in the coma.

Now, these four years of life . . . do you call it life? It is not death, certainly, but it is not life either. It is suspension of life; just the minimum of life is left, just the physiological phenomenon of breathing is left. The blood circulates still, but there is no consciousness.

Ramakrishna used to think that this is *samadhi*, and many people think that this is *samadhi*—and there are small tricks to create it. There are yoga postures, breathing exercises to create it. You can go into a coma and you will feel very silent, and when you come out of the coma you will feel very refreshed; you will feel rejuvenated, you will feel very alive, because it is such a deep relaxation—good for health but nothing to do with the fourth state, the enlightened state, the awakened state.

Ramakrishna came to know the real *samadhi* only in the last days of his life, through a mystic, Totapuri. Totapuri helped him to get out of this third state and to enter the fourth.

All the chanting of mantras is nothing but an effort to create suspension of awareness.

In Sanskrit we have two words for sleep; one is *nidra*. *Nidra* means ordinary sleep, natural sleep; every night you go into it. The other word is *tandra; tandra* means deliberately created sleep. It can be translated as 'hypnosis'. Hypnosis also means sleep, but a different quality is attached to hynosis: it is deliberate, it is created, it is not natural.

What do you do in hypnosis? You repeat certain things. For example, you repeat, "I am falling into deep sleep. My body is becoming numb and I am falling into deep sleep." You go on repeating, repeating, repeating, concentratedly repeating, and the idea slowly slowly sinks from the conscious mind into the unconscious, and the moment it reaches the unconscious you fall into deep sleep. It is a created thing.

The same happens with Transcendental Meditation and other methods which are nothing but chanting of mantras. *Any* kind of repetition can create *tandra*, hypnosis. And of course, afterwards when you are back you will feel very good, a certain well-being will be there, but this is not the realization of the ultimate truth. This is good for health purposes. . . .

That's why I call the Transcendental Meditation of Maharishi Mahesh Yogi a non-medicinal tranquilizer. It is good for people who are suffering from sleeplessness, who cannot fall asleep easily—it is good. Perhaps that's why only in America it has so many followers, because America is the country which suffers most from sleeplessness, from such a restlessness that it does not allow them to fall into sleep; they go on tossing and turning. But any kind of repetition, remember . . . it need not be a Sanskrit mantra, it need not be:

AUM
Purnamadah
Purnamidam
Purnat purnamudachyate
Purnasya purnamadaya
Purnameva vashisyate.

Anything will do—H_2O will do—it is an old method. People can simply count from one to a hundred and then backwards—from a hundred, ninety-nine, ninety-eight, ninety-seven, then come back to one, then again go up . . .up the ladder, down the ladder, up the ladder, down the ladder. . . . Four, five times you may be able to do it, and you will fall asleep—and you have done Transcendental Meditation!

You can create your own, there is no need to ask anybody—it is such a simple thing, it can easily be done. Your own name you can repeat and that will do. There is nothing special in Sanskrit words or Arabic words—*anything* will do, just go on repeating it.

But this creates only suspension of awareness, because repetition creates boredom and boredom creates sleep. If you are continuously nagging yourself . . . that's what Transcendental Meditation is—nagging yourself. Just go on torturing yourself with a mantra, go on chanting, don't listen to yourself. The mind will say, "I am bored with it! I am fed up with it!" but don't be worried, go on and on. Then there is only one escape left for the mind: to fall asleep, to get rid of you and your mantra and your Maharishi! So it falls into sleep.

The Mandukya Upanishad says it is not suspension of awareness either.

It is not knowing . . .

It is not knowledge, because it is not something there outside that you can observe and know. Science exactly means knowledge—the very word 'science' means knowledge. It is not science, it is not knowledge, it is not knowledgeability.

It is not unknowing . . .

But don't move to the other extreme. Saying that it is not knowledge you can think that maybe it is ignorance, unknowing. It is not that either—it is a very different kind of phenomenon. Ignorance and knowledge are two sides of the same coin: the ignorant can become knowledgeable, the knowledgeable can become again ignorant. They are convertible, they are not very different. What is the difference between the ignorant person and the knowledgeable? The difference of quantity. The ignorant person knows less and the knowledgeable person knows more. He is more informed, well-read, and the ignorant person is not so well-informed, not so well-read. But this is a difference of quantity, there is no qualitative difference.

Hence the Mandukya says:

It is not knowing,
It is not unknowing,
Nor is it knowingness itself.

The effort is to bring you closer to the inexpressible, so it is trying to avoid all the pitfalls. The first pitfall is that you may think it is knowing—it is not. You may think it is *un*knowing—it is not. You may think then it is knowingness itself—it is not.

It can neither be seen nor understood . . .

There is no way to see it because it is not outside, and there is no way to understand it because it is not *inside*. It is beyond both, hence it is beyond seeing and understanding. It is a mystery; it cannot be de-mystified.

It cannot be given boundaries.

When you say it is knowledge you have given it a boundary; when you say it is not knowledge you have given it a boundary; when you say it is knowingness itself you have again given it a boundary. Any word limits.

That's why I love the Upanishadic flight: it leaves behind everything. For example, the Vedas say it is knowing; that is the meaning of the word *veda*. *Vid* means knowing; from *vid* comes *veda*; *veda* means knowledge. The Vedas say it is knowing. The Mandukya Upanishad says:

It is not knowing . . .

Get rid of the Vedas, get rid of all the scriptures, get rid of all the words!

Socrates says: "I know only one thing, that I know nothing." He is saying that it is unknowingness. Dionysius says it is *agnosia*, unknowingness, but the Mandukya goes still further. It says it is better than the first—knowing is the lowest, unknowing is a little vaster, but still it defines, it gives a limitation. Socrates and Dionysius are better than the Vedas, but still lagging behind; one has to go a little further on.

And Mahavira says it is *kaivalya*, it is knowingness itself. The Mandukya Upanishad says Mahavira has come very close, but still, if we can deny that too, then we will be coming almost to it, to the indefinable.

> *It can neither be seen nor understood.*
> *It cannot be given boundaries.*
> *It is ineffable and beyond thought.*
> *It is indefinable.*
> *It is known only through becoming it.*

There is no other way to know it—neither from the scriptures, nor from traditions, nor from the gurus. It is not possible to know it from anywhere else, unless *you* become it yourself. And the way to become it is to dissolve into the whole, to disappear as a separate entity, as an ego; that is the meaning of becoming it. Don't be an island; disappear and become part of the infinite continent. Don't remain a dewdrop; slip from the lotus leaf into the lake and disappear. The moment the dewdrop disappears in the lake it becomes the lake, it becomes oceanic.

> *It is the end of all activity . . .*

At the very center of your being there is no activity; all activity is on the circumference, not at the center. The center is absolutely silent and unchanging. It is the supreme good, the *summum bonum*. *To be* it is to be moral, to *be* it is to be virtuous.

> *It is . . . one without a second.*

There is neither the known nor the knower; they have disappeared into one reality. So now there is nobody to claim, "I know," not even anybody to claim, "I don't know"—that too is a claim. Socrates' claim is far better than the claim of the knowledgeable people, the people who say, "We know"—they are the most stupid. Socrates is far better. He says, "I know only one thing, that I know nothing," but that too is a claim. At least one thing he knows—at least he knows that he knows nothing. Still he is . . . something of the ego may be just the shadow. If not the ego then the shadow of the ego is still lingering somewhere—a hang-up. But that hang-up has also to disappear, then you come to the real self.

> *It is the real Self.*
> *It, above all, should be known.*

The statement—the last statement—will look like a paradox, because we have been saying it cannot be known, it is not knowing, it is not unknowing either, it is not knowingness itself, it is ineffable, it is indefinable,and in the end the Mandukya Upanishad says:

> *Above all, it should be known.*

This is the trouble with language. It is not the fault of the Mandukya Upanishad—the language is faulty. The language cannot say what it is, the language cannot indicate correctly, but it *has* to be known. Now this known has to be given a special meaning: the meaning of becoming one with it. That is the only way to know it. To know means to disappear, to know means not to be.

Shakespeare says: The question is to be or not to be. If you ask the Mandukya Upanishad, it will say—and I agree with the Mandukya Upanishad—the question is not: To be or not to be? the question is: How not to be so that you can be? The way to be is not to be. Disappear as you are so you can appear *as you really are.* Let the mask fall so that the original face is discovered, let the mind go so that there is no interference from the mind . . . and you can be in silent blissfulness, one with existence.

Then you will find yourself in the flowers and their fragrance and you will find yourself in the birds and their songs, and you will find yourself in the sun and in the moon and in the clouds, in the people, in the animals . . . you will find yourself spread everywhere. You will be as vast as the universe itself.

All that you have to lose is this small ego. It is not much that you are asked to lose. It is rubbish! It is false! It is only an idea. If you are able to drop it, suddenly you explode into the whole, and then the whole splendor of existence is yours. All the songs are yours, all the blessings are yours, all the benedictions are yours.

That state of ecstasy is the fourth state, *turiya*. It has to be known! It has to be lived! That is the only way to attain to ultimate life. Unless it is found, life remains misery, life remains a hell. To find it is to enter into the kingdom of God.

Discourse 10

December 20, 1980

A CHALLENGE TO MY LOVE

The first question

Bhagwan:

"We're playing those mind-games together
pushing the barrier, planting seeds.
Playing the mind-guerilla,
chanting the mantra 'peace on earth'.
We've all been playing those mind-games forever . . .
Love is the answer, and you know that's for sure.
Love is the flower, you got to let it grow.
Yes is the answer, and you know that's for sure.
Yes is surrender and you got to let it grow . . ."

This song was written by John Lennon
about ten years ago.
Now he is dead.
Lennon was very much in love with you, even though
he declared that he was not ready
to become a disciple.
I can feel this connection myself.
I really would like you to say
something about his death.

Swatantra Sarjano

WORDS HAVE THEIR OWN MAGIC, and the poets, the singers, live in the magical world of words, not of realities. They are skillful, very skillful and efficient, as far as the delicate, subtle waves of words, imagination, dreams is concerned, but all that they go on doing is utterly unconscious.

John Lennon on the one hand sings:

"Love is the answer, and you know that's for sure."

He himself does not know it. He says:

"Love is the flower, you got to let it grow."

But to know it you have to be absolutely awakened, because love is the ultimate peak of consciousness. The poet can imagine about it, the singer can sing about it, the painter can paint about it, but they have seen only reflections of the moon in the lake; they have not seen the moon itself. And, of course, the moon reflected in the lake is just made of the same stuff as dreams are made of. The poets, the singers, are dreamers, they are not seers. So he says:

"Yes is the answer, and you know that's for sure."

But he himself is not sure. If he was sure then this statement that he was in love with me, yet he declared that he was not ready to become a disciple. . . .What does it mean to be a disciple? It simply means a love affair. It simply means the highest form of relatedness, of communion, of saying yes totally, not holding back anything.

He sings:

"Yes is surrender and you got to let it grow . . . "

His words sound true, but they are only reflections of the moon in the lake. If you dive in the lake you will not find the moon there. In fact, the moment you jump into the water, the reflection will disappear, will be broken into thousands of pieces. It will spread all over the lake; you will not be able to catch hold of it. The reflection *is* beautiful, but one has not to forget that it is only a reflection and it cannot transform your being.

So he sings: *"Love is the answer . . . love is the flower . . . yes is the answer . . . yes is surrender . . . and you know that's for sure"*—but he himself is absolutely unaware of it; he has not experienced it. A beautiful man, but still lost in dreams and imagination.

The poet lives unconsciously, the seer lives consciously. Sometimes their words are exactly the same—don't be deceived by the words. If you really want to know whether those words represent reality or just empty wishes you have to look into the life of the man.

Kahlil Gibran has written tremendously beautiful words. They come so close to Christ, to Zarathustra, to Lao Tzu, to Gautam the Buddha, that there is every possibility many people will think that Kahlil Gibran is enlightened. He may even surpass Lao Tzu and Buddha and Christ as far as expression is concerned; his expression may be far more beautiful because he is a skilled poet, a very skilled painter. He has the sensitiveness to appreciate beauty, but howsoever he is appreciating it is unconscious.

Buddha may not say things so beautifully, because he is not a poet in the ordinary sense, but whatsoever he says is the truth. His words may fall short of it . . . in fact, words always fall short of the truth; they are never adequate enough. So don't decide by words.

Sarjano, you are deciding by words. That's why you say:

I can feel this connection myself.

Sarjano himself has the quality of a poet, has the sensibility of a creative person. That's why I have given him the name Sarjano; *sarjano* means creativity.

But Kahlil Gibran or John Lennon have to be watched to know whether their truths are really truths or only fabrications of dream, fantasy, imagination; whether they have really experienced those things or they are only empty wishes. You have to watch the Buddha. . . .

Buddha is reported to have said: 'Don't be too bothered about what I say, rather look at me, rather watch me, rather feel me. Let the words disappear. Don't let the words stand between me and you. Experience my silence, feel the energy that surrounds me, resonate with me—only then will you be able to understand what I am saying."

If you want to understand a Buddha, his words, you have to watch his life.

Buddha has also said, very poignantly: "Don't follow my words, rather, follow what I am doing, follow what I am being."

Sarjano, I can see these words are beautiful:

"We're playing these mind-games together
pushing the barrier, planting seeds."

But Lennon was doing the same thing again, in this life also, playing the same games together. Once you *really* know that you are in a mind-game, it stops. Knowing it means it disappears, withers away. You cannot be in a mind-game if you are alert that it is a mind-game; you can be in it only when you think it is a reality. When you forget completely that it is a mind-game, only then can you get involved and identified with it.

"Playing the mind-guerilla,
chanting the mantra 'peace on earth'.
We've all been playing those mind-games forever . . . "

But there is no need to go on playing them forever. There have been people who stopped all those mind-games, but the only way to stop those mind-games is meditation; there has never been any other way. Meditation means entering into a state of no-mind.

If he was really in love with me, then there was nothing to prevent him from coming here. To be in love with me means to be in love with meditation, but he must have been afraid of meditation. If he said that he was not ready to become a disciple he must have been afraid of meditation, of surrender, of saying yes, of falling in love. Why?—because the poets, the singers, the painters, the sculptors, the musicians, are the most egoistic people in the world. They talk about egolessness, saying yes and surrendering and love, but that is *mere* talk.

They are very egoistic people, in fact they far surpass even the politicians and the priests, for the simple reason that they are *talented* people. The politicians are not talented people—they are third-rate, they belong to the world of the mediocres. But poets, singers, musicians, painters, they are talented people. They really have something which they can brag about—they have got something. Their ego has a solid support. The politician is making his house on shifting sands, but the poet—*any* kind of creative person—is making his ego on solid ground, on rocklike ground. His foundation is concrete; it is not made of just shifting sands. Hence he has every reason to feel egoistic, but then the danger is even far greater: he will be the last person to surrender, and his whole life he will talk about surrender and about egolessness and about love.

Kahlil Gibran talked about love, surrender, saying yes, but his whole life was quarrelsome. The people he loved, he always fought with them. He was talking about compassion, but he was a very angry man. He would go into childish tantrums for small reasons—any excuse would do. He would throw things, he would break things—he would go mad! The people who lived with him were always afraid of him, the women who loved him were continuously in misery.

And this is the man who wrote the great book, *The Prophet*. It stands as one of the ten great books of the whole world and it will remain one of the greatest ever; there is no possibility for somebody to surpass it. And this is coming from a man who was very angry, very violent, very jealous, very egoistic.

Wilhelm Reich has written about how to get rid of jealousy—because jealousy is *the* poison for love, it destroys the roots of love. And Wilhelm Reich is one of the greatest creative psychoanalysts after Sigmund Freud. But his wife writes something else—she writes about him: "I have never seen such a jealous person in my life. He was taking all kinds of freedom, he was moving with many women!"—because he was talking about freedom and that relationship should not be any kind of bondage, but about his wife he was very jealous. Almost twenty-four hours a day he was detecting, spying on where she was, with whom she was, what she was doing, was she looking happy with the man. When he went out of the town he would tell his friends to keep watch. . . .

Finally his wife had to divorce him—it was too much of a torture. He was taking every kind of freedom—he was moving with many women—and his wife was not even allowed to have friends, not to mention lovers.

You have to look into the *life* of the person, because only that is decisive.

Now, Lennon was continuously fighting with his own woman—many times they separated and many times they got together again—and he is talking about mind-games, and he was playing those mind-games himself!

Sarjano, the words are beautiful: *Love is the answer.* I also say love is the answer, but I *mean* it! He does not mean it, he is simply saying beautiful words. Beautiful words have their own hypnotic quality. They catch the mind of the singers and the poets and the musicians; they fall in love with beautiful words. He must be in love with the word 'love'—and remember, the word 'love' is not love, the word 'God' is not God, the word 'yes' is not yes.

Yes is a totally different existential experience. To say yes means to drop your ego entirely. Surrender means disappearing into the whole. He was a nice man, but as unconscious, Sarjano, as you are. That's why you say:

I can feel this connection myself.

You must be feeling it!

Now the poor man is dead. Somebody played the game—the mind-game—killed him. Many questions have come to me asking that I should say something about his death. To me, birth and death have no significance at all. There are many ways to die, and the best way is to be killed—at least *you* are not responsible! The worst is to die in your bed, and ninety-nine percent of people choose to die in their beds. Beware of the bed, because that is the *most* dangerous place in the world! All the accidents happen there: birth happens there, love happens there, death happens there. If you can simply renounce the bed you are enlightened!

He died a good death—somebody killed him. One has to die anyway; when one *has* to die one should choose a good way. I don't think he chose it and I don't think the person who killed him chose it either. People are living—all people are living—in utter unconsciousness.

A patient lying on the operating table started screaming, "I don't want to be cut open! You'll kill me! I don't want to die!"

The surgeon tried to calm the patient.

"Just take it easy, sir," he said. "Look at my long white beard. I've done thousands of operations and nothing has ever gone wrong."

"Oh, doctor, you're right! I know I can trust you!" replied the patient.

When the patient awoke after the operation, he looked around and saw the same white beard and said, "Oh, thank you, doctor! You are a saint!"

"It's okay, son, you don't have to thank me. I am not your doctor—my name is St. Peter!"

So what can I say about his death? It is perfectly okay! Everything is okay. Just . . . if he had *really* come here he would have died a totally different kind of death. He would have died celebrating, he would have died rejoicing. He would have died without any regrets, without any complaints. He would have died in love, in surrender, in yes. That he has missed this time—I hope next time he does not miss it.

The second question

Bhagwan:
Suppose you had experienced only negative
reactions from others
and had received no love in your life,
would you still be such a loving, happy man?
Or does happiness require a certain resonance
and response from others or from God?
Even Jesus Christ did not die happily,
as it is written in Matthew, Chapter 22:
"At the ninth hour, Jesus cried loudly,
'Lord, Lord, why have you left me?'"
Holger

LOVE HAS NOTHING TO DO with what others do with you. Love is not a response to a certain positive situation. You are born with love—love is the very stuff you are made of. You can go on giving it . . . it is a question of giving, not of getting. Of course, when you give it comes back—it comes back millions of times more, because the whole existence responds. But the basic idea, Holger, is not to get but to give.

The world is so loveless and full of hate for the simple reason that everybody wants to get love first—that is their condition for giving. And if everybody wants love first, then who is going to give it? And because nobody gets it—the first basic condition is not fulfilled—then nobody ever thinks of giving it.

And remember, love is alive only when you give it. If you don't give it, it goes sour, it becomes dead, it becomes a dead weight on you. It becomes hatred—it turns into its very opposite. It becomes fear, it becomes jealousy, it becomes possessiveness. Once your love is not alive then it turns into hundreds of monsters in you. And when you start giving those wrong vibes, naturally the whole existence reflects them back to you. Then one is in a vicious circle.

First you don't *give* love—love goes wrong, sour, bitter, becomes poisonous—and then you give it: you give anger, you give violence, you give hatred. For that you don't make any condition! You give those things unconditionally. Any small excuse is enough, and if there are no excuses you invent excuses. Then more and more hatred rebounds, and when hatred rebounds on you, of course you have every right to give more hatred. Then love is completely lost.

You ask me:

Bhagwan, suppose . . .

I never suppose anything! Philosophy begins with suppositions—I am not a philosopher. I am a very down-to-earth man, very pragmatic. I never suppose anything.

You say:

*Suppose you had experienced only negative
reactions from others . . .*

In fact, that's what I have experienced—and *still* I go on
experiencing the negative emotions. In fact, it will be
difficult to find you another man on the earth who
receives so many negative reactions from others. But I
enjoy it! I love it! By their negativity they are showing
they are interested in me, by their negativity they are
showing that they are not able to ignore me. By their
negativity they are taking a certain standpoint about
me. And if they are negative they can be positive too;
by being negative they have given the indication that
they are related to me.

Only the person who is neutral cannot be changed,
cannot be transformed. Negativity can easily turn into
positivity, hate can easily turn into love, just as love can
turn into hate, but a person who is absolutely neutral,
neither hateful nor loving, is beyond any change—he is
rocklike.

So I immensely enjoy people's negativity and I take it
as a challenge—a challenge to my love. If I can still love
them, only then do I know what love is. If I can love
only people who love me, then it is business, a bargain.
If I can even love people who don't love me, who certainly are hateful towards me, who would like to
destroy me, then it is true love, it is unconditional
love—it makes no demands on them.

I have experienced as much negativity, Holger, as one
can ever experience, and from my very childhood,
because my attitude has been that of a rebel. I have been
disobedient, rebellious. I have annoyed almost everybody: my relatives, the people of my village, my
teachers, my professors. I have annoyed everybody—I
enjoyed it!—but I have never hated anybody. Even the

people I annoyed, the people who took every kind of revenge on me . . . I have been expelled from colleges, from universities, but I have never hated anybody. Even the people who were the cause of my expulsion, my love for them has remained the same.

And they were puzzled by it, they were very much at a loss, because they were expecting that I would be angry. But I was never angry—rebellious certainly, but angry never; disobedient certainly, but disrespectful never. With all my respects I disobeyed! I remained always 'humbly yours'—rebelling, fighting, annoying them, doing every kind of thing that they would not like, but always 'sincerely yours'. About that even *they* were certain—that I was sincerely respectful.

I have experienced all kinds of negative reactions from others; that has not destroyed my love. In fact, on the contrary, it has made my love more integrated; it has made my love so centered and grounded that now I can say nothing can shake it, nothing can change it. Even if somebody kills me I will die loving him.

You say:

> *Suppose you had experienced only negative*
> *reactions from others*
> *and had received no love in your life,*
> *would you still be such a loving, happy man?*

Yes, I would be still the same. Whatsoever I am is not dependent on anybody else, it is my independence. It is the way I love to be, I enjoy to be; it has nothing to do with others. What others are doing with me or have done with me has nothing to do with what I am—they have not created me. I have *discovered* myself, nobody has created me. And a love that is created by others can be taken back. If it is only possible in a certain situation, the moment the situation changes your love will wither away. My love cannot wither away—because you have not created it.

Yes, I have received much love, but that has happened only because *I* loved, not before it. It was not a condition for the arousal of my love, it was only a response of existence.

All my sannyasins who have gathered around me from all over the world love me immensely, but that is not the cause of my love for them. Just the opposite is the case: because I have loved they have come to me; it is my love that has brought them to me. Now you will see me surrounded by so many loving people, but they have come to me because a certain magnetic love is in existence here; they are pulled by it. They are ready to do anything. I never *ask* them to do anything for me, but they are ready to do anything. They will be ready to die for me, although I would not like *anybody* to die for me. All that I would like is for them to *live* for me. Love cannot ask anyone to die, love can only ask: live in celebration!

But I have experienced and I go on experiencing all kinds of negativities. Millions of people would like me to be destroyed immediately, but that does not make any difference to my love. Love is something eternal, it is not temporal. It has nothing to do with time, nothing to do with others.

You say:

Does happiness require a certain resonance
and response from others or from God?

No, not at all. If it is dependent on others, then it is only pleasure and very momentary. And soon you will be frustrated by it because it will destroy your freedom; you will become dependent.

And remember: freedom is a higher value—higher than love. If love helps freedom only then is it of any value; if it destroys freedom then soon you will be tired of it, it will become a burden on you. If love becomes an imprisonment, howsoever beautiful, cozy, secure, comfortable, still you would not like to live in that prison. You would like to live under the sky, in the open, you would like to live in the unknown, you would like to live dangerously, because there you will have the ecstasy of freedom—the freedom of the bird on the wing, the freedom of the flowers.

Love is valuable only if it is in tune with freedom, but it can be in tune with freedom only if it is not given by others—not even by God—because if it is given by others it makes you a slave. And not only that: if it is given by others to you, you start *clinging* to others, you start expecting it, and every expectation brings a thousand and one frustrations. And that's what happened to Jesus Christ.

You say:

> *Even Jesus Christ did not die happily,*
> *as it is written in Matthew . . .*
> *"At the ninth hour, Jesus cried loudly,*
> *'Lord, Lord, why have you left me?' "*

According to me, up to this moment when Jesus cries to God, "Why have you forsaken me?" he is only Jesus, not Christ. He became Christ only in the last moment. That's why Christianity has been a dead religion from the very beginning, because Christ became a Christ only on the cross, at the last moment. He had no time to give his message, no time to sow the seeds, no time to help people to become enlightened.

Buddha lived for forty-two years after his enlightenment; naturally he managed to help thousands of people. He was the most fortunate Master *up to now*—underline it!—because hundreds of his disciples became enlightened before he left the world. He didn't die unhappily, he died fulfilled—fulfilled he was because he was enlightened and also fulfilled as a Master.

Krishnamurti is fulfilled as an enlightened man but is very much frustrated as a Master, and as his death is coming closer and closer and he is becoming older he is becoming more and more annoyed—annoyed because nothing is happening. Not a single human being has become enlightened. If Buddha up to now is the most fortunate enlightened man, then J. Krishnamurti is the most unfortunate!

Jesus had no time. Up to this cry he was only Jesus, because this cry shows—you are right, Holger—that he died unhappily, but you are not aware that something after this cry happened, just a few seconds later. You are missing those few seconds; those few seconds transformed his whole being. Up to this statement he is certainly a miserable man, and the misery is coming from expectations; otherwise why should he say, "Lord, Lord, why have you left me?"

He must have been hoping, expecting that some miracle would happen—that God would come down, something would save him at the last moment. The cross would suddenly change into a golden throne, hands from the sky would appear, and he would be saved. And at least one hundred thousand people had gathered to see the miracle.

There was no difference as far as expectations were concerned. Those people had gathered to see the miracle because they had heard so much about Jesus—that he walked on water, that he cured blind people, that he made the unhealthy healthy, that he had even raised a dead man, Lazarus, back to life. All that must have been sheer bullshit! Lazarus was his old friend—must have been pretending, may have been doing some yoga exercise, *pranayama*—holding the breath in. Yogis are known to do that very easily.

One yogi, Brahmayogi of South India, even gave demonstrations in Oxford, in Harvard, in Calcutta universities. For ten minutes even doctors had to certify that he was dead. He collected all those certificates from all the universities, from all the great experts who know when to declare a man dead, and he proved all of them wrong because after ten minutes he would start breathing again. He had become capable of stopping the breath for ten minutes. There are *pranayama* exercises, breathing exercises: you can stop breathing for a certain period of time, and in those moments you are as dead as one can be.

Lazarus must have been a yogi—he did well!

Brahmayogi also used to do another thing: he used to drink any kind of poison and he was capable of surviving. But in Rangoon he died, because he was capable of containing the poison for only thirty minutes, not more than that. He had learnt the yoga strategy of not allowing the poison to mix with the bloodstream. There *are* methods. . . .Yoga is a ten-thousand-year-old science; it has made many discoveries within the body, and these things are possible. And this is not an old story—it happened only in 1920, just sixty years ago.

But in Rangoon . . . you know, the traffic in the East is very strange. How people manage to go to their offices and come back home every evening is a miracle—a far bigger miracle than walking on water! You can see it in the Poona streets. . . .such crazy traffic that he got stuck. When he was coming back to his hotel from the university there was a traffic jam and he had to remain stuck in the traffic jam for more than thirty minutes. He came unconscious into the hotel and he died. The strategy was not workable for more than thirty minutes; that was as long as he was capable of containing the poison.

Lazarus must have been a friend indeed. And Jesus walking on the water must have known the rocks, where they were! In my own village I used to walk on water—I knew the rocks!

People had gathered to see: "Now the greatest miracle ever will happen." I can forgive the people, but I cannot forgive Jesus—even *he* was expecting, and nothing was happening. He was crucified and nothing happened, and everything was just going on without any miracle.

"Lord, Lord, why have you left me?"

Expectation brings frustration. This statement is enough proof that he was not yet a Buddha, not yet a man who has no expectations from life, no desires. He was still as unenlightened as the people who had gathered there—but he was certainly a very intelligent man. He immediately understood the point and immediately corrected it. He raised his eyes towards the sky and said, "Forgive me. Let *thy* kingdom come, let *thy* will be done."

The moment he said, "Let *thy* will be done," he became Christ. Before that he was only Jesus, son of Joseph and Mary, son of man. The moment he said, "Let thy kingdom come, let thy will be done," he surrendered his ego with all its expectations, his mind with all its desires. That *yes*, that total *yes!* And it could only be total at the last moment when he was dying. What was there to hold back? He totally surrendered; that was let-go. In that let-go he became Christ.

So, Holger, I will not say he died unhappily—he died blissfully. But you are right as far as it goes up to this statement, Matthew, Chapter 22; he is miserable, very miserable. But in the last moment the miracle happened—the *real* miracle—not that he was saved but that he surrendered. Resurrection is *not* the miracle, surrender is the miracle: "Thy will be done." The moment he said it totally there was no problem, no misery, no expectation, no frustration. He was at ease, at home. He was one with the universe. He attained to the fourth state, the *turiya*. He became awakened. He died an awakened man, but he could not give the message.

So Christianity is based on the teachings of Jesus— which are bound to be faulty, which are bound to be erroneous, which are bound to carry many flaws. And now I have decided to tell you what flaws they have! After *this* moment there is no flaw, no error—but he did not say anything at all! He died in absolute silence, blissfully.

That is the only moment which is precious in Jesus' life: for the first time he was absolutely free. When there is no desire there is freedom. For the first time he was absolutely free, because when there is no ego there is freedom.

Freedom does not mean freedom of the self: freedom means freedom *from* the self. And it brings immense bliss and benediction.

The last question

Bhagwan: It is really chilly again today.
Would you please tell us a few jokes
about Rajneesh sannyasins?
Okay, Shahido! First:

One night a great storm was raging; the wind was lashing waves up against the rocks and a boat foundered near the lighthouse. There was only one survivor, a Rajneesh sannyasin. The sannyasin, after swimming and sinking and swimming and sinking and being thrown against the rocks, finally reached the lighthouse. He crawled his way onto the shore and, exhausted, he made it to the door of the lighthouse and knocked on the door.

The lighthouse-keeper opened his small window and called out, "What do you want?"

"Nothing!" gasped the bruised sannyasin. "I was just passing by and I saw your lights on!"

Second:

The big game hunter was telling about his adventures to a group of sannysins. In describing some of his exciting experiences in Africa he said, "One night I remember being wakened by a great roaring noise. I jumped up and grabbed my gun, which I always kept loaded at the foot of my cot. I rushed out and killed a huge lion in my pajamas!"

At the close of his presentation he asked if there were any questions.

"Yes," said a sannysin sitting in the front row. "How did the lion get into your pajamas?"

Third:

Three men broke into the studio of a famous sannysin modernistic painter. They tied up the artist, forced open his wall safe and fled with all his money, tape recorder, tv, and all that they could put their hands upon. The next day the artist was found by other sannysins and released. He immediately called the police.

"Would you be able to identify the robbers?" the detective said.

"Oh, certainly," the sannysin said. "That's my business, remembering what things look like. I'll draw you a picture of them."

He drew the picture and gave it to the police. The next day they arrested a one-eyed go-go dancer, a buffalo, a garbage truck, and a Blue Diamond Hotel!

Fourth:

A sannysin was swimming in a river when he heard shouts coming from a drowning man up the river. He swam to the man and managed to save him. Afterward the sannysin found out that he had saved the Polack Pope.

"Now," said the Pope, "you can ask of me whatever you want."

The sannysin was nervous, he looked about furtively and whispered to the Pope, "just do me one favor—don't tell anyone that it was me who saved you."

Fifth:

The parents of a shapely teenaged sannysin noticed that their daughter was starting to fool around with men.

One evening before she went off to a disco they warned her of the perils she might encounter. "Darling, you must realize that men always try the same game. First he invites you to dance, then he offers you a drink. Soon he invites you up to his flat to listen to his record collection . . . once there, he throws you onto the bed. Then you are dishonored, your mother is dishonored, your father is dishonored."

The daughter went off on her date and returned home very late, with reddened face and disheveled hair.

"What happened?" asked her parents nervously.

"Well, you were right," replied the daughter. "He asked me to dance, he bought me a drink, and invited me to his place to listen to his record collection. But then . . . . *I* threw him onto the bed! And now *he* is dishonored, his mother is dishonored and his father is dishonored!"

Sixth:

A woman had just received her final divorce decree from a sannyasin and was chatting with a friend about it.

"He was terrible," she said. "At first he seemed so loving and understanding and romantic with his songs, but he turned out to be a tyrant!"

"Well," said her friend, "I hate to say I told you so but I said time and again that you should not marry him. Everybody knows that Rajneesh sannyasins make the world's worst husbands."

Six months later the divorcee fell in love and married another sannyasin. The next day she received this message with a bouquet of roses from her former husband: "Congratulations and best wishes for a happy marriage—signed: the Frying Pan."

The last:
A young woman sannyasin went to the chemist and said to the man behind the counter, "I want twelve condoms, please."

"What size would you like?" asked the man.

"Oh, assorted sizes," replied the young woman. "I'm going to a prick-nick!"

Discourse 11

December 21, 1980

EGO IS JUST A HABIT

The first question

Bhagwan: Would you please say something about the
relationship between spontaneity
and working on oneself?
Shouldn't we be loving as much as we can?
If there are certain things to do or ways to be
to increase our capacity for joy,
shouldn't we do them?
Shouldn't we let our egos drop?
Many good men have written
that love can begin as an impulse of the will,
and trying to be spontaneous
seems to be a contradiction.
Would you comment on this?
Mark Siegchrist,

ONE HAS TO WORK UPON ONESELF, but only in a negative way. One cannot work upon oneself in a positive way, because it is not a question of creating something but a question of discovering something which is already there.

When you paint, it is a positive act—you are creating the painting—but when you dig a well it is a negative act. The water is already there; you have only to remove a few layers of earth, stones, rocks. The moment you have removed them, the water becomes available. The water is there, *you* are here, and between the two there is a barrier: the barrier has to be removed. That's what I mean by negative work.

Man already has got whatsoever he is seeking and searching for. The truth is there, the bliss is there, the love is there—in one word, God is there. God is not a person, God is only the totality of all the values which are beyond mind. But the *mind* is the barrier, and you have to dig a well. You have to remove a few layers of thoughts, memories, desires, fantasies, dreams. The moment you have opened a door in the mind to the beyond, all that you always wanted becomes available.

The moment Gautam the Buddha became enlightened he laughed, and he said to nobody in particular—he said to himself—"This is ridiculous! I have been searching for it for thousands of lives, and it has been lying deep down within myself!"

The sought is in the seeker. Hence the Upanishads say the method to find it is *neti neti*. *Neti neti* means 'neither this nor that'; it is a process of elimination. You go on negating, eliminating. Finally, when there is nothing to be eliminated, nothing to be negated, when you have totally emptied yourself, it is found.

So the first thing to be understood, Mark, is: working on oneself gives you the feeling of some positive work, and that is wrong. Working on oneself simply means a negative process; it is emptying yourself. And the moment you are empty of the mind and all its processes, spontaneity explodes. Once you understand that the process is negative, then there is no contradiction between the process and spontaneity.

Spontaneity simply means now there is nothing to hinder your self-nature from expressing itself. All the rocks have been removed, all the doors have been opened. Now your self-nature can sing its song, it can dance its dance.

I use both the words: sometimes I say, "Work upon yourself," and sometimes I say, "Be spontaneous." And the logical mind is bound to find a contradiction, but there is no contradiction at all—because working on oneself means *neti neti*, neither this nor that.

Spontaneity has not to be created; if it is created it is not spontaneity. Then there is a contradiction: if it is cultivated then it is not spontaneous, obviously. A cultivated spontaneity cannot be true; it will be false, phony, pseudo, it will be only a mask. You may be simply acting, you will not be really spontaneous. And it cannot go very deep; it will remain only something painted from the outside. Just scratch the so-called cultivated, spontaneous person, and all his spontaneity will be gone. He was only acting, he was not really spontaneous.

Real spontaneity comes from the center; it is uncultivated, that's why we call it spontaneity. There is no way to cultivate it, no way to create it, no need either. But if you want to become an actor, if you want to act, then it is a totally different matter—but remember: any real situation will immediately provoke your mind. It will come rushing towards the surface; all spontaneity will disappear.

It was carnival time, and the gay guy dressed himself up as a lioness. A hunter carrying a rifle approached him. "Bang! Bang!" He pretended to shoot him. The lioness fell down dead. The crowd was amused.

As the hunter was about to leave, the gay guy pulled off his lion's head and said softly, "It's the law of the jungle, sweetie: if you kill, you eat!"

Anything cultivated will be only on the surface, it will be only a drama; it will not be your authenticity.

So I will say the first thing to remember is: spontaneity has to be discovered—or, it will be better to say, *re*discovered, because when you were a child you were spontaneous. You have lost it because so much has been cultivated—so many disciplines, so many moralities, virtues, characters. You have learnt to play so many roles, that's why you have forgotten the language of being just yourself.

The second thing you ask:

Shouldn't we be loving as much as we can?

Love is never a should, it cannot be commanded. You cannot *force* yourself to love as much as you can. That's what people are doing and that's why love is missing in the world. From the very beginning we start making the child false, and every falsity creates schizophrenia, it creates a double personality, it creates a split.

Every child is born whole, but we divide him in two. We tell him what to repress and what to express. We tell him what has *not* to be done and what *has* to be done. Whether he really feels it or not is irrelevant. And the child is so helpless, so dependent, that he has to listen to our dictates. And we have not yet been able to be democratic with children—we are dictatorial. We *talk* about democracy, but our whole way, our very pattern of life is dictatorial, it is non-democratic, it is really anti-democratic.

The child is not allowed to be himself; we start forcing him to be somebody else. And he *has* to follow us because it is a question of survival. If he does not follow us then he is in danger: he cannot live on his own, he has to compromise, and every compromise is a falsification.

We say to the child, "I am your father—love me!" as if just because you are a father there is some natural inevitability that love should flow towards you. And if it is inevitable, why say it? The very asking shows that it is not inevitable. The child may love, may not love; it will depend on you, on whether you are worth loving or not. Just being a father does not mean anything.

And the institution of father is something invented by man; it is not a natural thing at all, it is institutional. Some day it may disappear because there was a time when it was not there. For thousands of years humanity lived without the institution of fatherhood.

You may be surprised to know that the word 'uncle' is older than the word 'father', because matriarchy preceded patriarchy. The mother was there and the father was not known, because the mother was meeting, merging, melting with many people. Somebody had to be the father, but there was no way to find out. So all were uncles—all potential fathers were uncles. The word 'uncle' is older in *every* language than the word 'father'.

And it will be better to call God 'the Uncle' than 'the Father'—it is sweeter! But the Talmud, the Jewish scripture, says: "God is not your uncle, he is not nice. If you don't listen to him, if you don't follow him, he will throw you into hell." Exactly these are the words: "God is not nice, God is not your uncle." And I say to you, God is *not* your father, and he is *nice*, and it is better to call him 'Uncle'.

The institution of fatherhood came into existence with the invention of private property; they are joined together. The father represents private property, because when private property came into existence everybody wanted his own child to inherit it. "I will not be here, but a part of me should inherit my property." Private property came first, then came the father.

And to be absolutely certain that "The child is my own," the idea became prevalent in almost all the societies of the world that before marriage the woman has to be absolutely virgin—otherwise it is difficult to decide. She may already be carrying a child when she gets married, she may already be pregnant, and then the child will be somebody else's and he will inherit the property. To make sure that "It is *my* child that is going to inherit my property," virginity was imposed on women.

And you can see the difference: man was never expected to be virgin. They say, "Boys will be boys"—it is allowed—but the girl should be absolutely virgin. All kinds of stupidities have happened in the past because before getting married the woman had to provide proofs that she was really a virgin.

Sometimes by accident it can happen that the thin screen that proves the virginity of a woman is broken.

She may have fallen, or maybe it happened horse-riding, or something like that, or on a bicycle . . . these are dangerous things, avoid them! They are against virginity! The thin screen that proves that the woman has not been penetrated sexually. . . .In the West, particularly in the Middle Ages, if some accident had happened then the girl had to go to the doctors so they could put a false screen back to prove that she was a virgin, otherwise she would not get a good husband.

It is the whole idea of private property that has created the father, that has created the family, that has created the ownership of the woman by the man. If there was a time when there was no father, no private property, a day is *bound* to come when there will be no private property—the father will disappear.

But the father insists: "Love me—I am your father!" and the child has to pretend that he loves. There is not even any necessity for the child to love the mother. It is one of the laws of nature that the mother has a natural instinct of love for the child, but not vice versa—the child has no natural instinct to love the mother. He *needs* the mother, that's one thing, he uses the mother, that's one thing, but there is no law of nature that he should *love* the mother. He *likes* her because she is so helpful, so useful; without her he cannot exist. So he is grateful, respectful—all these things are okay—but love is a totally different phenomenon.

Love flows downwards from the mother to the child, not backwards. And it is very simple because the child's love will flow towards his own child, it cannot go backwards—just as the Ganges goes on flowing towards the ocean, not towards the source. The mother is the source, and love flows onwards to the new generation. To turn it backwards is a forced act, unnatural, unbiological.

But the child has to pretend because the mother says, "I am your mother—you *have* to love me!" And what can the child do? He can only pretend, so he becomes a politician. Every child becomes a politician from the very cradle. He starts smiling when the mother enters the room—a Jimmy Carter smile! He does not feel any joy, but he *has* to smile. He has to open his mouth and do some exercise of the lips—that helps him, that is a survival measure. But love is becoming false.

And once you have learnt the cheaper kind of love, the plastic kind, then it is very difficult to discover the original, the real, the authentic. Then he has to love his sisters and brothers, and there is no reason really. In fact, who loves his own sister and for what? These are all ideas implanted to keep the family together. But this whole process of falsification brings you to a point where when you fall in love that love also is false.

You have forgotten what real love is. You fall in love with the color of the hair—now, what has that to do with love? After two days you will not look at the color of the hair at all. Or you fall in love with a certain shape of nose or a certain kind of eyes, but after the honeymoon these things are just boring! And then you have to go on managing somehow, pretending, cheating.

Your spontaneity has been corrupted and poisoned, otherwise you would not fall in love with parts. But you only fall in love with parts. If somebody asks you, "Why do you love this woman or this man?" your answer will be, "Because she looks so beautiful," or, "Because of her nose, eyes, proportion of the body, this and that"—and all this is nonsense! Then this love cannot be very deep and cannot be of any value. It cannot become intimacy. It cannot have a lifelong flow; soon it will dry up—it is so superficial. It has not arisen out of the heart, it is a mind phenomenon. Maybe she looks like an actress and that's why you like her, but liking is not love.

Love is a totally different kind of phenomenon, indefinable, mysterious—so mysterious that Jesus says,

"God is love." He makes God and love synonymous, indefinable. But that natural love is lost.

And, Mark, you say:

Shouldn't we be loving as much as we can?

Do you think it is a question of *doing* something as much as you can? It is not a question of doing. It is a heart phenomenon. It is a kind of transcendence of the mind and body. It is not prose, it is poetry. It is not mathematics, it is music. You cannot *do* it, you can only *be* it. Love is not something that you *do*, love is something that you are. But these 'shoulds' are heavy on your spontaneity.

And you say:

If there are certain things to do or ways to be
to increase our capacity for joy,
shouldn't we do them?

The whole idea is of *doing* something, and the reality is discovered by being, not by doing. The question is not of doing anything; the question is of becoming silent and discovering your being. Doing is always extrovert.

Of course, if you want more money, you have to *do* something. Just sitting silently doing nothing, the spring comes . . . and the money does not grow by itself! The *grass* grows by itself, but not the money. You will have to do much: you will have to run after it, you will have to fight for it, you will have to be aggressive, ambitious, violent; it is a very competitive world as far as money is concerned. But your *being* is not something outside you.

If you want to be the president or the prime minister of a country you have to do much, you have to be constantly doing; there is no rest, no peace. And you have to be almost insane, because the fight is going to be tough. Unless you are utterly mad after power it is im--possible for you to reach.

But your being is not outside, there, and there is nobody competing with you for your being. And nobody can enter into your being; you are alone there. And it is already the case; you just have to turn in, you just have to look in.

So all that is needed is, Mark, sitting silently, doing nothing. . . .When you are not doing anything—physically, mentally—when you are in a *deep* interval, in a pause, all activity has ceased, then the being is discovered. Activity creates dust.

When Winston Churchill had become very old, his physician came and asked him, "How are you feeling?"

He was ill. He said, "I am kicking, but I am not creating as much dust as before."

In the world if you want money, power, prestige, you have to kick and create as much dust as you can. The more you kick, the more dust you create, the better. But for the inner world you have to stop kicking and creating dust so that all dust settles and you can see clearly who you are.

So it is not a question of doing anything. Bliss is your self-nature—just discover your being and you will find it *as* a consequence.

Jesus says: "Seek ye first the kingdom of God, and all else shall be added unto you"—and he is right. "Seek ye first the kingdom of God"—and that is within you, because he repeats again and again: "The kingdom of God is within you."

So just go withinwards and find your self-nature, and finding it all is found. Joy is found, truth is found, love is found, freedom is found, eternity is found, God is found.

And you ask:

Shouldn't we let our egos drop?

You are thinking as if ego is something that you are carrying and that you can drop. Ego is only an illusion, it is only an idea. It has not to be dropped, it cannot be dropped. How can you drop an idea?

For example, it is getting dark in the evening and on the road you see a rope, but it appears to you as a snake. Now, can you kill the snake? In the first place the snake is not there! Can you avoid the snake? In the first place the snake is not there. Can you be unafraid of the snake? In the first place the snake is not there, so all these things are irrelevant. All that is needed is a little light—just a candle will do—and you will see the snake has never been there. It was just an idea, an illusion, a projection.

The moment you find the rope, will you ask, "Now what to do with the snake? Should I drop it? Should I forget all about it?"

The moment you discover your being there is no ego found. Ego is only a projection: just as the snake is projected on the rope, ego is projected on the being. You don't know the rope, hence the snake; you don't know your being, hence the ego. Ego is not knowing your being; not being aware of your being is what ego is all about. So there is no question of dropping it.

But many people try to drop it, and the miracle is, they even succeed! They become humble. But humbleness is another trick of the ego, a very subtle trick—the ego has come from the back door—because to drop it simply means you have not understood it at all, so it is *bound* to come.

I used to live in a town where a man was very well known, almost as a saint, and many people had told me, "He is so humble!" Finally the man came to see me; he touched my feet and he said, "I am just dust underneath your feet!"

I looked at him—his eyes were saying something else, his nose was saying something else—so I said, "I can see you are absolutely right: you are just dust underneath my feet!"

He said, "What?!" He became very angry.

I said, "But I am simply agreeing with you! I have not said anything of my own! *You* started it and I have simply agreed with you, so why are you getting irritated?"

I told him, "Now close your eyes and sit silently and see the point! This is just another way of your ego trying to fulfill itself. The ego is there; now it is upside-down, doing *sirshasana*, the headstand. But it is the *same* ego; now it is pretending to be humble."

Three Christian monks met on a road. One said, "As far as scholarship is concerned, our sect is the most scholarly, the most philosophical. Nobody can compete with us in theological matters."

The second said, "You are right, but as far as ascetic practices are concerned, you stand nowhere compared to us!"

The third laughed and he said, "You are both right, but as far as humbleness is concerned, we are the tops!"

Now humbleness . . . "And we are the tops!" Even humbleness will play the same game.

Please, Mark, don't drop your ego! Understand it, be aware of it, bring the light of awareness and see—and you will not find it. You will not find it so there is no question of dropping it. *Don't drop it!* If you drop it, it will come back in some other form. It cannot leave you —it is just an old habit of unconscious mind.

The political situation in a South American country was very shaky. The military was worried. They managed to apprehend the country's greatest gossiper and they condemned him to death.

The gossiper was lined up for execution in front of a wall. When the order "Fire!" was shouted, the man fell down. After some minutes the gossiper realized that he was not dead.

The general approached him and said sternly, "You are such a fucking gossiper that I did this just to scare you. These bullets are blanks! Now I hope you have learnt your lesson—you can go free."

The gossiper ran hurriedly to the street outside where he was immediately approached by a friend. "Hey, Pablo," the friend asked him, "do you have any news?'

"Well," said the gossiper in a hushed voice, "don't tell anyone, but our headquarters don't have any ammunition!"

Old habits . . . they die hard!

Ego is just a habit, a habit of ignorance, unconsciousness; it will come back. Please don't drop it! Don't feed it, don't drop it, because in both ways you will be saving it. Just watch it, and you will not find it.

The Bishop received a large number of complaints about Father O'Reilly's bitter attacks on the British from his London pulpit.

"You can't go on speaking to your congregation in that fashion," his Lordship told the priest. "Remember the law of charity and the fact that you live in the country of which you speak so harshly. Next week I ask you to give a sermon on the Last Supper. With that topic you will not be able to indulge your bias."

Father O'Reilly accepted the rebuke mildly, but the Bishop discreetly attended the service the following Sunday to check that all went well. He had no cause to complain, and not once in the course of his sermon did the priest refer to the Base, Brutal and Bloody Saxon. The Bishop noticed with satisfaction that he was drawing to the end of what had been a very good and inoffensive piece of religious instruction: ". . . and having asked all the disciples, it was time to turn to Judas," Father O'Reilly said. " 'Judas,' came the question, 'wouldst thou betray me?' "

The priest paused and looked around. "Judas looked back without blinking an eyelid and then, with the treachery of his kind, he answered, 'Not bloomin' likely, guv!' "

The whole sermon went well, but his bias has come from the back door: "Not bloomin' likely, guv!" He has said it—he may not even be aware of it himself.

The only thing to remember is to watch where the ego is, and you will not find it—nobody has ever found it. Whosoever has looked for it has not found it, and those who have been trying to drop it have never been able to get rid of it.

Then you ask:

*Many good men have written
that love can begin as an impulse of the will.*

That is sheer nonsense! Love can *never* begin as an impulse of the will. Will means effort, will means imposition, will means compulsion, will means discipline. Will means forcing yourself to do something *against* yourself.

Love cannot begin that way, and if it begins in that way it will not be love but something else. And if the beginning is wrong, if the first step is wrong, the last step cannot be right.

And I know that many good men have written, Mark, but those good men are just phony. They are not Buddhas, they are not awakened people. They are as blind as anybody else, they are as blind as the whole of humanity. They are good—they have tried to be good, they have managed to be good—but they are boiling within. They have repressed themselves, that's all, and they have succeeded in repressing themselves. They have been able to create a beautiful facade and they are hiding behind the facade. They may be wearing glasses, but they are blind. And if you are wearing dark glasses, nobody will think that you are blind. Many blind people wear dark glasses just to hide their blindness.

"I want to go to the cinema, Mom! I want to go to the cinema! Let's go to the cinema," says the little boy very excitedly.

"Shut up and don't bother me!" says the mother irately. "You know very well that you are blind!"

But it is very difficult to know very well that you are blind! You can be good, you can be very disciplined, you can have a moral character, you can have a conscience, but unless you have consciousness you don't have any eyes. Those good people were good because they followed the rules of the crowd, and that's why one person may be thought good in one society, and the same person may not be thought good in another society.

Hindus think Ramakrishna is enlightened. Ask the Jainas and they cannot agree with you because he continued to eat fish, and according to the Jaina morality to eat fish and to become enlightened is impossible. One has to be absolutely vegetarian.

The Jainas have not conceded enlightenment even to Krishna, because he was the cause of the great war of *Mahabharat*. He persuaded Arjuna to fight. In fact, Arjuna was going to become a Jaina monk; he wanted to renounce the world and go to the mountains, but Krishna persuaded him—not only persuaded him, forced him in every possible way, gave him all kinds of arguments, and he argued well. It does not seem that he *convinced* Arjuna, but he silenced him. His argument was such, Arjuna tried in every possible way to escape, but Krishna would not give him any door to escape by.

Seeing that "This man is not going to leave and I cannot convince him," Arjuna thought, "it is better to fight and be finished." So finally he said, "Thank you, I am convinced"—but he was *not* convinced.

And the proof is that the *Mahabharat* has the story that when they were reaching the ultimate goal of paradise they all started melting on the way. Only Yudishthira with his dog reached the door of the ultimate. Even Arjuna melted on the way, disappeared on the way, evaporated on the way; even he was not able to reach the ultimate door. That shows perfectly that he missed Krishna's message—he was not yet enlightened, he was not yet awakened.

Evaporating on the way means getting born again into the world. Even the dog of Yudishthira reached, and the disciple of Krishna could not reach!

Jainas say Krishna has gone to the seventh hell because he created the greatest violence in the world. Now, who is good?

Do you think Jesus Christ is good? Ask Hindus, ask Buddhists, ask Jainas, and they will say, "No, not at all!" because according to *their* morality, according to *their* philosophy one suffers only because of past life sins—and the crucifixion is a great suffering. That simply proves that Jesus Christ must have committed great sins, may have murdered somebody, raped somebody, must have done something *really* bad, otherwise why should he get crucified?

Jainas say that when Mahavira—their *teerthankara*, their Christ—walks on a path, if there is a thorn lying on the path it immediately turns upside-down, seeing that Mahavira is coming by, because even a thorn cannot give pain to Mahavira. He is finished with all bad karmas, pain is impossible—so what about crucifixion? Jesus must have been a criminal in his past lives—may have been a Genghis Khan, Tamerlane, Nadir Shah, a Hitler—something like this!

And ask the Christians what they say about Mahavira or Buddha or Shankaracharya, and they will say these people are very selfish people—just meditating, not serving the poor. Jesus helped the blind, gave them eyes, turned stones into bread to serve the poor, even raised the dead back to life. His whole life was one of service to humanity.

Now what is there of service to humanity in Mahavira's life? Standing naked . . . is that a service to humanity? Just meditating with closed eyes and enjoying your inner self, being blissful—is that service to humanity? When the whole of humanity is suffering and you are enjoying yourself—is it human? It is inhuman!

Buddha, Mahavira, Krishna, these people cannot be thought good people according to the Christians. Now, what is this Krishna doing?—playing on the flute and girls dancing around him, and the whole of humanity is suffering! There are poor people and blind people, and hospitals are needed and schools are needed.

Do you think if Krishna was alive he would have got the Nobel Prize? Mother Teresa of Calcutta gets it, because she runs houses for orphans, serves the poor, feeds the poor. And this man Krishna, instead of serving the poor, was hitting with stones the poor girls carrying their milk-pots, so their pots would be broken, their milk would be spilt . . . and this man they call God! Instead of helping the poor he would take the poor women's clothes when they were taking a bath in the river and sit in a tree with the clothes. What kind of religiousness is this? This man has to be given to the police!

If you look around, who is good? Mohammed is good?—who carried a sword his whole life and killed many people and fought many wars? According to Buddha he is not good, according to Mahavira he is not good—he is violent. He married *nine* women. Now, is this the sign of a man of character? A man of character remains celibate! Shankaracharya is a man of character, remains celibate.

Jesus drinks wine. Now, Mohammed cannot agree with that—he is very much against wine. And this Krishna playing on the flute—Mohammed cannot agree that this man is good. He is as allergic to music as I am to perfume! He is very anti-music.

Now, who is good . . . ?

Mark, all our ideas of good are invented—only the awakened is good. So, according to me, the awakened person is good. Acts don't count at all, only consciousness counts. So, according to me, Mahavira is good, Krishna is good, Mohammed is good, Buddha is good, Ramakrishna is good, Christ is good, for the simple reason that they are all awakened. Now it is up to *their* consciousness to decide what to do and what not to do.

Jesus is so awakened that he can drink wine but he does not become drunk. What is wrong in it? There is nothing wrong in it. He has to decide for himself, nobody else can decide for him.

Mahavira is so awakened that he wants to be just as naked as a child; there is no need to hide anything, so he drops his clothes. Nobody else can be decisive. When you have your own consciousness, your acts are born out of that consciousness.

According to me, the only possible definition of good is: the act that comes out of a conscious being, whatsoever the act. But ordinarily we think about acts as good and bad; acts are neither good nor bad. The same act of drinking wine is good because *Jesus* is doing it, and it is bad if somebody who is not awakened goes on doing it. Both are doing the same act! Mahavira standing naked is good and a girl doing a striptease is not good. Consciousness is the only decisive factor.

You say:

> *Many good men have written
> that love can begin as an impulse of the will . . .*

Those good men are not *good* really; they are just traditional, orthodox. They have followed the scriptures, and when you are unconscious whatsoever you interpret is your interpretation.

A country bumpkin sort of fellow was elected Justice of the Peace in a backwoods town. Although he could count money, he had never learnt to read and write much beyond being able to sign his name. Not being able to read the law and also not wanting people to know how ignorant he was, he developed a system of fining people—not from a lawbook but from a Sears Roebuck catalog.

One day a stranger who was visiting a cousin in town was picked up for speeding. When he was found guilty, the judge solemnly fingered through his catalog and fined the man $9. The man was angry about the way he had been treated and was complaining about it to his cousin.

His cousin said, "You are lucky. He fined you the price of a parasol for only $9. If he had turned the page he would have fined you $385 for a piano!"

People are turning the pages of their scriptures, not knowing about their own selves. What can they understand? They are all catalogs! It may be the Gita or the Bible or the Koran, it makes no difference. What you are finding there is your own mind, it is your own reflection; it cannot be otherwise.

You are unconscious—you cannot be good.

A female voice on the phone at three a.m. begged the police to come as fast as they could. She said her husband was awakened by a noise in the back yard and when he went outside to investigate he was set upon and struck down by an unseen attacker.

A patrolman was dispatched from the police station at once and he was on the scene of the crime within minutes. Half an hour later he returned to headquarters with a sour look on his face and a huge lump on his forehead.

"Back already?" the desk sergeant asked. "Did you find the attacker?"

"Yes," the patrolman said, "I stepped on the rake too!"

In your unconsciousness what good can come out of you?

You say, Mark:

> *Many good men have written*
> *that love can begin as an impulse of the will . . .*

They don't know at all about love *or* about will. Will is another name for the ego and love means egolessness. How can egolessness begin through the ego?

A really religious person is not a man of will. A really religious person has dropped his will; he allows God's will to flow through him. That's what Jesus says at the last moment on the cross: "Let thy kingdom come, let *thy* will be done."

There are hundreds of books written all over the world about will power—that is nothing but ego power. The really religious person is absolutely egoless, will-less; he is just a hollow bamboo, a flute. Whatsoever God wants to sing he sings; if he does not want to sing, the flute remains silent. The flute has no will of its own because it is no more separate from existence.

The religious person is good—good in the sense that he is one with God. He has dissolved himself into God, he has forgotten all separation, he has attained to union with God.

Love cannot begin in will, as will, as an impulse of the will.

And you say:

> *. . . but trying to be spontaneous*
> *seems to be a contradiction.*

Of course if you think that love begins in an impulse of the will, then being or trying to be spontaneous will be a contradiction. But love does not begin as an impulse of the will and there is no contradiction. Love is spontaneity itself.

And I am not telling you to try to be spontaneous. How can you try to be spontaneous? That will be a contradiction! I am telling you to understand what you are doing, what you are thinking, what you are feeling—watch it.

That's what meditation is: watching all your acts, physical, mental. . . .When you can watch actions, thoughts, feelings—these three dimensions have to be watched—as your watchfulness grows, you will enter the fourth, *turiya*. The Mandukya Upanishad talks about the fourth. Watching the three you will enter the fourth—just by watching; it is not a question of trying. Trying means effort; watching means relaxedness, being utterly relaxed, just seeing whatsoever is passing.

Thoughts are passing always on the screen of the mind. Just be relaxed, sit in an easy chair as if you are watching the television. The mind is an inbuilt television! You can simply watch, and it is very colorful. Just by watching it you will see the watcher is not the watched, the observer is not the observed. A separation has started happening, a disidentification from the bodymind complex. And in that very disidentification you start centering, you start getting grounded in your very being. That will bring spontaneousness.

It is not a question of practising it. It is only a question of watching all that is happening *in* you, through you, so that you can see one day your seer, so that one day you can become aware of your own awareness. That is the ultimate peak of human growth; beyond that nothing else exists. One becomes a Buddha, and then whatsoever you do is good, whatsoever you do is love, whatsoever you do is service, is compassion.

The second question

Bhagwan: Is all esotericism nonsense?

Viramo,

Y ES! IT IS AN ESCAPE from reality into fantasy. People are thinking about heaven and hell, and they don't know who they are. And there are people who are describing detailed maps about heaven and hell. In the temples there are maps available, and these maps are very ancient.

Man came to know maps of the earth only recently; just three hundred years ago man discovered that the earth is a globe. Maps of the earth have been made only within the last three hundred years, and maps of heaven have been there for at least five thousand years. But it is easy because you are free to make your own map; nobody can refute it because it is only a question of fantasy and imagination.

Jainas have their maps, Buddhists have their maps, Hindus have their maps, and they are all contradictory.

One man came to see me, a follower of Radhaswami, and he said, "Bhagwan, what do you say? Our guru has said that there are fourteen heavens, and our guru has reached the fourteenth. And he has also said . . . " He had brought the whole list: Rama has reached only up to the fifth, Buddha and Mahavira have reached up to the seventh, Christ is only up to the fourth, Mohammed up to the third, Kabir, Nanak, they have reached up to the twelfth—and their own guru has reached up to the fourteenth. The fourteenth is called *Sachkhand*—the true heaven.

He asked me, "What do you say about it?"

I said, "Your guru is right—I know him!"

He said, "What do you mean?"

I said, "Because there are *fifteen* heavens and I am in the fifteenth! And he is always asking me, 'Bhagwan, somehow carry me to the fifteenth!' Your guru is in the fourteenth—I know him!"

He became very angry. He said, "What are you saying? You have reached beyond *my* guru?"

I said, "If he can reach beyond Buddha and Mahavira and Krishna and Christ, what is wrong in my reaching beyond him? And when there are fifteen, what can I do?"

I told him, "The name of the fifteenth is *Mahasachkhand*—the *great* land of truth. Your guru has reached only to the true land, I have reached to the *great* truth!"

These fools go on talking about all kinds of nonsense. Esotericism is just an escape from reality; it is a kind of madness.

The psychiatrist was very pleased with Sean's progress. "You're doing fine, Sean," he said soothingly. "You've improved much more than Barry. He's going around telling everyone he wants to buy the Bank of Ireland."

Sean suddenly grew very excited. "Oh, the ruffian!" he shouted. "I've told him a dozen times I won't sell!"

It is a question of insanity and nothing else—people talking about hells, how many hells there are. Hindus think there are three, Jainas think there are seven, and there was a contemporary of Mahavira, Sanjay Vilethiputta was his name—he must have been a man just like me; I love that man—he said, "Seven? There are seven hundred! Your Mahavira knows nothing! He may have only penetrated up to the seventh so he is talking about seven, but I have traveled the whole way. There are seven hundred, and there are also seven hundred heavens to balance!"

A man went to visit a madhouse and started talking with a madman. "You seem sane enough to me, why are you here?" he asked.

"Well, to tell you the truth, I don't know. Maybe it's because I like children."

"What's wrong with that? I like children too."

"Really? Fried or boiled?"

Once upon a time there was a guy called Urinjibhai Morarjibhai Desai who had become the Prime Minister of India. He was very esoteric. He was inaugurating direct telephone-links between heaven and hell. He called heaven first and talked to Saint Peter for about ten minutes. After that he called a few old friends who had gone to hell and talked to them for a few hours. When he had finished he called the operator to ask the charges of the calls.

"The call to heaven cost 780 rupees," said the operator. "The call to hell was fifty paise."

"My God!" Urinjibhai Morarjibhai Desai said. "Why do prices differ so much?"

"Well, it's simple, sir," stated the operator. "The call to heaven was long distance, while the one to hell was only a local call!"

Yes, Viramo, all esotericism is nonsense—except Almasto's esoteric questions. She has again asked. She says, "Bhagwan, can I ask a few more esoteric questions?" I love her esoteric questions—they are *really* esoteric!

First:
How many Gandhians does it take to screw in a lightbulb?
Almasto, five. First of all Urinjibhai Morarjibhai Desai to hold the lightbulb, and the other four to turn the table he is standing on. This is called non-violent Gandhian revolution!

Second:
How many communists does it take to screw in a lightbulb?
Almasto, two. One to screw in the lightbulb and one to pass out pamphlets.

Third:
How many Jews does it take to screw in a lightbulb?
Almasto, three. One to call the cleaning woman and two to feel guilty about calling the cleaning woman.

Fourth:
How many EST followers does it take to screw in a lightbulb?
Almasto, a roomful. They take turns as the leader tells them what rotten and worthless bulb-screwers they are. Nobody is allowed to leave to go to the bathroom while the screwing is in progress.

Fifth:

How many Indian mahatmas does it take to screw in a lightbulb?

Almasto, four. One to screw in the lightbulb and three to complain about how much better the old bulb was.

Sixth:
How many *brahmacharins*—celibate Hindu monks—does it take to screw in a lightbulb?

Almasto, two. One to screw in the lightbulb and one to keep his knee from jerking.

Seventh:
How many journalists does it take to screw in a lightbulb?

Almasto, two. One to screw in the lightbulb and one to give it a surprising twist at the end.

Eighth:
How many student radicals does it take to screw in a lightbulb?

Almasto, three. One to screw in the lightbulb and two to insist it be turned further to the left.

Ninth:
How many Union electricians does it take to screw in a lightbulb?

Almasto, thirteen. One to get the lightbulb, one to get the lightbulb to the screwer-inner, one to screw in the lightbulb, one to hold him steady, one to flick the switch to test the lightbulb, one to make sure that the other bulbs in the room will need fixing, one to supervise, one to shout, two to take a coffee break, one to eat lunch, one to nap, one to plot the best way of breaking into the apartment at night.

And the last:
How many Californians does it take to screw in a lightbulb?

Almasto, seven. One to screw in the lightbulb and six to share the experience.

Discourse 12

December 22, 1980

GET DISTURBED

The first question

*Bhagwan: I was brought up
in a moral and religious Hindu family,
hence I am very much disturbed
by your sannyasins' behavior.
Can't you give them some kind of moral discipline?*
Pratap Chandra Joshi,

IT IS YOUR PROBLEM, not *their* problem! You are suffering from a moral discipline, you want my sannyasins also to suffer. *You* are disturbed so *you* have to be cured. *They* are not disturbed!

But it always happens that you can see your own projections upon others' screens, but you can't see that they are *your* projections. Your religious and moral upbringing has been utterly wrong. If it had been true, nothing would disturb you, nothing at all; you would remain calm and quiet, centered, grounded.

It is none of your business what others are doing! They are not doing it to *you*, they are not interfering with you—who are you to decide how they should behave? Is it not a very undemocratic attitude? You want them to behave according to *your* mind, but *why* should they behave according to you? Who are you? You are free to do *your* thing, they are free to do their own thing. They are not disturbed by your moral and religious upbringing. They are not asking me, "Bhagwan, give this Pratap Chandra Joshi some discipline so he behaves like *we* behave."

The very desire that others should behave according to *your* ideology, according to *your* conceptions, according to your conclusions, is despotic—it is fascist. You are neither moral nor religious, you are simply a fascist!

And remember, morality has nothing to do with religion. Religion, of course, has much to do with morality, but not vice versa. Morality is a poor substitute for true religion; it is a plastic substitute for the real thing. It gives you a facade but not a new being. It does not change your center, your consciousness; it only paints your face. It is a mask. You can hide behind it and you can hide all kinds of repressed desires, longings, ambitions behind it. And whenever you see others behaving naturally, which *your* morality does not allow you, you will feel disturbed. The disturbance is coming from *you*, not from them.

> *The puritan people of Teeling*
> *Express all their horror with feeling.*
> *When they see that a chair*
> *Has all its legs bare*
> *They look away straight to the ceiling.*

Now, do you think chairs should be given some moral discipline, that their legs should be covered? They used to be covered in Victoria's days. In England it was very improper to leave your chairs' legs uncovered! But it simply shows a decadent society, a basically irreligious society.

Bhagwan removes a greeting card from His clipboard. On the card is drawn the cartoon figure of a woman with two holes punched through the card where her breasts should be. Bhagwan places two of His fingertips through the holes, thus giving the visual impression that her bare breasts are showing. He then places the card up in front of Him so everyone can see. The hall explodes in laughter.

Pratap Chandra Joshi, wake up and look at this picture . . . What can you see? Get disturbed! And it is nothing . . . just two holes! But you must have got disturbed, very much disturbed—and it was nothing but my two fingers! Don't be so foolish!

People go on seeing things . . . just now you have seen 'things' which are not there!

A mother and her daughter were in the kitchen when the mother noticed that little Mary was drawing a big prick. "Where have you seen that?" asked the mother, surprised.

"In your hands, Mummy!" replied little Mary innocently.

The mother hit the little girl and said angrily, "In *my* hands, hmm? You just wait till your father gets home!"

When the father got home he asked little Mary, "What did you draw that your mother has become so angry with you?"

"A pair of scissors, Dad," replied Mary sweetly.

Poor Mary, innocent Mary was just drawing a pair of scissors! Children are children—their drawings are not so accurate. But the mother read something else into it. And of course she had seen the scissors in her mother's hands—she was absolutely right.

That's what is happening to you. . . .

A man was dining out with his priest and they went to an Italian restaurant. As they were looking over the menu, the man said to the priest, "How do you pronounce that Italian dish that you are so wild about?"

Without looking up from the menu the priest said, "Gina Lollobrigida!"

It is *your* unconscious that crops up in moments when there is a certain situation—and here the situation is available. My people live out of freedom—that's my only discipline. They are not slaves to any moral code. They are religious people and you are not religious at all, whatsoever your so-called Hindu, moral and religious upbringing. You are *not* religious at all; you are simply carrying ideas implanted by others in your head.

You may have a conscience, but you don't have a consciousness. A conscience is a creation by others and a consciousness is a discovery by oneself.

My sannyasins are making every possible effort to throw out all the rubbish that their parents, priests and politicians have imposed upon them. That is part of the discipline of freedom: you have to become unconditioned.

Naturally, when conditioned people come they get very much disturbed. Perhaps in their disturbance there is some element of jealousy too—that they have not been so free in their lives. "How do these people dare? They should be prevented immediately! If we have been slaves, then everybody should be a slave!"

But the very desire that others should be disciplined is inhuman, ugly, violent, destructive, animalistic. What does it have to do with religion? Moralistic certainly it is, but morality is of no value at all. Morality simply means others have been telling you what should be done, what should not be done, and you have not been able to rebel against these impositions. They have been telling you, "If you do this, then you will have respectability, then you will have all the pleasures of heaven." You are greedy and they are exploiting your greed.

They say, "If you don't follow us then you will fall into hell, hellfire, and for eternity." And they depict the tortures of hell so colorfully that it shows only one thing: that they have *been* to hell—nothing else; they have *lived* there. Their description is so realistic. Just look into your so-called religious scriptures: hell is described in such detail that these so-called saints who are writing these scriptures must have been dwellers in hell and must have lived there really long enough to know all the details—with such minuteness, with such mathematical accuracy. They exploit your fear, they exploit your greed, and your religion or your morality is nothing but hidden greed and fear.

My religion has nothing to do with greed and fear; it is an adventure, a discovery of one's own true self. And once you have discovered your consciousness, you act in a totally different way. Then your actions have beauty; that beauty I call real morality. But that may fit with the conclusions of others, may not fit. The greater possibility is that it is not going to fit, because what others are telling you is in *their* interest; it is part of their vested interest. They are trying to make you a slave so that you can serve *their* purposes.

And when you discover yourself you become a master. You don't serve anybody else's purposes, you start living on your own. Every possibility is that your actions may be condemned, that you may be called immoral.

I am called immoral for the simple reason that I don't support the stupid morality that exists in India. It is just part of the establishment, it is part of the dead past; to carry it is simply to carry a corpse.

And then if you are simply following rules and regulations given by others, what will you do to your own desires, instincts, longings? You will repress them and they will come up in some way or other.

The boy was dating his schoolteacher. They had dinner, went to a dance, and on the way home he parked his car. She didn't think too much of that, but after quite a bit of conversation and petting she agreed. They had some fun.

Later she said, "You know, I'm worried."

"What's wrong?" asked the lad.

"I am wondering how I am going to face my class tomorrow with a clear conscience, knowing that I have sinned twice."

"You've only sinned once!" said the boy.

"I know, but you're going to do it again, aren't you?"

Pratap Chandra Joshi, be a little more aware, be a little more conscious. You must be carrying thousands of snakes and scorpions of repressed desire, of crippled instinct within you, and they are all struggling to come to the conscious; they all want to come out. You go on repressing them, but this is not a real way to live. You will live a phony life—a Hindu life, but not a life!

There are many lives available—the Mohammedan life, the Christian life, the Hindu life, the Jaina life. I teach *life* only, without any adjective, because I have seen it in my own self and I have seen it in thousands of sannyasins, that unless one starts living *life itself* one remains phony. Your shyness, your polishedness, your gentlemanliness, is nothing but a cover-up.

A very shy, moralistic, young British gentleman is confiding the difficulties he is having with his romantic life to a fellow public-schoolfriend. "Each day when I go horseback riding in Hyde Park I see this gorgeous damsel also going for her morning ride. She is absolutely beautiful and I am head-over-heels in love with her!"

His more experienced friend is not at a loss. "This is what you have to do. Tonight you paint your horse green, then tomorrow morning when you go for a ride and see her, she will be bound to say something about your horse and so introductions will have been made. Then after a month you can invite her for a drink, then after two months you can invite her for dinner. Then after three months you can invite her down for the weekend to your country cottage and show her your collection of silver snuffboxes. And then after a year she is bound to be yours!"

The shy gentleman excitedly rushes off and paints his poor horse green. The next morning on his ride he meets the lady, and sure enough, she can't help asking, "I say, why have you painted your horse green?"

Completely flummoxed, his face all red, the shy young gentleman manages to stammer, "Well . . . my dear . . . it's . . . it's because I want to fuck you!"

The second question

Bhagwan: The Mandukya Upanishad says—
Above all, it should be known.
And Jesus also says:
Seek ye first the kingdom of God.
Then how did the Christian church
right down to Mother Teresa change its meaning to:
Serve ye first the suffering humanity
and the kingdom of God shall be yours?
A German gentleman, Mr. Rheiner,
while speaking to me
violently accused the Rajneesh Ashram of being
a big money-making racket
and said that it should care
more for the poor
and that it should serve the downtrodden.
Bhagwan, how is it that even people
from the affluent West
continue to misunderstand you?
Ajit Saraswati,

I AM NOT AGAINST MONEY—I am against money-mindedness. I am not against possessions, I am against possessiveness. And these are two totally different dimensions, diametrically opposite to each other.

To be against money is stupid. Money is a beautiful means—a means of exchange. Without money there cannot be an evolved culture, society or civilization.

Just imagine that money has disappeared from the world. Then all that is comfortable, all that is giving you convenience will disappear with it. People will be reduced to utter poverty. Money has done a tremendous work; one has to appreciate it.

Hence I am not against money, but I am certainly against money-mindedness—and people don't make the distinction. The whole human past has lived in confusion.

Renounce money-mindedness, but there is no need to renounce money. Money has to be created, wealth has to be created. Without wealth all science will disappear, all technology will disappear, all the great achievements of man will disappear. Man will not be able to reach the moon, man will not be able to fly. Without money life will become very dumb, just as without language all art, all literature, all poetry, all music will disappear. Just as language helps you to exchange thoughts, to communicate, so money helps you to exchange things; it is also a form of communication.

But money-minded people cling to money; they destroy its whole purpose. Its purpose is to go on moving from one hand to another hand. That's why it is called 'currency': it has to remain like a current, moving. The more it moves the better, the richer the society becomes.

If I have only one rupee and it goes on moving and it moves to five thousand sannyasins, then one rupee becomes five thousand rupees. The more it moves, the more money is created. It has functioned as if there were five thousand rupees—just *one* rupee! But the money-minded person grabs it; he stops its being a currency. He holds it, he clings to it, he does not use it.

We certainly create wealth, and this is only a beginning; it is not yet a money-making racket. Just wait . . .

it will be! We are going to make as much money as possible, because I am not against money. But we use it, that's the point; we are not hoarding it. And the more we have the more we will be using; it will become more of a currency.

One of the reasons India is poor is because people are hoarders. And they are hoarding with beautiful rationalizations: they call it 'simplicity of living.' Sheer nonsense! If you have to live simply then give the money to somebody else who wants to live richly! Why are you hoarding it? Live simply, perfectly okay. It is your life; if you want to live simply, *live* simply—but why are you hoarding money? Then give it to people who can *use* it! But money should be used; it should be allowed to move as fast as possible.

Just wait a little! Tell Mr. Rheiner that once my commune is established you will see how wealth can be created and how wealth can be used, because I am not a one-sided person. I am neither for the inner nor for the outer, I am for both together. One has to be rich inside and one has to be rich outside too. Richness is beautiful; outer richness is beautiful just as inner richness is beautiful. Nothing is wrong in creating money.

We are not begging, we are creating, and we will never beg. When we can create, why beg for it? We have never asked anybody to give money to us.

Tell Mr. Rheiner he must be a greedy person, and a money-minded person. When the money-minded person comes here he sees only his own mind. This is a mirror! You will find it always: your face mirrored in thousands of ways.

But this has been the whole past. Mahavira renounced money, Buddha renounced money. I am *against* it— I am far more in favor of a man like Janaka who lived like an emperor and yet became enlightened. I am far more in favor of Krishna who lived the life of an emperor and yet was enlightened. These people are far more balanced.

Renouncing money simply shows one thing: that there is some fear in you. You are afraid that if you don't renounce you will cling. I am not afraid! And if you ask me . . . I don't have any money, not at all—not a single *paise*. I am just a guest in the commune, and of course you treat me like a guest—that's perfectly right: a guest should be treated as a guest—*you* are my hosts. But I don't have anything. That does not mean that I have to live like a beggar—that much intelligence I have! I need not live like a beggar; without having money I can live like an emperor. Is not that proof enough of enlightenment? I don't earn, I don't do a thing, I never leave my room. I can't even count money properly—you know my counting. After the first question comes the third, after the third comes the second. . . .

For years I have not seen money; I have not touched notes for at least twenty years. I have not touched any—not that I am against touching them, but notes are so dirty, particularly Indian notes—so dirty! that even when I used to travel I had somebody to accompany me, because who would touch those notes? So many hands have touched them and made them so dirty. They must be carrying all kinds of diseases!

And for ten years I have not even seen any, because no money comes into my room and I don't go anywhere. Unless the money walks into my room . . . but the guards are there, they won't allow!

But I am not against money. My commune has to be the richest commune that has ever existed on the earth. In fact, in the past many communes have come into existence and died because of this stupid idea that you should not create wealth. Then how can you exist?

Now, fifteen hundred sannyasins are working in the commune—how can they exist? They need food, they need clothes, they need shelter, they need medicines, they need everything. From where is it going to come? We *have* to create wealth. And this is just on an experimental basis, so that I can prepare you before the new commune happens, because in the new commune there will be at least ten thousand sannyasins living together.

All communes in the past have died. The longest a commune has ever lived has a fixed limit, three years—from three months to three years, that has been the minimum and the maximum life of a commune for the simple reason that if you insist on poverty, sooner or later you have to disperse.

This commune is going to live—and the only way for it to live is by being rich.

But these people who talk about serving the poor, Ajit Saraswati, who is preventing them? Why don't *they* go and serve the poor? Tell Mr. Rheiner *I* am not preventing him. He can go with all my blessings and serve the poor!

I receive hundreds of letters asking: "Why don't you serve the poor?" If there were so many people serving the poor, then you would not miss me—just one person not serving. But all these people want *me* to serve the poor! Follow your own idea, do your own thing— I am doing my own thing. *I* am not telling you to do anything, *I* am not writing letters to anybody saying, "You should do this, you should not do that." Why are these people trying to impose their ideas upon anybody? *I* will not prevent them, that much is certain. You can go—there are many poor people—and serve them.

What was Mr. Rheiner doing here? Wasting time! There are so many poor people; even in Poona you can find beggars. Go and serve them! Massage their feet . . . do whatsoever you want to do. Enjoy it!

Why do people go on writing to me as if *I* have made all these people poor, as if *I* am responsible? *They* are responsible! And the same people who are responsible for making this world poor go on insisting that I should serve them. You make them poor and I should serve them—a beautiful arrangement! *I* was poor, nobody came to serve me, so why should *I* bother?

I have my own approach to things: I am *not* here to serve the poor, I am here to destroy the poor completely. I have my own plans to do it, in my own way. I am not going to listen to such stupid Germans! In fact, just to say 'a German' is enough, but you may not understand—that's why I am saying 'stupid German'. Otherwise who has ever heard of a German being anything else?

I have my own plans to do things in my way, but if the poor insist on being poor then I cannot do anything. For example, I would like compulsory birth control methods to be used. If they don't want to be poor they have to listen to it; if they want to be poor then that is *their* decision, then I am not responsible.

Poverty can be destroyed within fifteen years—I am ready to take the challenge. Poverty can be destroyed within only fifteen years—the poverty of this country can be completely destroyed. But there is a difficulty: then what will your Christian missionaries, Mother Teresa, etcetera, do? They *need* the poor—the poor are absolutely needed—otherwise what will happen to the Nobel Prize, to Mother Teresa? If there are no poor people, whom are you going to serve? They need orphans, they need poor people, they need sick people. . . .

I can destroy this whole structure—simple methods are needed. And these fools have been serving humanity for at least ten thousand years—what is the result? Has poverty disappeared? Only the fruit shows what the life of the tree has been.

This idea of serving the poor is not new—it is not Mr. Rheiner's invention. For ten thousand years at least religions have been saying, "Serve the poor," and they have *been* serving the poor, but what has happened out of it?

I want to cut the very root! The first thing is: the population of all poor countries has to be reduced. America will be as poor as India if the same population is allowed. Any country will be poor if so many people are there, because the earth has a limitation; all our capacities to exist on the earth are limited. You go on producing children and you don't listen at all.

People are against me because they say I am teaching birth control. Their morality is at risk—because if people use birth control methods, then certainly *their* kind of morality will be at risk. Then their wife can have some love affair. Right now she cannot have any love affair out of the fear she may get pregnant; it is just fear that is preventing her. Their daughter may start having relationships before marriage. So these are the fears! But if these are the fears then *you* are responsible for your poverty, I am not responsible.

I am in favor of pre-marital relationships, I am in favor of all the latest methods of birth control, I am also in favor of extra-marital relationships. That will change the whole structure, but your poverty will go and with it will go your morality.

And I am continuously hammering on your morality for the simple reason that they are both joined together; it is a conspiracy of morality and poverty. Your morality has to be destroyed, only then will your poverty go.

It is very simple: bring more technology. Rather than opening orphanages bring more technology, bring more industry. That's what I am going to do—and that is called a 'money-making racket'!

In my commune everything of the latest has to be used so we can produce *more*! A machine can produce more than one thousand men or ten thousand men— then why use men? Men can be freed from labor. For the first time in the history of man, man can be more playful, can enjoy life more as fun, because the machine can do the work. But these 'workoholics', these people who are too much obsessed with the idea of work, won't allow machines to take their place. They are afraid. And they are far more dangerous than alcoholics—workoholics are more dangerous—because they are preventing machines and technology.

Mahatma Gandhi was a workoholic. He was against all technology, afraid that if man was free then life would become fun. And these so-called saints are against fun. Life should remain serious, it should not become fun. Life should be burdened with seriousness. If life becomes fun and people start enjoying it, who will bother about heaven?—because in heaven this is the only thing available: you will not have to work, you will only be enjoying. Have you heard about any work being done in heaven? The angels just simply go on playing on their harps, "Alleluia! Alleluia! . . ." day in, day out.

But that can be done *here*, right *now*! We are doing it! This can happen on the earth—but if this can happen on the earth, then who will bother about heaven and who will bother about the priests who show you the way to heaven? And who will bother about these so-called virtues through which you *earn* entry into heaven?

So all the religions need poverty. On the one hand they need poverty—all the establishments, the church, the state, they need poverty—and on the other hand they go on saying, "Serve the poor." Why do they say, "Serve the poor"? Just to keep the poor people consoled so they don't get rebellious, so they don't revolt against the whole structure. So go on throwing a few pieces to them, dregs, just a few pieces to keep them consoled. Go on giving them hope.

That's what Jesus did when he called the poor 'the children of God', when he said, "The last will be the first in my kingdom of God." Consoling the poor! That is just poisoning their minds.

I am not at all in any conspiracy with the establishment so I am not going to serve the poor. The people who have made them poor, they should serve them! I am totally ready to destroy poverty. I have no respect for poverty, I don't see any spirituality in poverty. It is ugly, it is inhuman. It is like cancer: it has to be uprooted, root and all. It has to be burnt—and it can be done.

I am ready to accept the challenge, but they don't even want me to have a commune because they are afraid that my commune will show the whole country, the whole world, that people can live in richness herenow, in *total* richness, both inner and outer, and that there is no need to be poor. And once my commune is there it will be an example, a model, and then we can start having communes in other countries. Already seeds have started spreading. Then we can spread the communes to all kinds of people, all cultures, all societies, and slowly slowly the whole earth can be transformed.

And I can do it quickly too, but it is not going to happen through serving the poor. Then the government will have to listen to me—I am ready to guide. I am not interested in politics so I don't want any power for myself. The government has to listen to me.

A fifteen-year plan . . . and I am ready to accept the challenge. All poverty can be destroyed, but with the poverty your Mother Teresa will go down the drain too!

The third question

Bhagwan: Every time I come to your lectures,
my ears go upright, especially when you tell a joke.
Often I don't get all the words and I miss it.
I then hope you will tell it again, but you don't.
I then try to get the next joke,
but I miss them again and again.
Then I realize the whole happening here
is one big joke
—and I miss it!
What do you say?

Henk van Hall

YOU DON'T SEEM TO BE A GERMAN, but some German blood must be in you!

It happened here: one Italian sannyasin needed a blood transfusion, and obviously the first person to jump ahead who was ready to donate the blood was a German. Now the Italian sannyasin is perfectly healthy, more healthy than ever before, very strong—German-strong!—but one problem has arisen: now she cannot understand jokes.

So either you or your parents or your parents' parents . . . some German blood transfusion has happened! By your name you appear to be Dutch. . . .Germans do miss the jokes—that's perfectly okay—but the Dutch are not allowed to miss the joke!

But I will tell a joke for you, very very slowly. . . .

A group of soldiers . . . get it? A group of soldiers were preparing for a parachute jump . . . Okay? The instructor opened the door of the plane and advised his troops for the last time, "Now remember, men, be sure to count to ten before opening your parachutes."

All of the men followed the instructions properly and were floating down towards the ground when, all of a sudden, one of the soldiers came whooshing past them, hurtling downwards, his parachute unopened.

"Oh, my God!" exclaimed one of the men, looking down. "There goes the new recruit— the one who stutters!"

Henk van Hall, do you stutter?—maybe not in speaking, but in thinking?

But one thing you have found perfectly rightly:that the whole happening here is one big joke!

You say:

> *. . . and I miss it.*

No, you have not missed it—that thing you have got completely right! It *is* a big joke because to me life is laughter, to me life is fun. It is not seriousness, it is not sadness. It is joy, it is cheerfulness, it is playfulness. There you have got the point perfectly. So there is nothing to be worried about if you have missed all other jokes—the *real* joke you have got!

A very very handsome man and his friend Peter went to the best nightclub in Paris. They sat at the best table and drank the finest imported wine. When the cabaret had finished, the handsome young man asked Peter to invite the most beautiful dancing girl to join them at their table. The girl approached them excitedly, her eyes sparkling, and sat down.

"Peter," said the Apollo-like man, "invite her to my suite!"

They left the nightclub, got into the Rolls Royce, and Peter drove them to the most expensive hotel in town. Peter left them in the suite and went away.

The next morning when the girl was leaving the room she met Peter in the hall and he asked, "How did you like it? Did you have a good night?"

"Oh, Peter," sighed the girl, "it was the most beautiful night of my life! Your friend is a god!"

Peter left her in a hurry and went inside the room. "Let's go back, Jesus," he said agitatedly. "I think she has discovered who we are!"

You *have* discovered, so forget all about the jokes!

The fourth question

Bhagwan:
I have a one-day stopover in Poland tomorrow.
Does Poland really exist or is it just a joke?
Deva Andrew

THAT'S VERY BEAUTIFUL and exciting—I would like to come with you! Poland is the only place I have a desire to visit. You are really fortunate that you are flying there, particularly because I have heard:

They are building a big new second airport north of Warsaw. To make matters simple, all arrivals will be at the new northern airport and all departures will be at the old southern airport.

It is not a joke—it really exists!

A Polish woman wearing only a shirt and underpants addressed the man in the lost-and-found: "Have you seen a red skirt with three kids holding onto it?"

A Polack drunkard fell into a puddle. A passer-by helped him to his feet.

"It'sh okay," replied the drunkard. "First you can save the children—I know how to swim!"

Two Polack hermits lived on adjoining hills, and after twenty years one of them got lonely and called on the other. After they had a ten-minute chat and Hermit B told Hermit A the latest news, they parted.

Fifteen years later Hermit B got the itch for more conversation and he went over to his neighbor again. As he entered the other's cell, Hermit A turned pleasantly and asked, "Forget something?"

A Polish couple got married and on their wedding night checked into a motel. They got themselves settled and in a few moments she called, "How about it, Chet?"

There was no answer. An hour later she repeated the question, "Chet, how about it?" Still no answer.

Soon it got to be five in the morning and by then she was fuming. "Chet, how about it?"

Finally he answered, "How about what?"

"How about going to sleep?"

And the last question

Beloved Bhagwan:
Can I ask a few more esoteric questions?
Almasto,

DEFINITELY NOT! Absolutely not, categorically not! How long are you going to screw in the poor lightbulbs? Baby, now do the real thing!

Discourse 13

December 23, 1980

MAKE IT
YOUR ONLY LONGING

सोऽयमात्माध्यक्षरमोङ्कारोऽधिमात्रं
पादा मात्रा मात्राश्च पादा
अकार उकारो मकार इति ॥

जागरितस्थानो वैश्वानरोऽकारः
प्रथमा मात्राऽऽप्तेरादिमत्वा
द्वाऽऽप्नोति ह वै
सर्वान्कामानादिश्च भवति
य एवं वेद ॥

स्वप्नस्थानस्तैजस उकारो
द्वितीया मात्रोत्कर्षादु-
भयत्वाद्वोत्कर्षति ह वै
ज्ञानसंतति समानश्च भवति
नास्याब्रह्मवित्कुले भवति
य एवं वेद ॥

सुषुप्तस्थानः प्राज्ञो
मकारस्तृतीया मात्रा
मितेरपीतेर्वा मिनोति ह वा
इदं सर्वमपीतिश्च भवति
य एवं वेद ॥

अमात्रश्चतुर्थोऽव्यवहार्यः
प्रपञ्चोपशमः शिवोऽद्वैत
एवमोंकार आत्मैव
संविशत्यात्मनाऽऽत्मानं
य एवं वेद य एवं वेद ॥

Sóyam ātmādhyakṣaram, oṅkaro'dhimātraṁ
Pādā mātrā, mātrāś ca pādā
Akāra ukāro makāra iti.

Jāgarita-sthāno vaiśvānaro'kāraḥ
Prathamā mātrā āpter ādimattvā
Dvā, āpnoti ha vai.
Sarvān kāmān, ādiś ca bhavati,
        Ya evaṁ veda.

Svapna-sthānas taijasa ukāro
Dvitīyā mātrā utkarṣādu-
Bhayatvād vā utkarṣati ha vai
Jñāna-santati, samānaś ca bhavati
Nāsyābrahma-vit kule bhavati
        Ya evaṁ veda.

*Suṣupta-sthānaḥ prājño
Makāras tṛtīyā mātrā
Miter apīter bā, minoti ha vā
Idaṁ sarvam, apītaś ca bhavati
Ya evaṁ veda.*

*Amātraś caturtho'vyavahāryaḥ
Prapañcopaśamaḥ, śivódvaita
Evam oṁkara ātmaiva
Saṁviśtyātmanātmānaṁ
Ya evaṁ veda, ya evaṁ veda.*

This pure Self and AUM are as one;
and the different quarters of the Self
correspond to AUM and its sounds, A—U—M.

Experience of the outer world corresponds to A,
the first sound.
This initiates action and achievement.
Whoever awakens to this acts in freedom and
achieves success.

Experience of the inner world corresponds to U,
the second sound.
This initiates upholding and unification.
Whoever awakens to this upholds the tradition
of knowledge and unifies the diversities of life.
Everything that comes along speaks to him of
Brahman.

The state of dreamless sleep corresponds to M,
the third sound.
This initiates measurement and merging.
Whoever awakens to this merges with the world
and has the measure of all things.

The pure Self alone,
that which is indivisible,
which cannot be described,
the supreme good,
the one without a second,
That corresponds to the wholeness of AUM.
Whoever awakens to that becomes the Self.

AUM
Pūrnamadah
Pūrnamidaṃ
Pūrnāt pūrnamudachyatē
Pūrnasya pūrnamadāya
Pūrnamēva vashisyatē.

THE SANSKSRIT LANGUAGE is the most ancient language in the world, hence it has a certain beauty, a certain flexibility, a certain poeticness which has disappeared in the modern languages. The modern languages are scientific; they are closer to prose, mathematics, logic. The modern languages insist on definite meanings, hence they are not flexible; they are solid blocks with clear-cut definitions.

The Sanskrit words have many meanings. Each word is a rainbow, a whole spectrum of meanings. Hence there is much scope to interpret in different ways, on different planes. So each Sanskrit word can be defined in many ways, multi-dimensionally.

This fundamental sutra, the *beej mantra*—

AUM
Purnamadah
Purnamidam
Purnat purnamudachyate
Purnasya purnamadaya
Purnameva vashisyate.

—consists only of one word: *purna*. This word *purna* can be translated in three ways. The first meaning can be 'perfection'; that's how it is being translated ordinarily by the scholars, pundits, professors. But that is the lowest meaning of it, the grossest meaning of it, for the simple reason that the idea of perfection is inapplicable to existence.

Only in one way can existence be said to be perfect, and that is that existence is perfect in its imperfectness. If existence were *really* perfect then there would be no possibility of evolution; perfection would mean death, absolute death. But life is growing, not only on the outside but on the inside too. Life is continuously moving like a river towards the ocean, towards the horizon—

which always appears to come closer and closer, but still a distance remains; one never absolutely arrives.

In other words, life is a pilgrimage without a goal—and that's its beauty, that's why it is alive. If the goal is achieved, then there is no meaning left; then there is no point in going on existing. Perfection will mean suicide; hence the meaning of *purna* as perfect is only scholarly. It is used by people who have not experienced existence, who have studied the scriptures but who have not merged into the ocean of life, who have not tasted it. It is a childish interpretation.

A first-grade schoolteacher was taking her pupils on a field trip to the local zoo. Each child was given a turn at guessing the names of the various animals. The camel, lion, giraffe, bear and the elephant all were named correctly.

"Now it's your turn," the teacher said to a little girl. She pointed to a deer and said, "What's the name of that animal?"

The little girl hesitated for a long time, and the teacher tried to prompt her by saying, "Think hard. What does your mother call your father at home?"

"So that's what a baboon looks like!" the little girl exclaimed.

That is the most childish meaning and it is dangerous too, because all perfectionism leads to neurosis. The perfectionist is not a healthy and sane person. He is bound to go insane because he is always trying to be perfect, and life is always imperfect. He is trying to go against the current, he is trying to go against the law, the universal law: *ais dhammo sanantano*. He is not flowing with existence, he is not in a let-go. He is trying hard to do the impossible—that is an ego trip.

So those who have interpreted the word *purna* as perfection have given it a wrong color. But the Sanskrit language allows it; its flexibility is such, its poetry is such that you can play with any word in many ways.

The second meaning is a little better than the first, and that is 'totalness'; *purna* can also mean 'the total'. But that is also lagging a little behind the real meaning. The concept of totality is mathematical, the concept of perfection is egoistic. Totality means 'the sum of all', but the sum of all may not have any intrinsic, organic unity. The total may be missing the soul, that which connects it, keeps it together.

'The total' simply means the sum total of all, but that is not enough. Existence is something more than the sum total; that plus point is the hidden secret of life. It is an organic unity. So we cannot just call it 'total'.

The third meaning is 'wholeness', which comes closest to the reality; closer than that one cannot come through language. If one wants to come closer than that then one has to be silent, then no language can help. But 'wholeness' is the most approximate meaning. Hence we translate this *beej mantra*, this seed, which contains all the Upanishads, the whole Upanishadic vision:

AUM
This is the Whole.
That is the Whole.
From wholeness emerges wholeness.
Wholeness coming from wholeness,
wholeness still remains.

The world is an organic unity. We are not parts in a mechanical sense, because in a machine the parts can be replaced. The part is not absolutely essential, it is dispensable; another part will do the same. But we are not parts in that sense. Even a small blade of grass is indispensable, irreplaceable; the whole existence needs it, it is not accidental. Hence the part is not only the part but the whole too.

P.D. Ouspensky, one of the very close disciples of George Gurdjieff, says that in lower mathematics—the mathematics that is taught in the schools, colleges and the universities—the part is always less than the whole. Obviously, the part cannot be equal to the whole, and the part certainly cannot be bigger than the whole. The part *means* smaller than the whole. How can my hand be equal to me or bigger than me? It is part of me! That being part itself is enough indication that it is smaller than the whole.

But Ouspensky says there is a higher mathematics too. The Upanishads belong to the higher mathematics. Then things start changing; then ordinary rules are no more applicable. Not only that—they are inadequate—they become absolutely contrary to the truth. In higher mathematics the part can be equal to the whole and in certain cases can be bigger than the whole.

You are equal to the whole—each part is equal to the whole—but when a part becomes a Buddha he becomes bigger than the whole. That's a totally different world of laws.

This universe is whole, the whole comes out of it, still the whole remains behind. You can take the whole out and nothing is lost; you can put the whole back, nothing is added.

This summarizes in essence the whole Mandukya Upanishad. I call the Mandukya Upanishad *philosophia ultima*—the philosophy of the ultimate. It is not an ordinary philosophy concerned with the mundane; it reveals the secrets of the ultimate. Hence you will have to be very very alert to enter these sutras—these are the last sutras of the Mandukya Upanishad.

This pure Self and AUM are as one . . .

By 'pure Self' is meant: when there is no content left in your consciousness, when the consciousness is contentless, when it mirrors nothing, when the mirror is left absolutely alone without any reflection. There is no thought, no memory, no desire, no imagination, no expectation—no ripple on the surface of your consciousness. The lake of consciousness is absolutely still, resting in itself. That is called the 'pure Self'; *you* are no more, you are dissolved as an ego entity; you have become part of the whole. The dewdrop has slipped into the ocean; it has become the ocean.

This pure Self and AUM are as one . . .

Remember the word 'as'—it is not saying that they *are* one. Many fools have interpreted it as 'they are one'. That's why all over this country people are chanting the mantra AUM, thinking that they are remembering the ultimate.

It is just like a thirsty man going on chanting the formula H_2O. H_2O is a formula: it represents exactly the constituents of water, but it is *not* water. It is *as* water, but if you are thirsty it won't help. And we are thirsty for the ultimate. Just chanting the mantra AUM is not going to help—this is sheer stupidity!

What Maharishi Mahesh Yogi calls Transcendental Meditation is only transcendental stupidity! Certainly it is transcendental—it is no ordinary stupidity, it is very sacred!—but stupidity is stupidity, and when it becomes transcendental it becomes more dangerous, more poisonous.

See the point:

This pure Self and AUM are as one . . .

Remember the word 'as'—don't forget it.

Jesus says: When you are *as* small children you shall enter into my kingdom. Only when you are *as* small children will the kingdom of God welcome you. Remember the word 'as'. He is not saying 'if you are children', he is saying '*as* children'. That simply shows, clearly shows, that it is not expected that you should be children; what is expected is that you should not be children but *as* children. You should be grown-up, you should be mature, ripe, yet you should carry some innocence of childhood within you—the same freshness, the same virgin consciousness, unpolluted, uncontaminated. The sage is not a child, but he is certainly *as* a child.

AUM is only a formula, just like H_2O. It simply represents the whole reality. Before we enter into this, the greatest formula invented ever by man, you have to understand a few things. First: AUM is not written in Sanskrit in the ordinary Sanskrit alphabet; it has a special symbol for itself. It is a code word. To make it clear, the ordinary Sanskrit is not used for it—a *special* symbol, hence it is untranslatable.

It consists of three sounds *and* the fourth, the soundless sound. It consists of four things: three are sounds and the fourth is only the harmony of those three sounds. Three sounds are *audibly* there, you can hear them. The fourth is heard not by the ears; it is heard only at the innermost shrine of your being.

So the symbol AUM consists of four things. Three are the basic sounds: aa-oo-ma—A, U, M. These are the basic sounds; all other sounds are branches of these three sounds. This is the real trinity, the trinity of sounds. All these three have arisen out of the fourth, but the fourth is inaudible, unhearable. The fourth is represented only by a dot; that dot is called *anuswar*.

If you go into an empty temple or a mosque or a church, or any empty house will do—a newly built house, utterly empty . . . go inside and start chanting the mantra AUM. "AUM, AUM, AUM. . . . " You go on chanting, then stop suddenly. Now you are no more chanting, but the vibe is still there, a humming sound . . . disappearing, disappearing . . . every moment disappearing, becoming more and more subtle . . . the humming sound, the tail-end of M. When you say, "AUMMMMM . . . " that tail-end of M will be heard when you have stopped chanting.

That is represented only by a dot; in Sanskrit that dot is called *anuswar*. Out of that dot arise three sounds, A-U-M. These four represent the whole existence, these four are the four dimensions of existence.

You can think of it in another way also: put a dot on a piece of paper—this is the center—then draw three concentric circles around it. The last concentric circle, the biggest will be A, the first. The second concentric circle, U, will be just in the middle between the first and the third. And then the third concentric circle, closer to the dot, the center, will be M. And the dot—the center of all these three concentric circles, these three circumferences—is the *anuswar*: the soundless sound; what Zen people call 'the sound of one hand clapping'. The Mandukya Upanishad calls it 'the fourth'—*turiya*—without giving it any name, simply a number.

The three, the first three, represent your three states, and the fourth, your self-nature. Man is also exactly as AUM; man is a miniature universe. If we can decipher man we will be able to decipher the whole of existence. If we can know a single dewdrop in its totality we will have known all the oceans, because we will have dissected a single drop which contains the secret of all the oceans. We will come to know the formula H_2O, and that's the secret.

Whether water exists on earth or it exists on other planets . . . it must be existing, according to scientists, on at least fifty thousand planets. Life is possible on at least fifty thousand planets, and that is the minimum; more are possible. This is a very orthodox number, the very minimum; less than that is not possible, more than that is possible. Fifty thousand planets: if they have life they must have water. Without water no life exists—neither plants, nor animals, nor man. But we know the formula; the same formula will be applicable anywhere and everywhere.

You are a dewdrop of God, of the whole, of this organic infinity, of this eternity. The best way to understand the universe, the truth, the existence, is to understand yourself. Socrates is right when he says, "Know thyself," because, knowing that, you will be able to know all.

This pure Self and AUM are as one;
and the different quarters of the Self
correspond to AUM and its sounds, A-U-M.

Experience of the outer world corresponds to A,
the first sound.

That is the outermost, the most superficial. And millions of people, unfortunately, die knowing only the A. Just their most superficial life and they think this is all there is to life: the Rotary Club, the Lions Club, the Blue Diamond Hotel . . . the family, the children, the market, money, power, prestige, respectability. All this consists of the most superficial life.

Experience of the outer world corresponds to A,
the first sound.

This first sound, A, represents your so-called waking state. Remember the word *'so-called'*—underline it in red. It is co-called waking, because a really awakened person becomes bigger than the whole. He becomes a Buddha, a Christ, a Krishna. Our waking is only so-called; only a very small fragment of our being becomes conscious.

When in the morning you wake up it is not much of a waking. You just open your eyes, you become capable of doing the most superficial things. You can prepare your breakfast and serve tea to your wife and make your children ready to go to school—and all these things are done in a very mechanical way. You are not really conscious of what you are doing because you have been doing it for many many days, for many many years, for many many lives; you can function like a robot.

I have heard:

The difference between the three Celtic races is that the Scot keeps the Sabbath and everything he can lay his hands on, the Welshman prays on his knees on Sunday and on everyone else the rest of the week, while the Irishman does't know what he wants but he'll fight to the death for it.

But this is how the whole of humanity is. People are living, dying, not knowing why they live, not knowing why they die. People are struggling to survive not knowing for what. People are rushing with great speed, not knowing where. They are not even aware of who they are—what kind of awareness is this?

Hence, call it so-called wakefulness. But this so-called wakefulness creates a world of its own.

This initiates action and achievement.
Whoever awakens to this acts in freedom and
achieves success.

This waking state is what Carl Gustav Jung calls extroversion. The extrovert person lives only outside himself, but because he lives totally outside of himself he is very active. He is so active, really, that he finds it difficult to fall asleep, he finds it difficult to rest. His life is more or less nothing but a restlessness.

A well-adjusted person is one whose intake of pep pills just overbalances his intake of tranquillizers, leaving enough energy for his weekly trip to the psychiatrist.

The extrovert lives in that way, but he achieves much: money, power, prestige, respectability. The great achievers—Alexander, Napoleon, Nadir Shah, Genghis Khan, Tamurlane, Joseph Stalin, all these people—they achieve much, but their achievements are almost like making sandcastles. They are bound disappear. Death will knock them down in a single blow.

At the Kremlin, the Moscow Communist Party headquarters, Joseph Stalin lay dying. He called his second-in-command, Nikita Kruschev, to his bedside. "I want to leave you something, Nikita," he whispered. "Any time something goes wrong for you as Party Head, open the first of these two envelopes."

A few years later Cold War problems arose; there was a political crisis with President Kennedy over Cuba, so Kruschev decided to open the first envelope. "Put everything on my back! Love, Joseph," was the advice.

Kruschev went straight ahead, throwing blame for the grave political situation onto Stalin, and his situation improved. But again a few years later the Kruschev government came under fire—the Corn Revolt was worse than ever, the Americans succeeded in landing the first man on the moon, the country was gripped with inflation. So he decided it was time to open the second envelope.

Inside were the words: "Prepare two envelopes!"

All achievement in the outside world is just like that. It is writing your name on water: you have not even finished and it starts disappearing. It is making a house of playing cards: just a little breeze and the whole palace collapses.

But the extrovert achieves, certainly. He makes many palaces—maybe they are only of playing cards; he launches many boats—maybe they are only paper boats, but he is capable of doing things and he achieves. He becomes a Nobel Laureat, he becomes a president, a prime minister. His whole mind is full of achieving more and more.

The West is living in that kind of state. That's why the West has achieved much—in technology, in industry, in affluence, in every possible way. The West has achieved much; the East has been an utter failure. As far as extrovert achievement is concerned, the West has defeated the East. And certainly the West has been more free; the East easily yielded to slavery. There was no resistance against slavery, no resistance against poverty—no resistance at all.

For twenty-two centuries India has been in slavery, with no resistance. Not a single revolution has happened here. Even what Indians call revolutions were not revolutions. India became free in 1947 and the revolution happened in 1942. This is rare! Revolution happens five years before, and freedom comes after five years— such a gap! Russia revolted in 1917 and in 1917 it became communist—it got out of the slavery of the czars. There was no gap.

This revolution of 1942 in India was nothing much; it has nothing to do with the revolution that India attained freedom. The freedom came because of the international situation. If Churchill had been in power in England the freedom would not have come.

When Lord Mountbatten, the last British Governor-General and Viceroy, went back to England, he met Churchill at a party. Churchill shouted at him, "You have slapped me in the face!" turned about and didn't speak with him for years. He was against giving freedom to India; if he had been in power there would have been no possibility of it.

India is very easily ready to yield to any pressure from the outside, for the simple reason that India has not lived extrovertly. Science was born in the West, not in the East, because science belongs to the extrovert mind, to the objective approach towards reality.

The poverty of the East and the richness of the West can be understood, according to the Mandukya Upanishad, very easily: the West is extrovert and the East is introvert. There is no need to go into any more details; it is very simple.

The West knows how to be free but it does not know what to do with freedom; the East knows what to do with freedom but does not know how to be free. The West knows how to create wealth but does not know how to use it, what to do with it. It has created immense power, and its own power is crushing itself.

Two cows in a pasture near a highway saw a tank truck pass by, with a sign on the side reading: "Pasteurized, homogenized, standardized, and Vitamin-D added."

One turned to the other and remarked, "Makes you feel sort of inadequate, doesn't it?"

The West has gone far ahead of nature and the reason is simple . . .

When coming up the stairs one evening, quite inebriated, the husband fell over backwards and broke the bottle of liquor that he was carrying. Not wishing his wife to know what happened, he went to the bathroom to make the necessary repairs.

Next morning when he woke up, his wife said, "Well, you came home drunk again?"

"No," he replied. "Whatever would make you think so?"

"Well," she said, "if you were not drunk, why is all that adhesive tape on the mirror in the bathroom?"

Simply looking around . . . and you will be able to decipher what the root cause of things is. The root cause of things is always very simple.

A psychologist took a poll surveying just how people sat in their tubs. He discovered that out of a hundred people, ninety-nine sat facing the faucets, only one sat facing away from the faucets.

He asked the lone man why, and he said, "Very simple— I have no plug for my tub!"

Experience of the inner world corresponds to U,
the second sound.

This initiates upholding and unification.
Whoever awakens to this upholds the tradition
of knowledge and unifies the diversities of life.
Everything that comes along speaks to him of
Brahman.

The second is the state of dreaming. The first is the so-called waking state, the second is the dreaming state —it is introversion. The first creates science, the second creates art. The first is an objective approach towards reality, the second is a subjective approach towards reality. The poet, the painter, the singer, the dancer, the musician, they all belong to the second: the introverted state.

The East has given great poets, great musicians, great dancers to the world. It has shown great aesthetic sensibility, which is lacking in the West, but it has not shown any scientific growth, it has not developed any technology.

The introvert person is closed within himself; he is a dreamer. He is very skillful in dreaming, but only in dreaming. If he clashes with the extrovert he is bound to be defeated. It is like a fragile, soft, delicate poet wrestling against Mohammed Ali—there is no possiblilty of winning over Mohammed Ali! The poet is like a rose-flower and Mohammed Ali is like a rock. If the rose has to fight against the rock it is going to be defeated.

That's why the East has remained in slavery: it knows how to grow roses, it does not know how to throw rocks. It knows how to dream, but it does not know how to industrialize things, how to bring more technology. So it goes on dreaming—beautiful dreams, sweet dreams—but it goes on suffering in the outside reality. It knows how to be more satisfied; it is more satisfied with less than people in the West are with so much more. They have all that man can have, yet there is no satisfaction. The East is satisfied—without anything; you can see that satisfaction on people's faces, but it is nothing to brag about. Both are lacking because both are half. Both are unfinished, both are missing.

And unless the extrovert and the introvert meet to create a new world we will not be able to survive long. We have gone different ways. Your left leg has gone on one side, your right leg has gone another, and you are continuously falling apart and the distance between your two selves is becoming too big—every moment it is becoming bigger and bigger.

Rudyard Kipling says: West is West and East is East, and the twain shall never meet. Man has to prove Rudyard Kipling wrong; if Rudyard Kipling is *not* proved wrong, there is no hope for humanity at all.

My work here consists in proving Rudyard Kipling absolutely wrong. East and West *can* meet, *should* meet; there is no reason why they cannot meet, because extroversion and introversion are two sides of you. You can easily shift your gears. You just have to learn how to shift your gears, so when you are needed in the outside world you become an extrovert and when you are finished with the outside world you change your gear and you move into the innner world—the world of poetry and music and dance. The inner world will bring you closer to God and the outer world will bring you closer to matter; both are immensely needed.

Whoever awakens to this upholds the tradition
of knowledge . . .

That's why in the East people are so traditionalist, so orthodox—fanatically orthodox, very intolerant of things new and very much obsessed with the old. The old is gold in the East—howsoever rotten it is, that does not matter, it has to be old; if it is old then it is good. The older the better! And, obviously, the older it is the more rotten it will be—it will be stinking! But people are obsessed with it.

A man walked into a bar, trailing an extremely foul odor behind him. He sat in a corner all alone. All evening he sat there nursing his beers.

Finally a lady felt so sorry for him that she held her nose and went over to him.

"Yes," he said, "it is always like this, I am always alone. Nobody talks to me because of the smell—it is my job at the circus. I pick up the shit after the elephants, and the stench is terrible. I have no friends and feel terribly lonely."

"In that case," she asked, "why don't you quit your job?"

"What!" gasped the man. "And give up showbiz?"

Nobody wants to give up anything. People become attached to the old because they become efficient with it. The West is always for the new, the East is always for the old. The West is continuously discovering the new, and the East is continuously trying to prove that "Our scriptures are older than you think."

Historians say that the Vedas can be at the most three thousand to five thousand years old, not more than that, but Hindus don't agree. Lokmanya Tilak tried to prove that the Vedas are at least ninety thousand years old. Why this obsession?

The Mandukya Upanishad says in this sutra:

*Whoever awakens to this upholds the tradition
of knowledge . . .*

Tradition becomes more important than discovery. Past-orientation becomes the very life-pattern of the introvert. And the extrovert is future-oriented; he is always looking to the future, his golden age is yet to come. And the introvert? His golden age has passed long before—*Ramarajya*, the kingdom of Rama. The golden age has passed; now there is only deterioration, every day man is falling.

The Eastern calculation is that the best days were in the beginning and now we are living in the worst days. The Western vision is totally different: the past was nothing important; now we are starting to live, beginning to live. So there is hope in the West; in the East there is a kind of hopelessness, a despair, a fatalist, determinist attitude that nothing can be done. The time is such: this is *Kali Yuga*, the worst time. The most you can do is to make as much good out of it as possible. Nothing much is possible, but do whatsoever you can do. Decorate it a little, arrange things in a better way, just somehow pass the time. Soon this creation will be dissolved and a new creation will begin, again there will be the first age: *Satya Yuga*, the age of truth. But this is the age of darkness.

Beware! Future-orientation has its own difficulties, because you cannot live in the present. Past orientation also has the same problem: you cannot live in the present. So neither does the West live in the present nor does the East; the East lives in the past and the West lives in the future.

The explorer heard the sound of drums coming from deep within the jungle, so in the spirit of discovery he slashed his way through the thicket in search of the drums. At last he came to a clearing where a witchdoctor of a strange tribe was beating on a hollow log.

Through his native interpreter the explorer said to the witchdoctor, "Why doctor make boom-boom?"

'We need water, we want water," the witchdoctor said.

"So," the explorer said, "witchdoctor beat drum for rain?"

The interpreter did not bother to translate that question. Instead he turned to the explorer and said, "Don't be silly! He is calling the plumber."

If people who are obsessed with the past are given modern technology they will go on living with their old ideas. Even with the latest technology they will not have the *mind* of a scientist.

That is happening every day in India. People go to the West to learn science, but their superstitions remain with them. They come back with Ph.D.s and D.Litt.s, but still they will do the *yagna*—the fire worship—when it is not raining. They will go to the temple of Hanuman, the monkey god, and worship there. Even doctors, scientists, all kinds of people who are well-versed in technology . . . but their minds don't change, they remain the same.

Church was over and the lady was backing out of the parking lot when she discovered she did not have her handbag. She quickly parked her car again and rushed back to the pew where she had been sitting. Sure enough, her handbag was gone.

As she stood there trying to think what to do, the minister walked up to her and said, "I am sure you are looking for your handbag. I saw it there and I thought I had better pick it up for safe-keeping."

"Ah, thank you," the woman said. "But surely no one would steal my handbag in church?"

"No, I don't suppose so," the minister said. "But knowing my Indian congregation as well as I do, someone might have seen it and considered it an answer to a prayer."

But this introvert has come a little closer to the center:

Everything that comes along speaks to him of Brahman.

A man went to the hospital to get a cardiogram. After the cardiogram had been taken he was given a sheet of paper with a whole bunch of jiggly lines on it. He took it home and put it into his player piano and it played back 'Nearer, my God, to thee'!

The introvert is nearer; he has not reached, and if he remains an introvert he will never reach, but he is nearer.

The first can be called, according to modern psychology, consciousness; the second, subconsciousness; and the third, unconsciousness.

The state of dreamless sleep corresponds to M,
the third sound.
This initiates measurement and merging.
Whoever awakens to this merges with the world
and has the measure of all things.

The third is a negative state of transcendence, *jad samadhi*; it is not true *samadhi*, but very close. The man has fallen into a deep unconsciousness, but he is silent; there is no turmoil within. But it is a negative state; there is no light, there is only darkness. Even dreams have gone. There has happened a certain merging. He has tasted *the measure of all things*, but in a deep unconscious state.

It is just as when you wake up in the morning and you say, "I slept a very deep sleep last night. It was so beautiful!" But it is only later on that you say it. When it was there, the *deep* sleep, you were not aware of it. It is only a later reflection, a later glow. In the morning you feel yourself so refreshed that you can see, you can infer, that you must have gone into deep sleep.

But this is not true *samadhi*. We call it *jad samadhi*—unconscious *samadhi*—but it has come very close. This is the closest to the fourth, *turiya*.

The first man becomes scientific, objective; the second becomes introvert, a dreamer, poetic, aesthetic; and the third becomes a mystic. He knows but he cannot say anything, because his knowing is still lost in a deep darkness. He *feels*; there is a certain experience hovering around him, but he cannot define it, he cannot pinpoint it, he cannot show it to the world.

You will find many people in India—if you go to the caves and the monasteries you will find many people —who look immensely blissful, but very stupid at the same time. I have come across a few persons who were very very blissful, but at the same time very stupid too. Their eyes don't give the indication of a Buddha—not that awareness, not that sharpness—but they are very innocent. Their innocence is more like ignorance than wisdom.

Beware of the third, because many seekers have got lost in the third and thought they have arrived. This is the *most* dangerous place. The extrovert can *never* feel that he has arrived; he knows that his life is insane, feverish. The introvert cannot accept the idea that he has arrived, because all that he has is a vague dreamworld. He cannot catch hold of those dreams; there is nothing to catch, only vapor, only clouds.

But the third person, one who has experienced dreamless sleep, he is neither extrovert nor introvert; he has slipped out of that duality. He has had a certain merging with existence, hence the danger: he can think that he has arrived. And people can start worshipping him, seeing his innocence, seeing his childlike qualities. They will call him Paramahansa. But he has yet to go one more step. . . .

> *The pure Self alone,*
> *that which is indivisible,*
> *which cannot be described,*

> *the supreme good,*
> *the one without a second,*
> *That corresponds to the wholeness of AUM.*
> *Whoever awakens to that becomes the Self.*

The third has only tasted of God, the fourth has become God himself. He can say, *"Aham Brahmasmi*—I am the Supreme, I am the Absolute!" He can say, *"Ana'l haq!"* like Mansoor Al Hillaj—"I am the truth." Only then . . . but this can be said only when your unconsciousness becomes luminous, when the darkness of the third disappears, when its negativity disappears and it becomes a positive experience in full awareness. We call this state Buddhahood. And reaching the fourth, *turiya,* the part becomes bigger than the whole. The miracle has happened. The miracle is so immense that it cannot be described—words fall short.

No song can sing it, no poetry can contain it, no music can define it! And it is indivisible; you cannot divide it into parts. In fact, unless you achieve the fourth you should not call yourself an individual.

The root of 'individual' is the same as the root of 'indivisible'; they both mean the same: that which cannot be divided. Unless you attain to the fourth you are not an individual; you are only a person, a personality —and a person is a phony thing. A personality is a mask, individuality is your true nature. It is the supreme good, the *summum bonum.* All virtue flows out of it.

Then you need not follow any morality, then you need not follow any discipline. Then you need not listen to any scripture—you *are* your own scripture. Your own consciousness gives you every commandment. And because now you are fully conscious you can live spontaneously, moment-to-moment. Only the fourth lives in the present and lives consciously.

The third is also in the present, but unconscious. The first is in the future, the second is in the past, the third *is* in the present but unconscious, the fourth is in the present *and* consciously in the present. The fourth is the state of a Buddha, of a Christ, of a Krishna, of a *Jina*.

This is the goal of all sannyas. Unless this is achieved life has been a sheer wastage. Unless this is known you have not known anything at all. Unless you have reached this fourth state, the center, the very center, the innermost shrine of your being, your life cannot have meaning and significance. Then you missed the spring. Then you lived only a so-called life—futile, ugly.

The fourth brings you to the optimum. You become the Everest, the peak, the fulfillment, the flowering; the one-thousand-petaled lotus opens up. Then all the blessings of existence are yours, all the love of existence is yours, all the freedom of existence is yours.

And the most remarkable thing to be remembered is: the fourth contains all the three. So the fourth can be scientific, can be poetic, can be restful. It is possible for the person who has achieved the fourth to move in all the dimensions, all the other three dimensions.

Man has come to a point where he needs the fourth; only with the fourth will we be able to give birth to a new man. And the new man is urgently needed—the old man is finished, he is outdated. He is just lingering somehow, stale and dead. Out of old habit he goes on and on. But this century's end will be very decisive: either we will be able to give birth to a new man or we will have to commit suicide.

My effort here is to prepare the ground for the new man. Sannyas, according to me, is only a preparation to herald the new man. Hence I am teaching you the *philosophia ultima*. This is the ultimate philosophy: the method, the technique, the device, to reach the fourth. Make it your only longing, your only desire. Become this longing, that you have to reach the fourth. And once you are committed, involved, there is no reason why you cannot reach—it is your potential, it is your birthright.

Discourse 14

December 24,1980

WHOLENESS —
A SINGLE WORD
CONTAINS IT

The first question

Bhagwan:
Are Krishna, Mahavira, Buddha and Lao Tzu
also responsible for the poverty in the world,
just as Jesus Christ is?
I myself want to serve
the poor and the downtrodden.
Can I do it with your blessings?
Sangam Lal Pandey

Y ES, THESE PEOPLE ARE RESPONSIBLE for the poverty in the world. Krishna, Buddha, Mahavira, Lao Tzu, are as much responsible as Jesus Christ, for the simple reason that they all insisted on the inner *against* the outer. And the outer has to be developed as much as the inner, otherwise man loses balance. If you only grow in the outside world you become rich, but inside you become just a beggar. And vice versa is also true: if you emphasize only the inner journey you certainly become rich in meditation, in awareness, but you become poor on the outside.

It is certainly easy to take care of one side—easy because you don't have to be continuously balancing between two polar opposites. But life consists of polar opposites. Life is like a tightrope walk: the tightrope-walker has to balance himself each moment; not for a single moment has he to stop balancing. The moment he stops balancing he falls from the rope. Yes, sometimes he will lean to the left so that he does not fall to the right, but when he leans too much to the left again the danger of falling. . . .He immediately has to balance it by leaning towards the right, but not too much. A constant alertness is needed, only then can one remain total, whole. And to be whole is to be holy.

That's the message of the Upanishadic philosophy, of the Mandukya Upanishad: wholeness—a single word contains it. Albert Einstein is not whole, neither is Mahavira whole. Both have chosen one part, one aspect of the coin, but the neglected aspect is bound to take its revenge. And humanity has lived up to now in a very lopsided way.

It hurts, I know, when I say that Jesus Christ, Krishna, Mahavira, Buddha, Lao Tzu, are responsible for the poverty of the world, but what can I do? I have to say the truth *as* it is. I feel sorry for you because it is going to hurt you, but *my* responsibility is towards truth, my commitment is towards truth. And the truth is that in different ways all these people *have* helped man to remain retarded.

Krishna is a fatalist, a determinist. He believes that things happen because God has decided them to be so, so nothing can be done about it. He helps you to settle with things as they are. Certainly it helps inner growth, because on the outside the struggle ceases. If you are poor, you are poor—God has determined it so. It is your fate to be poor; there is no possibility of avoiding it, you cannot escape it. You have to accept it, you have to be satisfied with it.

Yes, it helps in a way—in that it turns your whole energy inwards. Outside there is no freedom; then your whole energy can have freedom only on the inside. You are free to grow towards enlightenment, towards God-consciousness, but the outside world will remain the same. You are impotent as far as the outside world is concerned— and poverty and richness *are* in the outside world.

Krishna certainly helped this country to remain poor.

Mahavira and Buddha both believe in the theory of karma: you are poor because in your past lives you have committed grave sins; you are suffering as a consequence. It is better to suffer silently than to complain, because if you complain you are again creating bad karma for the future; in the next life you will again suffer. So the poor person has to accept that he is poor because of his past lives.

Now, you cannot undo the past—it has already happened. It is a different kind of determinism, fatalism —only a different kind, a different sort, with a different logic behind it, but the total outcome is the same. The rich person is rich because of his past lives and the poor person is poor because of his past lives. As far as the present is concerned you have to live in total acceptance. Again, this acceptance will help you to become more meditative, because there is nothing to do on the outside. The energy involved in the outside is released; it becomes available for inner growth. But without a subtle balance with the outside world, the inner growth makes you only half, it never makes you whole.

Buddha and Mahavira both renounced their kingdoms, their palaces, their riches. By renouncing their palaces, their kingdoms, their riches, they condemned wealth. It did two things. One: if wealth is condemned, the poor feel very good; their egos are nourished because then poverty has something spiritual about it: "Look! Mahavira and Buddha renounced their wealth!" So what is the point of creating more wealth for yourself? If people are already renouncing, it simply stops you going in the same way from where people are coming back and telling you that it is a cul-de-sac, that it ends and leads nowhere, that soon you will come to an abyss and you cannot go further. The path is suicidal!

And when Buddha and Mahavira dropped out of the world it gave a tremendous satisfaction to the poor; it helped their egos: "Somehow we are already spiritual." Poverty started having a flavor of spirituality; being poor became equivalent to being spiritual: "Nobody can be spiritual without being poor—so poverty is good, poverty is great virtue!"

Jesus calls the poor 'the children of God', and down the ages all the saints, except the Upanishadic seers, have been insisting on this point again and again, hammering it. It has gone deep into the very soul of man that poverty has something beautiful about it.

So the poor felt good, and because Mahavira and Buddha made them feel good . . . they had nothing else to feel good about. They were hungry, starving, undernourished, without shelter. Buddha and Mahavira became tremendously supportive; millions of poor people worshipped Buddha and Mahavira for the simple reason that they made them feel at ease with their poverty. *And,* on the other hand, their renunciation of their kingdoms and their wealth made the rich people feel guilty, and whenever you make somebody feel guilty he is bound to respect you.

You have to understand the psychology of guilt. Whenever you make somebody feel guilty he has to compensate to get rid of the guilt. He starts respecting and worshipping Buddha and Mahavira because these people have done what he is not yet capable of doing but hopes someday to do—if not in this life then in some other life that blissful moment will arrive when he will also renounce all the riches, all the wealth, the whole kingdom, the whole outside world. As far as the present is concerned he can do a little bit by donating his money to the poor. So the rich people started donating a little bit of their money to the poor to get rid of the guilt. And they started worshipping Buddha and Mahavira; that too was a way of getting rid of the guilt.

Both religions, Buddhism and Jainism, flourished on these two things. The poor person felt good because his poverty started having the color of spirituality, and the rich person became guilty and donated. Of course, all the Jaina scriptures say: "Donate only to the Jainas, because they are the right people. You should not donate to the unworthy—donate to the worthy. Donate to the Jaina temples."

And you can see it. There are very few Jainas, just thirty-five *lakhs;* in a country of seventy *crores,* thirty-five *lakhs* is just nothing—just salt in your vegetables, just a little bit of salt in your soup. But go and see their temples—they are the richest temples in India. And there are thousands of Jaina temples: the most architecturally beautiful, the richest, for the simple reason that they made the rich people feel so guilty that they started donating.

The Buddhists say the same thing: "Don't donate to anybody else, donate to the Buddhists—because unless you donate to the *right* person your donation is futile." And who is the right person? One who follows the Buddha!

Brahmins say, "Donate only to the Brahmins, to the Hindus. Don't donate to the Jainas and the Buddhists. They are atheists, they don't believe in God."

These religions helped the poor to remain poor and helped the rich to feel guilty. And donations also help the poor to remain poor because they cannot revolt against those who are donating. How can you revolt against such well-wishers? How can you revolt against those who are creating beautiful temples for you, *dharmashalas,* poor-houses, orphanages, schools, hospitals? How can you revolt against such good people, such virtuous people?

So this strategy of donation became a shelter, a shield for the rich, and it became a consolation to the poor.

In India in the past ten thousand years there has never been any class struggle for the simple reason that the richer class was always helping the poorer ones in small ways. They looked, appeared friendly. They were exploiting, they were making them poor; they were the cause of the poverty. With one hand they continued to suck their blood, and with the other hand they were providing a little bit of food to them. And it was good to give a little bit of food and nourishment to the poor, otherwise how can you suck their blood? From where is the blood going to come? They should not die, they should be kept alive! To keep them alive, go on giving them a little bit in donations; then they *are* alive and you can go on sucking them.

Lao Tzu says to remain in a let-go. It is beautiful for the inner growth, but not good for the outside world. Let-go means no struggle, no revolution, no rebellion, just going with the river wherever it is going, not trying to decide the direction.

Mathematics was first discovered in India; that's why the mathematical digits from one to ten are basically of Indian origin. You can even see the similarity in the words: three is *tri* in Sanskrit, six is *shasht* in Sanskrit, nine is *nav* in Sanskrit, eight is *asht* in Sanskrit, two is *dwa* in Sanskrit; *dwa* became *twa* and from *twa* it became two.

Mathematics was discovered for the first time in India, but it was not developed, it was not followed up, for the simple reason that the world is illusory, it is *maya*; all that is required of you is to renounce it.

In fact, the young drop-outs in the West should not be called hippies—they are not. The real hippies are the people who renounce the world, they are the *real* drop-outs. The word 'hippie' means one who has shown his hips to the world and escaped. In that sense, Mahavira, Buddha, Lao Tzu, all are hippies—literally! They all escaped from the struggle of life.

Mathematics was developed, but mathematics can be applied only to the outside world because it is a way of measuring. Do you know?—the English word 'matter' comes from a Sanskrit root which means 'measure'; matter means 'that which can be measured'. Now, mathematics is needed only for matter, that which can be measured. The inner world is immeasurable, you cannot measure it, hence it is beyond matter; mathematics is not needed there.

The people who called the world illusory stopped all scientific growth.

The first technological devices were invented in China, but science did not develop there. And the sole cause was Lao Tzu, because Lao Tzu said that to invent a machine is to cheat nature.

The story is that an old man, a gardener, was drawing water from a well with his young son. Both were perspiring—it was a hot summer day—and they were pulling up the water and watering the trees.

A man of scientific mind, a Confucian, was passing by. He looked—the old man was really old, must have been beyond ninety. At this age he was working so hard, from the early morning to the evening, and the well was very deep, sixty, seventy feet deep. "He has wasted his whole life just watering trees, and now the same will happen to his son. His whole life from the morning to the evening, he will be pulling up water." And when you have done so much work in the day, what can you do in the night? You cannot sing, you cannot play on the sitar or the guitar, you cannot play on the flute. No energy is left. You can just fall asleep, and in the morning again the same routine begins.

The Confucian scholar of scientific bent went close to the old man and said, "Have you not heard that now we have found a device which can bring the water out of the well very easily? You need not waste your life. Just a horse will do it, and far more efficiently and far more quickly."

The old man said, "Stop all this nonsense!"

The young man had gone home to bring bread, butter and a few vegetables for the old man and for himself.

He said, "And you go away from here before my son comes back. If *he* hears you talking about a device, he is so young—he may become seduced by your idea. Get lost immediately! I have heard about that device, but I believe in Lao Tzu. He is my Master and he says machines are devices to cheat nature, and I don't want to cheat nature. Nature means Tao! If you cheat nature. . . ."

And of course, in a way it is right: when you invent a machine and it starts doing the work of man you are doing something which is not natural. Machines are not natural, and if a machine can do the work of a hundred people that simply means you have cheated nature. It is not good.

This is a famous story and significant, because China developed the first devices five thousand years ago but because of Lao Tzu and his influence all that growth was stopped. Certainly if you relax with nature you can grow inwards easily, very easily. Let-go is the secret of growing inwards, but that is not the secret of growing outwards.

These people have kept the world in poverty. And these are the people, on the other hand, who go on saying to you, "Go and serve the poor!" They are the cause of all poverty. I respect these people: as far as the inner world is concerned they have given great diamonds to the world, treasures, secret keys. But that makes man only half; the other half remains undeveloped.

My effort here is to help you to grow in a balanced way. Life is not illusory and the outside world is *as* significant as the inside world, and you have to live richly in both worlds when one can live richly in both worlds. Why choose to be rich only in one aspect of your life? And only when you are rich on both the sides does a great harmony, a great balance arise in you.

Sangam Lal Pandey, you must have thought that I would not speak so about Mahavira, Krishna, Buddha and Lao Tzu. I have no commitment to any individual. I respect truth wherever it is found, but *only* truth, and if something untrue is hanging around it I am the last person to allow it—I will destroy it immediately.

You are asking me:

I myself want to serve the poor and the downtrodden. Can I do it with your blessings?

A man in a high-powered car swung off the highway onto a gravel patch in front of a typical back-country store. Several old-timers were sitting on the porch, chatting and chewing tobacco.

As the driver braked the car to a fast stop, he yelled at the men on the porch, "I want to go to Farmingdale!"

After ten or fifteen seconds when no one had responded he shouted again, "I want to go to Farmingdale!"

The men on the porch seemed to be holding a whispering consultation for a moment, and then one of the old fellows walked over to the car and said, "Mister, we just had a committee meeting and we have no objection!"

I can only say that much—that I have no objection—but if you are asking me for my blessings, then you will have to understand my conditions. If you want to serve the poor in the way they have been served for thousands of years, then I cannot give you my blessings, because thousands of years of public service has not helped the poor at all—in fact it has helped them to remain poor. It may give you a good feeling, that you are doing great work; it may give you a good ego—that you are a public servant, that you are a great reformer, that look! you have sacrificed your life for the poor and the downtrodden.

I cannot give blessings for your egoistic trips, because service has not helped the poor and the downtrodden; now that is an absolutely recognized fact. How long are you going to serve the poor? Ten thousand years is enough—nothing has happened. There have been servants and servants and they have been doing great work—missionary work—and nothing happens out of it.

So at the most I can say to you that I have no objection. It won't make much difference, so why should I object? If you feel like doing it, go by all means and do it—but remember it is not going to help the poor. It may help *you*, but it is not going to help the poor.

Just an old habit, just an old conditioning . . .

A Jewish man put five hundred dollars cash on the counter for a one-way ticket to Israel. "Such a deal!" he kept saying to himself.

Later on he was escorted to a boat where fifteen other retired Jewish garment-workers were sitting. The harrowing journey began when two athletic looking Anglo-Saxons jumped aboard the rowboat. The first WASP acted as captain and screamed, "Row!" and the other stood over the poor Jewish fellows with a whip.

Three months passed, and lo and behold! the rowboat reached Israel. On the way into the mooring, one old Jewish garment-worker said to the captain, "Excuse me, sir, I have never traveled this way before—how much should I tip the guy with the whip?"

Old habits die hard!

Sangam Lal Pandey, if you want to serve the poor, I feel sorry for you—but okay!

A minister had a habit of preaching on whatever words he happened to point his finger to when he opened the Bible. This particular Sunday morning, he opened the Bible and the finger pointed to the words: "And Judas went out and hanged himself."

He was not in such a pessimistic mood, so he violated his procedure and thumbed through an additional few pages of the Bible and dropped his finger and it read: "Go ye and do likewise."

Sangam Lal Pandey, I have no objection: Go ye and do likewise! But if you want *my* blessings then you will have to understand *my* conditions. I cannot give blessings without conditions, because enough nonsense has been done in the name of service. If you really want to do service to the poor, to the downtrodden, then the first thing is: spread the message that life is not illusory, that it needs your attention, that wealth is not sin, that wealth has to be created.

And the person who creates wealth should be respected as much as a painter, musician, poet. The painter creates the painting, the poet creates the poetry—and I don't think that poetry, painting and music can feed people. The man who creates wealth—a Morgan, a Rockefeller, a Carnegie—should be respected more than any Picasso, but they are condemned. These people—Rockefellers, Morgans, Carnegies—are condemned for the simple reason that they have been creating wealth. And you want to serve the poor people. How are you going to serve them without wealth?

So create respect for wealth, create respect for wealth-creating people, create respect for a wealth-creating system of society. Create respect for capitalism because that's what capitalism is—a wealth-producing economic structure. Socialism is impotent. Sixty years of experimentation in Russia has proved it enough, that the people are utterly poor. Of course, now the poverty is distributed equally! So there is no jealousy because there is nobody richer than you, everybody is as poor as you are.

The American poor person is in a far better condition than the Russian commissar. But in Russia one thing has happened: you cannot rebel, you cannot go against the system. You are constantly watched.

Two pins are walking along the Red Square in Moscow. Suddenly one says to the other, "Watch what you're saying, Ivan, there's a safety-pin behind us!"

The communist party in Russia had a membership drive. The rules were as follows: any communist who could recruit a new member would no longer have to pay dues. If he got two members he would be permitted to leave the party. And if he recruited three members he would receive a certificate stating that he had never belonged to the party in the first place.

The statue of Stalin in Lenin Square is so big that it gives shade from the sun in the summer, protection from the wind in winter, and the birds an opportunity to speak for all.

Sangam Lal Panday, create an atmosphere in the poor that the world is not illusory, that wealth is not a sin, that creating wealth is one of the most creative activities. *I* am teaching my sannyasins . . . believe me, in the new commune we are going to grow money on the trees!

Secondly, help the poor to understand that no more children are needed. This will be real service. I don't call Mother Teresa's service real service. First you help them to create orphans, because the Catholic church is against contraceptives. If you are against contraceptives there are going to be orphans. First create orphans by being against contraceptives, then open orphanages and win the Nobel Prize. Such simple arithmetic! Allow the beggars to reproduce children, as many as they want, because to prevent nature is not good. And these same people go on opening hospitals.

If preventing nature is not good, then if somebody is ill, don't give him medicine—that is preventing nature. In fact you are murdering amoebas . . . and in millions! It is not good. All germs that you kill are souls, potential Buddhas. Sooner or later they will all become Buddhas, and you are killing them. On the one hand open hospitals so people can be prevented from dying, people can be prevented from getting diseases, and then tell them that reproducing children is their birthright.

So beggars will create more beggars. And you will have to open more hospitals, and you will have to open more orphanages, and you will have to feed the poor . . . and you will enjoy the trip! How good it feels when you are feeding the poor, serving the poor.

I have visited many Rotary Clubs in this country many times. Rotarians seem to be the most stupid people in the world—that's my experience. They are the richest of every town, every city, the topmost people. But on the Rotarian desk, the president's desk, there is a board saying 'We Serve'. And what do they do? They distribute medicine, food packets, clothes.

These things are not going to help. This is not service, this is a conspiracy to keep the poor hoping that somehow things are going to be better—one just has to wait. And they have been waiting for thousands of years.

So if you really want to help the poor, Sangam Lal Pandey, teach them to use contraceptives, help them to use all kinds of birth control methods. Help them to be operated upon: help the women to be sterilized, help the men to be sterilized. This will be *true* service. Then I can give you my blessings. Help the people to understand more about technology, more about science. They don't need the Bible, they don't need the Gita, they don't need the Koran—they have had those things long enough. They need better technology, they need electricity, they need machines. Help them to become more science-oriented. That will be *real* service.

If we can reduce the population, if millions of people can decide not to have children at all. . . .Look at my sannyasins. Five thousand sannyasins are here and only three hundred children. And my sannyasins are not celibates: they are celebrants! So what has happened? They have simply understood the fact that the world is already overpopulated. It is an ugly act to go on reproducing children. Those three hundred children are also here because they were born before these people became sannyasins. Once a person becomes a sannyasin, his first duty is to understand what the situation is. The world is already overpopulated, it is *bound* to be poor. Withdraw, don't reproduce. Drop that old stupid idea that you have to leave a few children in the world. You are enough! Your parents have done a great service to the world, now you be more compassionate.

Sangam Lal Pandey, if you really want to serve the poor, then you will have to understand my conditions. And then, certainly, go and help them—but first you will have to practice what I am saying.

In India, unless you produce at least one dozen children you are not thought to be man enough. Stop producing children! In fact, to use sex only for reproduction, as Mahatma Gandhi says, as the Polack Pope says . . . Mahatma Gandhi also seems to be a hidden Polack—they all say you have to use sex only for reproductive reasons, otherwise it is sin. I say just the opposite: if you use sex as fun, it is virtue; if you use it for reproduction, it is sin.

The second question

*Bhagwan: Have you forgotten poor Murphy
and his great sutras completely?*
Suneeta,

No, I WAS JUST WAITING for you to ask. I can forget Buddha, Christ, but not poor Murphy. He is such a beautiful guy, so wise. Listen to his sutras . . .

First: Love is not enough, but it sure helps.

Second: We have only ourselves and one another. That may not be much but that's all there is.

Third: Murphy's two political principles. First: No matter what they're telling you, they're not telling you the whole truth. Second: No matter what they are talking about, they're talking about money.

Fourth: Fact is solidified opinion.

Fifth: Facts may weaken under extreme heat and pressure.

Sixth: Truth is elastic.

Seventh: The other line always moves faster. This applies to all lines—bank, supermarket, tollbooth, customs. If you change lines, then the other line, the one you were in originally, will move faster.

Eighth: The only thing worse than work is looking for work.

Ninth: Men do not stumble over mountains, only molehills.

Tenth: Some people can't tell a lie, some people can't tell the truth, and others can't tell the difference.

Eleventh: There are three ages to all of us—youth, middle-age, and "You are looking fine!"

Twelfth: If drinking is bad for you, why are there so many old drunks and so few old doctors?

Thirteenth: Somebody asked Murphy what he considers an ideal audience. Murphy said, "The ideal audience is one that is highly intelligent, well-educated and just a little bit drunk."

Fourteenth: One friend asked Murphy, "Were any of your boyish ambitions ever realized?" "Yes," said Murphy, "when my mother used to cut my hair, I often wished I might be bald."

Fifteenth: Don't put off until tomorrow what you can do today. If you enjoy it, you can do it again tomorrow . . . if you're young enough.

And the last: The man condemned to die in the electric chair asked his friend Murphy if he had any parting words of wisdom for him. Whereupon the great Murphy replied, "Yes, don't sit down."

Discourse 15

December 25, 1980

TRUTH AS IT IS — NAKED

The first question

Bhagwan: A Zen saying is:
Better to see the face than to hear the words.
Wouldn't it be better to see the face
and to hear the words?
Casper Vogel,

IT IS ONE THING TO UNDERSTAND words, it is a totally different experience to understand the statements made by mystics. The words are simple. Anybody can understand them, but the implications can be understood only by those who have experienced the same kind of consciousness out of which those words have flowed.

This Zen saying is one of the most significant sayings: *Better to see the face . . .*

By 'the face' is meant your original face—not the face tha* is reflected in the mirror, not the face that is reflected in other people's eyes, but the face that you had even before your parents were born, the face that you will have when your body has gone back to the dust, when you are dead. 'The original face' is a Zen way of speaking about your spiritual reality, about your innermost truth, about your individuality. The face that you are acquainted with is your personality. The word 'personality' comes from a Greek root *per-sona*. *Persona* means a mask.

Personality is a mask, and you don't have one personality either, you have many, for different purposes. You are continuously changing your personalities every moment. As the situation changes, your personality changes. Your mask is not one, there are many masks. When you are in need and you approach a friend, you have a different face. Wher you' friend is in need and he approaches you, you have a totally different face. These two faces are not the same at all, and for each situation you have a mask appropriate for it. And amidst this crowd of masks your original face is lost. You are more concerned with what people say about you. Why?—because their eyes, their opinions, their ideas give you your face. Your face is borrowed. If somebody says you are beautiful, you are happy. If somebody says you are ugly, disgusting, you are unhappy.

Your face is dependent on what others say about you. If they call you a saint you start flying above the clouds. And if they call you a sinner, you are crushed below the earth. You don't know who you are, hence so much concern with other's opinions, so much concern with mirrors.

Your whole idea about yourself is borrowed—borrowed from those people who have no idea who they are themselves. It is a very strange world, very insane.

The saying can be understood very easily. That's what Casper Vogel has done, he thinks he understands.

Better to see the face than to hear the words.

Thinking that he has understood it, he asks:

Wouldn't it be better to see the face
and to hear the words?

Once you have seen the original face there is no need to hear the words. The original face is encountered only in absolute silence. Words have no business there. Words are left far behind, far away. You have to go beyond the mind, only then can you see the face.

Mind consists of words. The moment you go beyond the mind you have gone beyond words. There is nothing to hear, but only to see. That's why we have called the great mystics the seers. And in the East, particularly in India, philosophy is called *darshan. Darshan* means the art of seeing.

It is not right to translate philosophy as *darshan* or *darshan* as philosophy. It is a mis-translation. But people like Casper Vogel go on doing these things. Scholars like Dr. Radhakrishnan and others have translated the Indian vision into other languages, and they have called it 'Indian philosophy'.

In India philosophy has not really existed at all—philosophy in the Greek sense of the word, philosophy in the sense Plato, Aristotle, Descartes, Kant, Hegel, Russell or Wittgenstein will understand. Philosophy in the East is not philosophy, it is *philousia*. Philosophy means love for knowledge, love for wisdom; *philousia* means desire for essence or isness.

Truth is not something to be thought about, it is something to be experienced, seen. The Zen people call it your original face. It has nothing to do with the face, with your body, with your mind; it has nothing to do even with your heart.

The ordinary Indian religious person thinks there are three ways to reach God: *gyan yoga*—the path of knowledge; *karma yoga*—the path of action; and *bhakti yoga*—the path of devotion. Vivekananda also agrees with the ordinary mind, and he says these are the three paths to God. None of these is really a path to God. Action belongs to the body and the body has to be left behind. Knowledge belongs to the mind and the mind has to be left behind. Devotion belongs to the heart and the heart has to be left behind. Only when you have transcended these three do you know what Zen is.

Zen comes from the Sanskrit word *dhyana*; it has a beautiful history. Gautam the Buddha never used the Sanskrit language for two reasons. One, it was the language of the scholars, the pundits, and they are the most stupid people in the world. Buddha never wanted to use the language of the scholars and the pundits and the priests. He used the language of the people.

Of course Sanskrit is very sophisticated. The exact meaning of 'sanskrit' is: that which is very sophisicated, cultured, refined. But it became so refined that it lost all contact with reality; it became so refined that it became abstract, it lost aliveness; it became conceptual, it became philosophy in itself.

Buddha dropped Sanskrit; he never used it. He used Pali, the language of the people. It is more raw but closer to the earth; more pragmatic, more primitive, but closer to reality. Primitive languages are always closer to reality. They are not yet in the hands of the scholars, the professors, the philosophers. In Pali, *dhyana* is pronounced *jhana*. From *jhana* has come the Japanese word *zen*.

Zen is the only path. Vivekananda is utterly wrong in saying that there are three paths; there is only one path. There is only one reality and one path to it, and that is *dhyana*—meditation. Meditation is not knowledge, it is not action, it is not feeling: it is transcendence of all these three. And when you have transcended the three you enter the fourth—*turiya*.

We have been meditating over the Mandukya Upanishad all these days. The Mandukya Upanishad is concerned with the fourth, *turiya*. Zen is the fourth, meditation is the fourth. And the original face is discovered only when all the turmoil of activity, thinking, feeling, has ceased, when you have fallen into a tremendously silent space. There are no words to hear, there is only to see—or even better will be, only to be. One simply is. And in that isness is revealed all that is hidden. There is no need to say anything. When you have tasted yourself, what is the point of saying anything.

Two mystics, Farid and Kabir, met by coincidence. Farid was traveling and his disciples said to him, "We are very close to the commune of Kabir, and it will be a great experience for us if we can see you both being together, talking to each other, sharing your experiences with each other." Farid agreed.

The same happened to Kabir's disciples. They heard Farid was passing by; they prayed to Kabir, "It will be good if we invite Farid and his followers to be with us, just for a few days. It will be of tremendous significance for us just to see you two together, talking, sharing."

Kabir said, "That's beautiful! Invite him." Farid was invited. Kabir himself came outside the village to receive him. They hugged each other, they laughed loudly. Holding hands they walked together to Kabir's community. Two days they stayed together, and the disciples of Kabir and Farid were utterly disappointed because not a single word was uttered by Farid or Kabir. They sat together, smiled at each other. Sometimes they held each other's hands. Now how long could the disciples sit and wait and wait? Two days appeared like two years! And they became very tired and bored. And what happened to these people? They all were puzzled because Farid had been talking to the disciples for years. Kabir had been talking to his disciples for years—and suddenly both have become dumb?!

After two days they parted. They again hugged each other, laughed. . . . The moment Farid was left with his disciples and Kabir was left with his disciples—the disciples were really boiling within—they jumped on their masters and they said, "What happened to you? Why did you suddenly become silent?"

Farid said, "But there was nothing to say. The moment I saw him, I also saw that he has seen. So what is there to say? He knows, I know, and we know the same reality."

And Kabir said to his disciples, "Do you want me to appear stupid? I could see that he knows, so there was no need to say anything. Words are needed to show you the path, but he has arrived, so we shared our arrival by hugging, smiling, laughing. We have both arrived at the same space. We enjoyed! We really loved to be together. These two days were tremendously beautiful. But when two zeros come together they become one."

It is natural. When two absolutely egoless beings come together, there is no separation, there is no wall, there is no barrier between them. A merger, a melting into each other starts happening. Kabir and Farid must have enjoyed those two days of tremendous understanding. But there is nothing to say!

Casper Vogel, the moment you have seen the face there is no need for any words. If you are too attached to the words, then avoid the face; then don't search for reality. Then it is better to go on *thinking* about reality; then you are capable of hearing only as much as you can.

Just the other day I was reading a statement of Rudolf Steiner: "If a German comes to a crossroads and sees that one road has a signboard saying: 'To Heaven,' and the other road has another sign saying: 'To the Lecture Hall About Heaven,' he will go to the second—to listen to the lecture *about* heaven."

Germans are philosophical people; they have given birth to great philosophers. Who bothers about heaven? First let us *hear* about it, discuss it, analyze it, whether it exists or not, go through all the theories, ponder over it. And heaven can always wait. Tomorrow the lecture may be there or it may not be—who knows?—but heaven is always there. You can always go to heaven whenever you want, but about the lecture. . . . One has to rush immediately! Once the clock says eight, the doors are closed and the German is left out. And he has to sit in the front. Look!—Haridas, just sitting by my side. . . . Do you think Haridas will go to heaven? Never! He will go to the lecture.

If you want to hear the words, Casper, then it is better not to bother about the orginial face. If you have seen the original face you are finished with all words, all philosophy, all religion.

The second question

Bhagwan: Dolly Diddee showed me a passage
from one of your earlier books where you say
that no saint is against any other saint,
and that they deliberately speak against each other
to drive away people who are not suited to them
and to push their buttons.
Does this mean
that you don't really mean your criticism of
possible saints like Muktananda, Nityananda,
Maharishi Mahesh Yogi,
Swami Prabhupada of Hare Rama, Hare Krishna,
and Nobel prizewinner
Mother Teresa of Calcutta?
Are you non-serious when you criticize them
or are you earnest in your criticism?
It does somewhat upset me
when you talk against Mother Teresa
every other day.
Ajai Krishn Lakhanpal,

It IS A LONG STORY. The moment I became capable of seeing I started talking about truth as it is—naked. But nobody was ready even to listen to it. I was puzzled: I had found the original face, I had seen it, I wanted to share with those who were searching for it, but they were not ready to listen to it.

For a few years I struggled hard, but then I saw that they were not wrong, I was wrong. They could not digest truth raw and naked; when you have been eating cooked food for many many lives you cannot digest raw food. I was wrong, they were not wrong.

Then I started cooking things! Then I started saying things which they could digest. I became less and less concerned about truth and more and more concerned about the people who were to digest it; I had to see how much they could digest. And I had to prepare the food in such a way that it was sweet, not bitter, that it tasted good, it looked good. Whether it was nutritious or not, that was secondary. Who bothers whether Deeksha's cakes are nutritious or not? whether the ice cream is going to make you healthy or ill? Who bothers about these things? It *tastes* good. It may destroy you finally . . .

And I was amazed—when I started serving cooked food people became very much interested and excited. That was a device: that's how I have been able to hook you all! Otherwise I was sitting on the riverbank day in, day out—not a single fish! Once I started serving cooked food—cooked according to your desires, not according to your needs. . . . I didn't need to think at all about the truth in the beginning days, I forgot all about it. I stopped going to the river—the fish started coming to me on their own, walking long distances.

So don't be too bothered about what I have said in my earlier works. I have said many things which I don't mean! What I am saying today is closer to truth than what I said yesterday, and every day it will become closer and closer to the truth. Before I am gone I will again have told you the naked truth.

I had to take such a long route because there was no other way; I had to be very indirect. The moment I became enlightened I started telling people that there is no God—and they were shocked! Then I cooked it. I said, "There is God, but God is not a person, only a presence." This is cooked food. I am simply saying there is *no* God. But now it tastes sweet—no person, only a presence.

But what else can you do? If people are foolish you have to be careful with them. So I have certainly said, Ajai Krishn Lakhanpal, that no saint is against any other saint—but that is absolutely wrong.

Buddha was as much against Mahavira as anybody can be, Mahavira was as much against Gosala as anybody can be. Krishna was against the Vedas, Buddha was against the Vedas, Mahavira was against the Vedas. Mahavira was against Krishna. . . . Do you think Jesus Christ was supporting the Old Testament? Of course, he was serving cooked food, but the Jews are very clever people: they found it out! He was saying: "It has been told to you before an eye for an eye. If somebody hits you with a brick you have to answer him with a rock, it has been told before. But I say to you that if somebody slaps you on the right cheek, give him the left too."

Now what is he saying? It is cooked food. He is saying that the old prophets, the old so-called prophets, were wrong. The Jewish God and the Christian God are totally opposite. The Jewish God says: I am a very jealous God. And Jesus says: God is love. Now love and jealousy never meet, there is no possibility. Jews immediately found out: "This man is destroying our past. Before he succeeds it is better to destroy him." They killed him; he was only thirty-three when he was killed.

Jews found him out far more quickly than anybody else has ever been.

Lao Tzu lived long, Buddha lived long, Mahavira lived long. They went on saying things, but in such a way that you could not find them out—it was impossible for you to find them out.

I wanted to say the naked truth from the very beginning, but to whom to say it? I had to drop that. For a few years I tried my hardest, but all the doors remained closed; nobody was even ready to listen. Then I changed the whole strategy, I became a little more diplomatic. Then whatsoever I wanted to say I started saying through Mahavira, through Buddha, through Zarathustra, through Lao Tzu, through Jesus. . . . I continued to say things but I was using other people's names. And Christians became very much interested when I said the same things in the name of Jesus! Whatsoever I said in the name of Jesus is simply my own; it has nothing to do with Jesus at all. And if I meet Jesus there is going to be a great argument. They all must be waiting for me—let this guy come!—because I have been telling things in the name of Buddha which he never meant . . . but Buddhists became very happy.

Fools are fools! The earth is so full of them.

I started saying things in the name of Mahavira which are absolutely the opposite of what he said—because if I had to live with Mahavira in the same room, either I would leave or he would leave! We could not have tolerated each other. First, his smell . . . because he never used to take a bath. He was against taking baths because when you pour so much water on your body, so many small germs in the water die; that is violence. So he never took a bath.

And he used to live naked—you know the Indian roads—he was walking because he was not using any vehicle, he could not according to his ideology. To ride on a horse is violence, to ride in a bullock-cart is violence. He had to walk, and without shoes, because shoes were made out of leather—that is violence. And twenty-five hundred years ago . . . even *now* Indian roads are not contemporary, at least one thousand years behind. Twenty-five centuries ago, walking in Bihar—which is still very dusty—he must have been gathering dust in the hot summer, perspiring and gathering dust, layers upon layers of dust.

He was not even ready to clean his teeth, he was against washing his mouth, rinsing his mouth. Always that violence—if you rinse your mouth you are killing germs in the water, and there are millions of germs in the water. His breath must have been smelling really foul!

One thing is certain: I could not have tolerated him in the same room. And he would not tolerate me either. He would simply go mad seeing my air-conditioned room, my Rolls-Royce—he would simply go mad!

He was an ascetic. According to me he was a masochist—now this is raw food!—he was torturing himself, he enjoyed torturing himself. And I am not a masochist or a sadist; neither do I want to torture myself nor do I want to torture anybody else. He was both, a sado-masochist: he was torturing himself and teaching people to torture themselves.

But I have spoken on Mahavira. I had to play with words to manage my meaning in his words. It was a difficult task but I *did* it, and the Jainas were very happy.

The same I have done with Krishna. I think my commentary on Krishna is the biggest in the whole of history. Lokman Tilak's commentary on Krishna, his Gita, was thought to be the biggest—it must be more than one thousand pages. But my commentary is twelve times bigger. And I *don't* agree with Krishna really! Whatsoever I have said—the words are his, the meanings are mine.

But this can be done very easily with the saints who are dead. What can they do? And when we meet later on somewhere—if that meeting ever happens—then I can simply apologize; there is no problem in it. And I hope they will understand—because they themselves had done the same thing, and I am doing the same thing. There is no problem in it.

So one thing, Ajai Krishn: whenever you want to try to understand me, don't bring in what I have said in the past; that is not going to help. The *latest* has to be taken into account. And when tomorrow I say something, that will be even better. Before I enter into my grave, my last statement will be just the naked truth.

But I had to take this long route for the simple reason that—whom to get hold of, with whom to share your experience? With whom? There are Hindus, there are Mohammedans, there are Christians, there are Buddhists, there are Sikhs, there are Parsis . . . not a single human being is available, all are already divided. The only way is to catch the Christians through Jesus and the Jews through Moses and the Hindus through Krishna. Once they are with me then they will be able to understand.

And now I have found my people so I don't care much. Now I can start giving you my original experience.

You ask me:

> *Does this mean
> that you don't really mean your criticism. . . ?*

I really mean it!

> *. . of possible saints like Muktananda,
> Nityananda. . . ?*

You say 'possible saints'? These are impossible saints!

Muktananda is a very ordinary person; I have met him. I was passing by his ashram and his disciples invited me, just for a few minutes' stay, to take a cup of tea. So I said, "Okay."

The man was so flat, just like a flat tire, nothing in him, nothing of any worth, not even junk. And it was not only apparent to me: one of my disciples, a woman follower, Nirmala Srivastava, was with me—even she could see, even she proved to be far more intelligent than Muktananda. We stayed only fifteen minutes; it was a sheer wastage of time. And the moment our car moved away, Nirmala told me, "This man is absolutely common, very ordinary. Why did you waste your time?—even fifteen minutes is an unnecessary wastage!"

I looked at her, and immediately I knew that some idea had entered into her head—and it had entered. The idea was: "If such a fool like Muktananda can become a saint, then why can't I become a saint?" And the idea worked out well. Now Nirmala Srivastava is a great saint, is traveling around the world, having many devotees. That day it transpired, looking at Muktananda. Now she is 'Her Holiness, the World Mother—*Jagaj-janani*— Mataji, Nirmalaji Deviji Srivastavaji. Now she has many followers, doing the same thing that Muktananda is doing—raising people's kundalini. Once she could see that this fool can raise people's kundalini, then "Why can't I raise it?" And she is certainly far more intelligent than Muktananda, far more capable, far more skillful, far more intellectual. Muktananda is not a saint.

But this has not happened only once.

You must have heard of the name Yogi Bhajan. In America he has many followers; he has turned many American fools into *sardars*. He preaches the Sikh religion; he is the head of the Sikh religion for the Western hemisphere. And do you know what he was? He was just a porter at the Delhi airport.

But what happened to Nirmala Srivastava happened to him too. His name was Sardar Haribhajan Singh. Muktananda came to Delhi airport with his followers, and this porter was simply carrying his luggage. He looked at this man; he said, "If this fool can lead, then what is wrong with me?" And of course Sardar Haribhajan Singh is a taller man, healthier, more robust, and far more intelligent. He immediately escaped to America, became Yogi Bhajan, and gathered a big following.

Just a few days ago he was in Delhi, and one of the highest authorities of the airport told Laxmi, "I was passing through the Taj Mahal Hotel in New Delhi—I had gone to see some friend—and I saw on the lawn there a very saintly man surrounded by many Americans. I asked, 'Who is this man?' and I was told that he is a great guru, Yogi Bhajan. I thought he must be a great yogi, otherwise how can you get such a gathering?" This man felt happy because he is also a *sardar*, and Yogi Bhajan has made all these people *sardars*; they were all sitting around him with turbans and *kirpans*. He was very happy.

When he was passing by this crowd of Yogi Bhajan's people—Yogi Bhajan seems to be really a good man, a simple man—he said, "Hey boss!" This officer could not believe that he was calling him, so he thought he must be calling somebody else: "How can such a great mahatma say, 'Hey boss!' to me?" So he went on.

He again shouted, "Hey boss!" so he turned back. Yogi Bhajan took him inside his suite in the Taj Mahal, closed the doors and said, "Have you forgotten your poor porter, Sardar Haribhajan Singh? I am Sardar Haribhajan Singh and nobody else. Have your forgotten your poor servant?"

Then he remembered. But he said, "How did this happen? How did you become such a great mahatma?"

He said, "It is due to Muktananda. When I saw Muktananda I said, 'If this fool can get a following, then what is wrong with me? Why should I go on wasting my time being a porter at Delhi airport?' Now I am the head of the Sikh religion in the Western hemisphere. I have thousands of followers. But," he said, "to you, I say that I am simply the same man—I know nothing. But these people are greater fools than I am."

And you can always find greater fools than you are. The world abounds in them.

Muktananda is not a saint or anything. Nityananda, Muktananda's guru, was simply a traditional, conventional person. He fulfilled the expectations of the Hindus, hence he was a saint. Anybody can manage it; all that you need is a lack of intelligence. You can do it. You have to be stupid—only a stupid person can be traditional, conventional, only a stupid person can fulfill other people's expectations. A real saint can*not* be traditional.

Listen to these words of Meher Baba, a real saint, an authentic sage. He says: "Not only is the perfect Master not necessarily bound to any particular technique in giving spiritual help to others, but also he is not bound to the conventional standard of good. He is beyond the distinction of good and evil. But although what he does may appear lawless in the eyes of the world, it is always meant for the ultimate good of others. He has no personal motive."

These people all have personal motives. If you want to be worshipped as a saint, then you have to fulfill the expectations of the people you are living with. If you are living with Hindus, fulfill their expectations of what a saint is supposed to be; if you are living with Mohammedans, fulfill their expectations—and you will be a saint. It needs no intelligence, no art, no diligence, nothing at all—just fulfill their expectations. If they think that you should eat only once a day, eat once a day. And it can be managed, it is not much of a problem; it is just a question of creating a habit. If they want you to fast for three days and then eat only once after three days, you can do that. Nityananda must have been doing such things—his big belly is enough proof.

Have you seen a picture of Nityananda? If you have not seen one you have missed something really worth seeing. There are people who have bellies, but here the case is just the opposite: the belly has the person! The belly is all, just a little head on top of it, two hands by the side, two legs—but the belly is the real thing. It is a belly with a head, hands and legs. This is bound to happen. If you have to eat only once after three days then you have to take the whole quota for three days, you have to accumulate it. Nityananda looks permanently pregnant. Just look at his picture and you will see it. He is not a saint, just a conventional Hindu, a traditional Hindu.

A saint is always revolutionary, a saint is basically a rebellion.

And Maharishi Mahesh Yogi . . . . I know him well, because we come from the same part of India. The distance between my village and his village is only six miles. I used to go to his village every morning just for a morning walk. He is absolutely phony. There is nothing in him. What he is teaching is just an ancient, simple method of chanting a mantra. You can use any word repetitively; it creates a kind of auto-hypnosis. It gives you a good sleep, but a good sleep is not enlightening; a good sleep is good for your physical health so nothing is *wrong* in it, but there is nothing valuable either.

And Swami Prabhupada . . . if Muktananda is a very ordinary person, Prabhupada is extra-ordinary. He is an extra-ordinary idiot! Muktananda can be helped, Prabhupada cannot be helped at all.

But you can judge by the people they attract. You can just see the people who are part of the Hare Krishna movement. You will find the most idiotic people of the world gathered together. Here you will find just the opposite—the most intelligent people of the world are coming here. They are *bound* to come, they *have* to come—it is inevitable. You will find your polar opposites in the Hare Krishna people. I have never come across such idiots! But they also need a saint. Of course, their need should be fulfilled—Prabhupada did that.

And you ask me:

> *Are you non-serious when you criticize them,*
> *or are you earnest in your criticism?*

I am absolutely earnest, but serious I cannot be—that is impossible. I am always non-serious. Even when I am utterly honest, sincere, I am non-serious. Serious I cannot be; that is not my nature.

And why should I be serious just because there are a few fools in the world? Why should I be serious? I enjoy! In fact, a few fools are always needed in the world. They serve a certain purpose: they keep the world laughing. They are so ridiculous—without them we would be missing something. They are so absurd—they are needed. They keep your sense of humor alive; that is their purpose. God—and you know what I mean by God: just a presence, no person—God always creates whatsoever is absolutely needed, he never creates anything unnecessary. So these people *are* needed.

And, Ajai Krishn, you say that you are disturbed because I talk against Mother Teresa every other day. Do you want me to talk about her *every* day? I can do that too—for your peace of mind. Don't get upset! You seem to be a devotee of Mother Teresa, saying that I only mention her every other day. She is not a saint, she's just an agent of the Catholic Church; she is just trying to convert people to Roman Catholicism.

A few days ago I mentioned a Protestant couple who wanted to adopt a child; the couple is childless. The organization was ready to give them a child but when the husband filled out the form they came to know that he is not a Roman Catholic; he is a Protestant Christian. Both are Christians—the Catholics and the Protestants—there is not much difference between them—but he was refused. And when I said this, I have seen angry letters against me in the newspapers saying that there must be some reason why Mother Teresa and her organization refused the couple; that couple must have been a hippie couple—just because of her compassion she refused them.

That is utter nonsense!—because they were willing to give a child, they had accepted to give, they were absolutely ready to give. Only when the form was filled out and he mentioned that he was not a Catholic but a Protestant Christian was he refused. And he is not a hippie—the couple is a well-established, well-to-do, well-educated couple. The husband is a professor in a big university in Europe.

So when people write these letters against me, they should check what they are saying.

The husband's letter was published in *The Times of India*. He was shocked because he had believed that Mother Teresa believes in universal brotherhood. What to say about *universal* brotherhood?—even Protestants and Catholics are not brothers.

Then a follower of Mother Teresa replied: "Mother Teresa and her organization refused to give the child, not because of your religion but because the orphan child has been raised according to the Roman Catholic discipline. It is out of compassion for the child because if he goes to a Protestant family there will be a disturbance. His lifestyle with Mother Teresa will have to be radically changed, and that will be a shattering experience for the child. That's why they have been refused."

Now so many questions arise. First, the child basically is Hindu. Mother Teresa has disturbed the child in the first place by giving him a Catholic training and discipline. And now, giving the child to a Protestant family . . . which is not very different from a Catholic family. Both believe in Christ, both believe in the Bible—what differences are there? Just very nonessential differences: that a Protestant priest is allowed to get married and a Catholic priest is not allowed to get married. How is this going to disturb the child? What nonsense!

There are certainly great differences between Hinduism and Christianity, and the child would have had to go through a drastic change. That is perfectly okay—compassionate towards the child. And if Mother Teresa thinks that changing religion is disturbing a person, then why are millions of Hindus, poor Hindus, being converted to Christianity? They should be stopped. And they are not children—they are grown-up people; their conditioning is bigger. In fact, they will have to go through a deeper crisis. If compassion is there, then converting anybody from one religion to another is inhuman. But that is perfectly okay.

The whole Catholic Church is after people, how to make more Catholics. She is simply an agent of the Catholic Church, of the hierarchy of the Roman Catholic organization. She's not a saint at all—far more clever than Muktananda, not as idiotic as Prabhupada, more cunning, more clever; so clever and so cunning that she goes on doing this conversion business behind a facade of serving the poor. Even Hindus are befooled,

Mohammedans are befooled, and nobody can see the trick and the politics—the politics of numbers.

I am going to say whatsoever I feel is the truth, and every day I will go on sharpening the truth. I have spoken so much for all kinds of people—three hundred books are there. Now I have to create three hundred more books to get rid of all that I have said! But I am capable of doing it—I have planned it already. For seven years I have been speaking non-stop, just seven years more speaking non-stop and I can put you in a real jam!

The last question

*Bhagwan: Can you share with us
a joke about Christmas today?*

Satyarthi

ACCORDING TO THE ANCIENT AKASHIC records, Mary had just given birth to her son. She was lying back in the hay exhausted, when the door opened and in walked half a dozen shepherds, and half a dozen kings, and half a dozen wise men from the East.

She raised her eyes to her husband and said, "Jesus, what a way to spend Christmas!"

Discourse 16

December 26, 1980

THIS IS FAR OUT

The first question

Bhagwan: The other day you said
that sex for reproduction is sinful.
I have also read your words saying that
the greatest creative act of a woman
is in producing a child,
and that there is a vast difference
between a mother and a woman.
If this is so, then is there sin in participating in sex
and in love in the hope of creating a child
and experiencing the joy of creation
and the renewing energy of the universe?
Satdharma,

ONE THING has always to be remembered about me: never bring in what I have said before. I live only now and here, so whatsoever I say now is *the* truth; there is no guarantee about it for tomorrows. I live absolutely in the moment, so don't bring the past in and don't bring the future in either.

Be with me totally immersed in *this* moment. To be in this moment without any hangovers from the past, without any dreams about the future is the only way to be with me—to be in communion. Go on dying to the past; that's the only way to remain alive.

So please never quote me, what I have said before, because the context changes every moment. Much water has gone down the Ganges since I made the statement that the greatest creative act of a woman is in producing a child. I was not talking at that time to my own people; I was talking to the common masses, to the crowd.

Now I am talking to my own people there is no need for any kind of rationalization. I can give you the truth in its utter nudity, and the truth is beautiful only in its utter nudity.

Yes, up to now the greatest creative act of the woman has been giving birth to a child, but it is not going to be so any more. The earth was not so populated in the past; it was a need, a great need, and the woman fulfilled it. But now she has to grow new dimensions of creativity, and only then will she be able to be equal to man. Otherwise, she has been in the past only a factory and man has used her only to create more children. Having more children was economically beneficial, it was business, because they help you in every possible way; they were not a burden in the past.

In poor countries still the old idea continues that the more children you have the better off you will be economically. In the past it was true—it is absolutely false today. Mohammed married nine women and he allowed Mohammedans to marry four women, simply to create more Mohammedans, because there was constant war between the Mohammedans and the non-Mohammedans and it was a question of power—the politics of numbers. Whoever was more powerful was going to win, and power belonged to numbers. Now it is simple arithmetic: if you marry nine women to a single man, a single man can produce nine children in a year. But do just vice versa—marry one woman to nine men—and you may not even have one child. They will mess around . . . they may even kill the woman!

So it was economically, politically significant that men should marry more women, and people were stealing women from each other's tribes. It was more significant to steal a woman than a man because man is not so reproductive; one man is enough to serve many women and one man can produce many children.

But now the whole thing has changed—the world is overpopulated. Now the need of the day is to divert women's creativity into new dimensions: into poetry, into literature, into painting, into music, into architecture, into sculpture, into dancing. She should be allowed now the whole spectrum of creativity. To create a child now is dangerous. To overpopulate the earth now is suicidal; already we are more than are needed.

In Cairo, a city which is suffering from a severe housing shortage, a man was drowning in the river Nile. He was screaming for help, and a passer-by walking across the bridge heard him and called out to the distressed man, "What's your name?"

"Never mind my name!" gasped the drowning man. "Just save me!"

"First your name, please!" insisted the man on the bridge.

"Mr. Hussein," blubbered the struggling unfortunate before he went under for the second time.

"Quick," urged the man on the bridge, "now your address!"

"Forty-nine Kasr el Nil Street," gasped the man with his last breath.

Hearing this, without hesitation the man on the bridge rushed off to the address mentioned, leaving the poor man to drown in the river. He located the owner of the apartment building and told him excitedly, "There's a vacant apartment in your house—can I rent it?"

"Gone already," mumbled the apartment owner. "Sorry, but I just let it to the guy who pushed him in!"

Now giving birth to children is not creative, it is destructive! The whole context has changed and we have to learn new ways to live in a new context. And the woman could not create great poetry, great music, great art, great literature; she could not be a scientist, a mystic—she could not do anything, because she was constantly pregnant in the past. She was undernourished, tortured by so many children, dozens of children, always pregnant, sick. She had not yet lived totally— she had not time enough to live.

For the first time it is possible through contraceptives and birth control methods and sterilization that the woman can free herself from getting pregnant unnecessarily carrying the long long burden of giving birth to children, then raising them up. Her energies can be freed. Now she can also become a Buddha, a Zarathustra, a Jesus, a Krishna. Now she can also create like Mozart, Wagner, Leonardo da Vinci, Michelangelo, Shakespeare, Kalidas, Rabindranath, Tolstoy, Chekhov, Gorky, Dostoevsky.

And *my* feeling is: once the energies of the women are freed totally from giving birth to children she may be able to create greater Buddhas. Why?—because she is a far more creative force than man. But her creativity has remained confined to giving birth to children, and that is not much of a creativity—it is just biological. Animals are doing it perfectly well, so what is great about it? Giving birth to a child is not anything conscious, deliberate, meditative. You are just being used by nature, by biology as a means to propogate the race, the species.

That's why there is a certain undercurrent of guilt in everybody, even without the priest. The priest has used it, exploited it, but he has not really created it. There is an underlying guilt about sex; priests have magnified it very much because it became a source of great exploitation for them. They could dominate man more powerfully by making him feel guilty. But there must be a cause within man himself, otherwise without any background inside him no guilt can be imposed upon him. Man feels it deep down in a subtle way, in an unconscious way—he knows. It is vague, hidden behind layers of mist, but it is there: that sex is not something conscious, it is unconscious, that it is mechanical, that you are being used as a means, that you are not the master, that it is a biological force, that it is not really you who are wanting a woman or a man, it is just the hormones.

That's why we can change a man into a woman—and a man can be changed into a woman or a woman into a man just by changing a few of their glands. So that's what sex is all about—a few glands. Once your hormonal system is changed, a man becomes a woman, a woman becomes a man; there is not much difference. There are two sides of the same biology. And when you know that you are being used and you find yourself incapable of getting rid of this slavery, a guilt arises that you are not being man enough, that you are not really a master, you are a slave. Hence we hide sex.

For thousands of years man has been making love in darkness, in the night, behind the doors, for the simple reason that it looks so ridiculous making love under the sky in the sun, and people watching. You will feel so embarrassed, you will look so ugly. Even in the darkness the woman has more sense of grace—she immediately closes her eyes; while making love she never opens her eyes. Even in darkness she is afraid to see the face of the man because he looks so animal-like. He *is* like an animal!

Sex is an animal act. That's what I mean when I say that sex for reproduction is sinful; the word 'sin' is not used in any moralistic sense. I am simply saying it is sinful because it is unconscious, unmeditative. You are not *doing* it, you are forced to do it by some unconscious forces.

In fact, the word 'sin' is beautiful; it comes from a root which means 'forgetfulness'. You may not be able to see the connection between forgetfulness and sin, but there *is* a connection: forgetfulness means unawareness, unconsciousness.

The sex act in itself is so animal that for centuries we have been hiding it, repressing it, covering it in every possible way.

A middle-aged Australian couple went on a boat trip

to England. They did not participate in the social activities each night, but one evening the wife went to bed and the man joined in one of the games. A member of the audience was chosen at random to speak on a subject pulled out of a hat.

The Australian man was chosen, and he was given the subject 'sex' to speak about for five minutes. He really got into it and the audience roared with laughter.

When he returned to his cabin, his wife sleepily asked what he had been doing. He told her everything, except that the subject for his talk was sex—he told her it was sailing.

The next day the wife was stopped by a buxom young woman who said, "Your husband's speech last night was hilarious and full of unusual insights!"

The wife looked puzzled and said, "That's strange . . . in his whole life he has only done it twice; the first time he got seasick, and the second time his hat blew off!"

We don't even want to mention the word! Even the word is avoided. We have other words for it: 'making love'. . . .Now making love is not possible at all; love is not something that you can make or manufacture or do. Sex can be done—it is just an activity—but love is far deeper. But we want to avoid the word 'sex'; it reminds us of our animality.

That's what I meant when I said sex for reproduction is sinful. One: now the earth needs no more people. If we are bent upon making a hell out of this earth then it is okay—then go on reproducing. Then listen to the Pope and Mother Teresa. . . .Ajai Krishn Lakhanpal, mind you, I have mentioned her again—just for your sake, for your peace of mind! . . . Then listen to all these stupid guys who are telling you to avoid contraceptives, avoid birth control, avoid sterilization, because they are irreligious acts; avoid abortion because that is very immoral. But if you avoid abortion, avoid contraceptives, avoid sterilization, you will be responsible for global suicide and that will be real violence—and we are approaching closer to it every day. That is the first reason I say that sex for reproduction's sake is sinful.

But the Pope, Mahatma Gandhi, and the so-called other saints, they say sex is moral only if you are indulging in it for reproductive reasons. In fact they are telling you sex is good only if it is animal, because animals enter into sex only for reproductive reasons. That's why no animal goes into sex *all* the year around; it is man's dignity, it is man's freedom—it is only man who has the capacity to make sexual contacts all the year round. Animals are living in a kind of bondage: there are seasons, their sex is seasonal, and after the season is over their sex is over—their sex life is finished. Then they don't have any interest in the other.

That's why no family or any kind of intimacy has arisen in animals; it is seasonal. Once in a while they are possessed by natural forces to reproduce. When the time is good and the climate is good for their children to grow up they go into sex, otherwise they forget all about it. They are saints according to the Polack Pope and Mahatma Gandhi—they are the real moral people!

To me, going into sex for reproductive reasons is sinful because it is animal, it is unconscious, it is biological. Going into sex for the sheer joy of sharing energy with anyone you are intimate with . . . it is a way of communing energy to energy, heart to heart. It is melting and merging into each other . . . for no other purpose. If a purpose is there—that you want to create a child—then it is business. If there is *no* purpose, if it is purposeless fun, then only does it have beauty, and then it does not create any bondage. And you are getting free of biology, you are rising higher than biology, you are going above the animals, you are reaching the peaks of humanity.

So to me sex is beautiful only when it is non-purposive, when it is just playfulness, when you are not in it for any other ends, when to be in communion with a woman or a man just for the sheer joy of it is enough. Then you have transcended the lower animal life and you have entered into a higher dimension.

And remember, reproduction is not creation. Once the woman is freed from the unnecessary burden of reproduction she will be able to create more powerfully than any man, because if she can give birth to a child why can't she give birth to beautiful music? But it has not been possible up to now, and man has been trying to rationalize. . . .

Sigmund Freud says that man creates music, art, poetry, just to compensate for his inferiority complex. Because he cannot produce children, he cannot carry children in a womb, he cannot be a mother, he finds other ways to be a mother. He becomes a mother to a painting, to a statue, to the Taj Mahal, to Ajanta, Ellora, to Khajuraho. He tries to mother in some way or other so that he can compensate and he can show to the woman: "You are not the only one who can be pregnant —I can also be pregnant with great ideas."

Sigmund Freud has a great insight there, but the insight is only half; the other half he has not talked about at all. He is as much a male chauvinistic pig as anybody else! The other half has also to be told. The other half is that if the woman is freed . . . and she can be freed now, almost completely freed. Only a few women should be allowed to have children; then we can have a better humanity. And as far as children are concerned the consideration should not be that it has to be from your husband, that it has to be from your wife. That is stupidity—we have to get rid of it. Where children are concerned, then your child should be the *best* possible.

When you want to have a beautiful dress made you don't think, "It should be made only by my wife"—you search for the best tailor. When you want your car to be fixed you don't think, "It has to be fixed by my husband"—you search for the best German mechanic!

And that you are already doing as far as animals are concerned. English bulls are being imported into India for Indian holy cows! We are far more scientific about that—it is far better. Indian bulls are exhausted, tired. When you can get English bulls, why bother about Indian bulls? Why torture them more? And better cows and better bulls can be produced easily by crossbreeding. Man has to be scientific about himself too.

In the future I predict it is going to happen, because I trust in the intelligence of humanity, I have not lost hope. I am not a pessimist, I am absolutely optimistic. This is *going* to happen, this *has* to happen, this is inevitable, that one day a father will brag: "For *my* child I have got the life cells from Albert Einstein. My child is no ordinary child: the male part comes from Albert Einstein, the female part comes from Marilyn Monroe! It is *my* child, no ordinary child!" And I can *see* the point: your child should be the best.

Why should one insist that the female part of the child has to come from *your* wife—for what?—and the male part has to come from you? When you can get better male chromosomes, female chromosomes, when you can get better life cells, healthier ones, more intelligent, then it is perfectly compassionate, loving, that you should manage it.

Sooner or later children can be produced in the labs; they have already succeeded in having test-tube babies. The woman need not carry the child in the womb for nine months; we can create a better womb in the laboratory, we can create better children through scientific methodology—and the woman can be completely freed from the burden of remaining pregnant. And once her energies are released she will be able to be creative. But I think man is afraid of her creativity. She can certainly surpass man's creativity; naturally she is more endowed with creativity.

I am all for creativity but remember, reproduction is not creativity; they are not synonymous. Creativity is something conscious, reproduction is unconscious. Creativity is meditative, reproduction has nothing to do with meditation at all.

But man has just been using the woman almost like cattle. He has been using the woman to raise *his* children; he has been using the woman just as a farm. That's exactly the meaning of the word 'husband': husband means 'the farmer'. Agriculture means husbandry: the wife is the field and the husband is the farmer, and the wife's only function is to give a good crop every year.

The woman can never be liberated unless this is understood: that she has to stop this past pattern. And man has been telling her, "You are great because you give birth to children!" This is a rationalization, this is a consolation. Beware of such tricks. Man has exploited woman in every possible way and it is time to finish this exploitation.

A luxury cruise was proving to be very boring. One evening, just to liven things up a little, a British gentleman called everybody together in the Grand Saloon to propose a game.

"All the gentlemen are to line up on one side of the room and all the ladies on the other. When I clap my hands, everybody has to undress *as* quickly as possible. When I clap my hands a second time, the gentlemen have to race across the room and rape the ladies as quickly as possible. The winner of the game is the man who finishes first and the prize: a kiss from one of our lovely lady passengers!"

What a great idea! But man has been practising this idea down the ages, in different forms.

You ask me, Satdharma:

> *The other day you said*
> *that sex for reproduction is sinful.*

Yes, absolutely sinful.
You also ask:

> *I have also read your words saying that*
> *the greatest creative act of a woman*
> *is in producing a child. . .*

I contradict those words!

> *. . . and that there is a vast difference*
> *between a mother and a woman.*

Certainly there is a vast difference between a mother and a woman. A mother is one who paints, creates poetry, music, art. Just giving birth to a child, any woman can do it; that is nothing of much value. To mother is a totally different phenomenon. Man can be a mother, woman can be a mother; the moment you are creative you are a mother.
And you ask:

> *If this is so, then is there sin in participating in sex*
> *and in love in the hope of creating a child*
> *and experiencing the joy of creation. . . ?*

I don't think anybody has ever experienced the joy of creation by making a woman pregnant. In the first place you don't know whether you have made the woman pregnant or not, so how can you experience the joy of creation? After two, three months you will be able to experience the joy—when it is discovered that the poor woman is pregnant. Do you think you know exactly at the time that you are enjoying the bliss of being creative? Don't be foolish, Satdharma. Be a little sensible, a little intelligent.

. . . and the renewing energy of the universe?

If you are playful then certainly you are renewing the energy of the universe. Every play, every fun, every laughter, every cheer, every dance, every love, renews the energy of the universe—but not by making a poor woman pregnant. It is very unjust really of nature; nature is not just.

If *I* were to make the creation again, then I would decide it in this way: one time the man will become pregnant, one time the woman will become pregnant, and then you will know how much joy there is in being pregnant. Nine months carrying the child in the womb, and all kinds of children . . . they kick around and they do all kinds of things. They even affect your moods, your thoughts, your feelings; they overshadow you. And you are continuously sick, being nauseous, vomiting; you cannot eat, you cannot rest, and all kinds of nightmares . . . just think, for nine months! And then the child is born at last—that too is painful—and then the upbringing of the child which is the most painful thing in the world.

It is very easy for man to say to the woman, "This is great joy and we are renewing the energy of the universe!"

The woman has simply listened up to now; because she has been totally dependent on man she has had to listen to whatsoever nonsense he says. Just try one night to sleep with your child in the bed: either you will kill the child or you will commit suicide. As far as I am concerned I know perfectly well I cannot sleep in the same room where a child is sleeping, because children have strange ideas: in the day they will sleep and in the night they will create trouble!

It is the woman who has somehow tolerated it; man cannot tolerate that. Just try one day: let the woman go for a holiday and manage your twelve children—and the next day you will have to visit the psychoanalyst. They will drive you crazy!

And, Satdharma, you are calling it:

> *. . . experiencing the joy of creation*
> *and the renewing energy of the universe.*

You can renew the energy of the universe by being playful. Love just has to be fun—it has been much too serious. And out of seriousness jealousy has arisen, out of seriousness continuous nagging by the woman has arisen; out of seriousness you are continuously watching the woman—whether she is mixing with somebody else . . . talking to whom? Was she laughing with the neighbor? What was she doing the whole day when you were at the office? This seriousness has destroyed all joy; it has not renewed the energy of the universe, it has simply destroyed the very energy of the universe.

Men can also be like flowers. Certainly you can enhance the energy of the universe, but the way you have behaved up to now this has not been the case.

Four friends meet one winter's evening by the fire and start talking about their adventures.

"Once I has hunting on a mountain alone," says one. "The night was so silent I could not sleep because of the noise of my beard growing!"

"That's nothing!" replies the second one. "I was hunting with a friend up north on the mountain. It was so cold that when we spoke our words would become ice. We had to melt them on the fire to hear what we were saying!"

"Ah, that's nothing!" boasts the third. "Just last month my stomach had to be operated upon because of my sex life!"

"Your sex life?!" the others exclaim in wonder.

"Yes, you see, day after day I have licked and sucked so many women that I had an enormous lump of hairs in my stomach!"

After a few moments of silence the fourth guy says, "Well, your experiences are just games compared to what has happened to me! Years ago with five other friends I crossed Canada, an unexplored country at that time, and we were attacked by wild Indians. One by one all my friends were killed until only I remained alive—a lone figure surrounded by corpses. Then after a bloody fight. . . ."

"What happened?" ask the others in awe.

"The only thing that could have happened—I was killed. And here I am in spirit!"

Love has to be more in the spirit than in the body; it has to become a little more unearthly. It has to become more fun. It has to become more part of the cosmic joke that the universe is.

Satdharma, you are too serious about it—drop your seriousness. Seriousness is irreligious, immoral! Laughter is prayerful. Make your love-life full of laughter—and for the first time this is possible. It was not possible in the past because no scientific technology was available; we had to wait for scientific technology. But now scientific technology is available, only the mind of man is not yet ready to be scientific; it is still superstitious.

In science we are living in the twentieth century, and as far as our superstitions are concerned we are living three thousand years back. We are almost like Mohenjodaro. In Pakistan, the most ancient civilization that has been excavated up to now is that of Mohenjodaro, a city that has been discovered. The city was destroyed at least seven times, and the city must have been at one of the peaks of civilization because seven layers have been discovered. Seven times the city flourished and was destroyed—maybe some natural calamity, maybe some war, earthquake, flood; nothing can be determined now. One thing is certain: that seven times the city flourished, seven times it was destroyed; again it flourished on top of the old city, again it was destroyed.

Mohenjodaro, the word itself, simply means *murdon ka teela*—'a hillock of the dead'. It is a hillock, a seven-layered hillock, and millions of dead people are buried there. Mohenjodaro is seven thousand years old—your superstitions are also that old. A statue of a naked man has been found in Mohenjodaro and Jainas think, "That belongs to our religion"—of course: they worship naked *teerthankaras*, so Jainism is seven thousand years old. One of the statues of a brahmin priest has been discovered with the thread that brahmins wear around their necks—*yagno paveet*— so they claim that their culture and religion are seven thousand years old.

We are living in the past as far as our psychology is concerned and we have not gone beyond Mohenjodaro, that hillock of the dead. Our psychology is full of corpses. Scientifically we are in the twentieth century, psychologically we are lagging far behind. And this is one of the causes of misery on the earth, of poverty on the earth, of illness on the earth, of sadness. This whole sadness and misery can disappear once we decide to be contemporary as far as psychology is concerned; in fact, psychology should be a little *ahead* of scientific technology.

And that's my whole effort here. My sannyasins have to be psychologically *ahead* of the time, psychologically far more developed than the scientific technology is. Only then can you use it, otherwise you are bound to misuse it. Now science has made possible everything which can transform the earth into a paradise. There is no need to look for a paradise in the afterlife—it can happen now and here. And for the first time it is possible: it can happen *now*; you need not wait for it any more.

This is my whole problem: I am talking of a religion, of a philosophy, of a metaphysics, which is absolutely contemporary or a little bit ahead; and the people who are your saints, your mahatmas, your popes, they are living in the dead past. The gap is big, unbridgeable. And of course, *I* cannot compromise because that would be suicidal. *They* have to compromise! They have to come to the twentieth century, I cannot go back; that is not possible. And you have to be ready to fight for the present against the past.

My sannyasins have to be rebels against the past—for a new present, for a new future. We are very close to the sunrise. Just a little effort and the earth can be transformed, totally transformed into a beautiful place—it has never been, but man has always dreamt about it.

The second question

Bhagwan: I laughed at everything you said
the other day
until you said that Mahavira smelt.
I felt personally offended. It hurt.
If not even being born an American Jew
has helped me to drop my attachment to Mahavira,
if not even your outrageous statements

about him have helped,
what to do?
Am I stuck with this conditioning forever?
Perhaps a few more outrageous remarks
from you would help.
There is a part of me that goes on
being identified with a Jaina part of me
that I don't even know (intellectually) anything about.
I have tried all my life
to hide my asceticism in hedonism,
but I can see that it is still there.
Satya Bharti

THAT ASCETICISM is in everyone, and your insight is right that you have been hiding it behind a facade of hedonism. Millions of people are doing that. A real hedonist is not a hedonist at all. *I* am a real hedonist, but I am not a hedonist at all! The person who thinks he is a hedonist and tries to live the life of a hedonist is simply trying to suppress the deep-rooted asceticism, the deep-rooted sado-masochistic tendencies which have been created in the whole of humanity for millions of years.

Man has lived in such suffering that he had to start worshipping suffering, because there was no other consolation; there was no way to get rid of it. It was so much there that the only possible way was to cover it up, to give it a beautiful color, to paint it beautifully. And the best way was to worship suffering. That's what asceticism is: worship of suffering, worship of torture. When a man starts torturing himself, people worship him; this is worshipping a very ill kind of man, a very sick mind.

This part exists in everybody; Jainism is only the full-fledged philosophy of it. But everybody carries a Jaina within himself; a part of everyone around the earth . . . whether you are a Jew or a Christian or a Hindu or a Mohammedan does not matter, a Jaina is bound to be there because the whole past has been one of such misery that we have all accepted misery as the way of life. And the best way to accept it as the way of life is to worship it, is to give it the color of spirituality. That's what Jainism has done.

You say that you were shocked when I said Mahavira smelt. I am not saying it—Jaina scriptures are saying it. Of course they say it in such a way that you will not be able to discover it. They say that Mahavira did not smell at all—but why do you mention it? He did not perspire—but why do you mention it? And how is a body which is alive able not to perspire? Perspiration is an absolute necessity for an alive body because it keeps the temperature of the body at a fixed point, ninety-eight degrees or something. When it is too hot your body perspires and your perspiration evaporates; that evaporation takes the heat of the body away. It evaporates because of the heat of the body, but in the evaporation the heat is taken away and your body remains at a fixed temperature. Without perspiration you will die.

And Mahavira was not made of steel; he was made of bones, blood, skin, just as *you* are. He was not manufactured by a Ford company on an assembly line; he was born of a mother. He was as much a human being as you are, as I am, as everybody is. It is impossible not to perspire. But Jainas make it a point that he did not perspire for the simple reason that if he perspired and he did not take any bath, then he would smell. To avoid the fact that he smelt, all these fabrications. . . .

You will be surprised to know Jaina scriptures mention that he did not urinate, he did not defecate. What nonsense is this? I have come across a case in the medical history that seems to be the longest period of constipation: eighteen months. One man remained constipated for eighteen months; that is the record. But it seems the people who write medical history are not aware of Mahavira: for forty-two years. . . . That is the greatest chronic case of constipation!

Why didn't Mahavira defecate?—because if you defecate, certainly there will be problems. It is better to deny it, because the problems will be that either he will have to use tissue paper—which Indians don't use and at that time nobody was aware of—or he will have to use a toilet, a septic tank, but there was no septic tank in those days, and even if there were he would not have used it because the water in the septic tank, your turd falling into the water, can kill small germs in the water!

Jaina scriptures say: Never defecate on wet ground, never defecate in a river, never defecate in water! So even now Jaina monks don't go into the toilet; in the modern toilet they cannot go. They have to go outside the city and find a dry place. In the rainy season it is very difficult to find a dry place!

He could not use water after defecating to clean himself because water . . . he was very much against water because water contains germs and they will be dying and that will be violence. So it is better to cut the root of the problem: he never defecated. Such control! Such discipline!

And you say Jesus did miracles! Walking on water you think is a miracle? This is a miracle: forty-two years, holding, holding, holding . . . twenty-four hours!I don't think he had any time to meditate or do anything. Even in sleep he must have been holding, holding! This is sheer greed.

And Sigmund Freud again has the insight. He says the color of shit and gold is the same, so the people who are interested in gold become constipated. Mahavira renounced gold, but must have renounced grudgingly, reluctantly. He took revenge—he gathered all the gold inside!

And, Satya, you say that you were shocked when I said Mahavira smelt. Just think of forty-two years of constipation, no urination, no bath, no cleansing of the mouth. How can you avoid smelling! But Jaina scriptures say this is the miracle a *teerthankara* can do. They had to invent these miracles.

There is a story that a snake bites Mahavira on his foot and instead of blood, milk comes out. And Jainas say this is a real miracle. I don't think this can be milk. It may have looked white, but it can be only pus, it cannot be milk. How can milk come out of the feet, because milks needs a certain mechanism in the body; it exists only in the woman's breasts. The milk has to be created, it is a chemical process. How can the feet create milk? Either he had breasts on the feet . . . but then the problem arises that he must have been in a very distorted state! And my feeling is, even if a snake bites on the breast of a woman, milk won't come out, blood will come out. So it must have been pus—this man must have been full of pus. No urination, no defecation— what else can you have inside?

And, Satya Bharti, you say you were shocked. I myself am shocked, but what to do?

And the last question

Bhagwan:
I feel like the guy with the green horse.
Help!

Big Prem

A GREEN HORSE WON'T DO HERE—paint it orange. And, moreover, if you can find a donkey that will be far better, because in a poor country like India riding on a horse is a luxury. People will not forgive you—they cannot forgive me. It will be better if you choose a donkey.

The donkey represents the poor and it also represents the religious. It is a very religious animal—sad, serious, always in a philosophic mood. And once you paint it orange it is a saint, a mahatma! And then you can write on your donkey 'His Holiness, Paramahansa, Donkey-ji Maharaj'. Then you are sure to find a man—that's what she is asking for.

Now Big Prem is really big, and to find a man bigger than Big Prem is a little difficult. But right now one man is free . . . and be quick! Divya has really given total freedom to Hamid, *real* freedom! First she was insisting, "You have to live in the room so that I can give you total freedom, because if you live in another room then how will I give you total freedom! I have to practice total freedom and you have to live in my room!" But finally he escaped, so now he is free, Big Prem. Before some other woman gets hold of him . . . and sooner or later somebody is going to get hold of him, it won't be long. Somebody may have already caught him, because men are so foolish—and particularly Iranians—how long can they remain free?

So from this lecture, Buddha Hall, you immediately rush towards Ayatullah Rahullah Hamidullah! Catch hold of him! But if he is already caught then it is difficult. There is only one thing you can do: you can go with your donkey, painted orange, into the Blue Diamond's manager's office. I have received his research —he may be of great help to you. He seems to be a really alive man in this town of Poona—in this Mohenjodaro, the city of the dead! He must be an alive man because he has sent his research work. It is printed on a simple card—his whole research. He has sent it to me, but I will give it to Big Prem because she can use it. I will read this research paper to you:

Dear Bhagwan:
Scientists report . . . a stroke of genius:
Scientists have determined that the average time of love-making is four minutes. The average number of strokes per minute is nine, making the average love-making thirty-six strokes. Since the average length is six inches, the average girl receives two hundred and sixteen inches or eighteen feet per love-making. The average girl does it three times per week, fifty-two weeks annually—one hundred and fifty times eighteen makes 2,700 feet, or just over half a mile. So, my girl, if you are not getting your half a mile every year, why not let the man who gave you this card help you catch up?

The name of the Blue Diamond's manager is Mr. Pandit—you take this card to him. If you cannot get hold of Hamidullah, then you get hold of Mr. Pandit! Of course you will not be satisfied by half a mile . . . Big Prem is really big!

And the really last question

Bhagwan: I got so excited today when you dropped
Mahavira, Buddha and Jesus
in the wastepaper basket.
It was like a breath of mountain air.
You gave us a glimpse of yourself
that was so intimate and so mischievous.
Would you like to play Puck
in our next production of
'A Midsummer Night's Dream?'
Prem Pramod,

That's just far out!

AUM
Purnamadah
Purnamidam
Purnat purnamudchyate
Purnasya purnamadaya
Purnameva vashisyate.

This is far out.
That too is far out.
From the far out emerges the far out.
The far out coming from the far out,
the far out still remains behind.

BOOKS PUBLISHED BY
RAJNEESH FOUNDATION
INTERNATIONAL

For a complete catalog of all the books published by
Rajneesh Foundation International, contact:

Rajneesh Foundation International
P.O. Box 9
Rajneeshpuram, Oregon 97741 USA
(503) 489-3462

EARLY DISCOURSES

A Cup of Tea
letters to disciples

From Sex to Superconsciousness

THE BAULS

The Beloved (2 volumes)

BUDDHA

The Book of the Books (volume 1)
the Dhammapada

The Diamond Sutra
the Vajrachchedika Prajnaparamita Sutra

The Discipline of Transcendence (4 volumes)
the Sutra of 42 Chapters

The Heart Sutra
the Prajnaparamita Hridayam Sutra

BUDDHIST MASTERS

The Book of Wisdom (volume 1)
Atisha's Seven Points of Mind Training

The White Lotus
the sayings of Bodhidharma

HASIDISM
The Art of Dying
The True Sage

JESUS
Come Follow Me (4 volumes)
the sayings of Jesus
I Say Unto You (2 volumes)
the sayings of Jesus

KABIR
The Divine Melody
Ecstasy: The Forgotten Language
The Fish in the Sea is Not Thirsty
The Guest
The Path of Love
The Revolution

RESPONSES TO QUESTIONS
Be Still and Know
The Goose is Out
My Way: The Way of the White Clouds
Walking in Zen, Sitting in Zen
Walk Without Feet, Fly Without Wings
and Think Without Mind
Zen: Zest, Zip, Zap and Zing

SUFISM
Just Like That
The Perfect Master (2 volumes)
The Secret
Sufis: The People of the Path (2 volumes)
Unio Mystica (2 volumes)
the Hadiqa of Hakim Sanai
Until You Die
The Wisdom of the Sands (2 volumes)

TANTRA

The Book of the Secrets (volumes 4 & 5)
Vigyana Bhairava Tantra

Tantra, Spirituality & Sex
Excerpts from The Book of the Secrets

The Tantra Vision (2 volumes)
the Royal Song of Saraha

TAO

The Empty Boat
the stories of Chuang Tzu

The Secret of Secrets (2 volumes)
the Secret of the Golden Flower

Tao: The Pathless Path (2 volumes)
the stories of Lieh Tzu

Tao: The Three Treasures (4 volumes)
the Tao Te Ching of Lao Tzu

When The Shoe Fits
the stories of Chuang Tzu

THE UPANISHADS

The Ultimate Alchemy (2 volumes)
Atma Pooja Upanishad

Vedanta: Seven Steps to Samadhi
Akshya Upanishad

Philosophia Ultima
Mandukya Upanishad

WESTERN MYSTICS

The Hidden Harmony
the fragments of Heraclitus

The New Alchemy: To Turn You On
Mabel Collins' Light on the Path

Philosophia Perennis (2 volumes)
the Golden Verses of Pythagoras

Guida Spirituale
the Desiderata

Theologia Mystica
the treatise of St. Dionysius

Be Realistic: Plan For a Miracle
(March 13 - April 6, 1976)

Get Out of Your Own Way
(April 7 - May 2, 1976)

Beloved of My Heart
(May 3 - 28, 1976)

The Cypress in the Courtyard
(May 29 - June 27, 1976)

A Rose is a Rose is a Rose
(June 28 - July 27, 1976)

Dance Your Way to God
(July 28 - August 20, 1976)

The Passion for the Impossible
(August 21 - September 18, 1976)

The Great Nothing
(September 19 - October 11, 1976)

God is Not for Sale
(October 12 - November 7, 1976)

The Shadow of the Whip
(November 8 - December 3, 1976)

Blessed are the Ignorant
(December 4 - 31, 1976)

The Buddha Disease
(January 1977)

What Is, Is, What Ain't, Ain't
(February 1977)

The Zero Experience
(March 1977)

For Madmen Only (Price of Admission: Your Mind)
(April 1977)

This Is It
(May 1977)

The Further Shore
(June 1977)

Far Beyond the Stars
(July 1977)

YOGA
Yoga: The Alpha and the Omega
(10 volumes)
the Yoga Sutras of Patanjali
ZEN
Ah, This!
Ancient Music in the Pines
And the Flowers Showered
Dang Dang Doko Dang
The First Principle
The Grass Grows By Itself
Nirvana: the Last Nightmare
No Water, No Moon
Returning to the Source
A Sudden Clash of Thunder
The Sun Rises in the Evening
Zen: The Path of Paradox (3 volumes)
ZEN MASTERS
Hsin Hsin Ming: The Book of Nothing
Discourses on the faith-mind of Sosan
The Search
the Ten Bulls of Zen
Take It Easy (2 volumes)
poems of Ikkyu
This Very Body the Buddha
Hakuin's Song of Meditation
INITIATION TALKS
between Master disciple
Hammer On The Rock
(December 10, 1975 - January 15, 1976)
Above All Don't Wobble
(January 16 - February 12, 1976)
Nothing To Lose But Your Head
(February 13 - March 12, 1976)

Zorba the Buddha
(January 1979)

Won't You Join the Dance?
(February 1979)

The Sound of One Hand Clapping
(March 1981)

OTHER TITLES

Rajneeshism
an introduction to Bhagwan Shree Rajneesh and His
religion

The Sound of Running Water
a photobiography of
   Bhagwan Shree Rajneesh and His work

The Orange Book
the meditation techniques of
   Bhagwan Shree Rajneesh

BOOKS FROM OTHER PUBLISHERS

ENGLISH EDITIONS
UNITED KINGDOM

The Art of Dying
(Sheldon Press)

The Book of the Secrets (volume 1)
(Thames & Hudson)

Dimensions Beyond the Known
(Sheldon Press)

The Hidden Harmony
(Sheldon Press)

Meditation: The Art of Ecstasy
(Sheldon Press)

The Mustard Seed
(Sheldon Press)

Neither This Nor That
(Sheldon Press)

No Water, No Moon
(Sheldon Press)

Roots and Wings
(Routledge & Kegan Paul)

Straight to Freedom (Original title:
Until You Die)
(Sheldon Press)

The Supreme Doctrine
(Routledge & Kegan Paul)

The Supreme Understanding (Original title:
Tantra: The Supreme Understanding)
(Sheldon Press)

Tao: The Three Treasures (volume 1)
(Wildwood House)

UNITED STATES OF AMERICA

The Book of the Secrets (volumes 1-3)
(Harper & Row)

The Great Challenge
(Grove Press)

Hammer on the Rock
(Grove Press)

I Am The Gate
(Harper & Row)

Journey Toward the Heart (Original title:
Until You Die)
(Harper & Row)

Meditation: The Art of Ecstasy
(Harper & Row)

The Mustard Seed
(Harper & Row)

My Way: The Way of the White Clouds
(Grove Press)

Only One Sky (Original title:
Tantra: The Supreme Understanding)
(Dutton)

The Psychology of the Esoteric
(Harper & Row)

Roots and Wings
(Routledge & Kegan Paul)

The Supreme Doctrine
(Routledge & Kegan Paul)

Words Like Fire (Original title:
Come Follow Me, volume 1)
(Harper & Row)

BOOKS ON BHAGWAN

The Awakened One: The Life and Work
of Bhagwan Shree Rajneesh
by Swami Satya Vedant
(Harper & Row)

Death Comes Dancing: Celebrating Life
with Bhagwan Shree Rajneesh
by Ma Satya Bharti
(Routledge & Kegan Paul)

Drunk On The Divine
by Ma Satya Bharti
(Grove Press)

The Ultimate Risk
by Ma Satya Bharti
(Routledge & Kegan Paul)

Dying For Enlightenment
by Bernard Gunther (Swami Deva Amitprem)
(Harper & Row)

Neo-Tantra
by Bernard Gunther (Swami Deva Amitprem)
(Harper & Row)

FOREIGN LANGUAGE EDITIONS
DANISH

TRANSLATIONS

Hemmelighedernes Bog (volume 1)
(Borgens Forlag)

Hu-Meditation Og Kosmisk Orgasme
(Borgens Forlag)

BOOKS ON BHAGWAN

Sjælens Oprør
by Swami Deva Satyarthi
(Borgens Forlag)

DUTCH

TRANSLATIONS

Drink Mij
(Ankh-Hermes)

Het Boek Der Geheimen (volumes 1-4)
(Mirananda)

Geen Water, Geen Maan
(Mirananda)

Gezaaid In Goede Aarde
(Ankh-Hermes)

Ik Ben De Poort
(Ankh-Hermes)

Ik Ben De Zee Die Je Zoekt
(Ankh-Hermes)

Meditatie: De Kunst van Innerlijke Extase
(Mirananda)

Mijn Weg, De Weg van de Witte Wolk
(Arcanum)

Het Mosterdzaad (volumes 1 & 2)
(Mirananda)

Het Oranje Meditatieboek
(Ankh-Hermes)

Psychologie en Evolutie
(Ankh-Hermes)

Tantra: Het Allerhoogste Inzicht
(Ankh-Hermes)

Tantra, Spiritualiteit en Seks
(Ankh-Hermes)

De Tantra Visie (volume 1)
(Arcanum)

Tau
(Ankh-Hermes)

Totdat Je Sterft
(Ankh-Hermes)

De Verborgen Harmonie
(Mirananda)

Volg Mij
(Ankh-Hermes)

Zoeken naar de Stier
(Ankh-Hermes)

BOOKS ON BHAGWAN

Bhagwan: Notities van Een Discipel
by Swami Deva Amrito (Jan Foudraine)
(Ankh-Hermes)

Bhagwan Shree Rajneesh: De Laatste Gok
by Ma Satya Bharti
(Mirananda)

Oorspronkelijk Gezicht,
Een Gang Naar Huis
by Swami Deva Amrito (Jan Foudraine)
(Ambo)

FRENCH

TRANSLATIONS

L'éveil à la Conscience Cosmique
(Dangles)

Je Suis La Porte
(EPI)

Le Livre Des Secrets (volume 1)
(Soleil Orange)

La Meditation Dynamique
(Dangles)

GERMAN

TRANSLATIONS

Auf der Suche
(Sambuddha Verlag)

Das Buch der Geheimnisse (volume 1)
(Heyne Verlag)

Das Orangene Buch
(Sambuddha Verlag)

Der Freund
(Sannyas Verlag)

Reise ins Unbekannte
(Sannyas Verlag)

Ekstase: Die vergessene Sprache
(Herzschlag Verlag, formerly Ki-Buch)

Esoterische Pyschologie
(Sannyas Verlag)

Die Rebellion der Seele
(Sannyas Verlag)

Ich bin der Weg
(Rajneesh Verlag)

Intelligenz des Herzens
(Herzschlag Verlag, formerly Ki-Buch)

Jesus aber Schwieg
(Sannyas Verlag)

Kein Wasser Kein Mond
(Herzschlag Verlag, formerly Ki-Buch)

Komm und folge mir
(Sannyas Verlag)

Meditation: Die Kunst zu sich selbst zu finden
(Heyne Verlag)

Mein Weg: Der Weg der weissen Wolke
(Herzschlag Verlag, formerly Ki-Buch)

Mit Wurzeln und mit Flügeln
(Edition Lotus)

Nicht bevor du stirbst
(Edition Gyandip, Switzerland)

Die Schuhe auf dem Kopf
(Edition Lotus)

Das Klatschen der einen Hand
(Edition Gyandip, Switzerland)

Spirituelle Entwicklung
(Fischer)

Sprengt den Fels der Unbewusstheit
(Fischer)

Tantra: Die höchste Einsicht
(Sambuddha Verlag)

Tantrische Liebeskunst
(Sannyas Verlag)

Die Alchemie der Verwandlung
(Edition Lotus)

Die verborgene Harmonie
(Sannyas Verlag)

Was ist Meditation?
(Sannyas Verlag)

BOOKS ON BHAGWAN

Begegnung mit Niemand
by Mascha Rabben (Ma Hari Chetana)
(Herzschlag Verlag)

Ganz entspannt im Hier und Jetzt
by Swami Satyananda
(Rowohlt)

Im Grunde ist alles ganz einfach
by Swami Satyananda
(Ullstein)

Wagnis Orange
by Ma Satya Bharti
(Fachbuchhandlung at für Psychologie)

Wenn das Herz frei wird
by Ma Prem Gayan (Silvie Winter)
(Herbig)

GREEK

TRANSLATION

I Krifi Armonia (The Hidden Harmony)
(Emmanual Rassoulis)

HEBREW

TRANSLATION

Tantra: The Supreme Understanding
(Massada)

ITALIAN

TRANSLATIONS

L'Armonia Nascosta (volumes 1 & 2)
(Re Nudo)

Dieci Storie Zen di Bhagwan Shree Rajneesh
(Né Acqua, Né Luna)
(Il Fiore d'Oro)

La Dottrina Suprema
(Rizzoli)

Dimensioni Oltre il Conosciuto
(Mediterranee)

Io Sono La Soglia
(Mediterranee)

Il Libro Arancione
(Mediterranee)

Il Libro dei Segreti
(Bompiani)

Meditazione Dinamica:
L'Arte dell'Estasi Interiore
(Mediterranee)

La Nuova Alchimia
(Psiche)

La Rivoluzione Interiore
(Armenia)

La Ricerca
(La Salamandra)

Il Seme della Ribellione (volumes 1-3)
(Re Nudo)

Tantra: La Comprensione Suprema
(Bompiani)

Tao: I Tre Tesori (volumes 1-3)
(Re Nudo)

Tecniche di Liberazione
(La Salamandra)

Semi di Saggezza
(SugarCo)

BOOKS ON BHAGWAN

Alla Ricerca del Dio Perduto
by Swami Deva Majid
(SugarCo)

Il Grande Esperimento:
    Meditazioni E Terapie Nell'ashram
Di Bhagwan Shree Rajneesh
by Ma Satya Bharti
(Armenia)

L'Incanto D'Arancio
by Swami Swatantra Sarjano
(Savelli)

JAPANESE

TRANSLATIONS

Dance Your Way to God
(Rajneesh Publications)

The Empty Boat (volumes 1 & 2)
(Rajneesh Publications)

From Sex to Superconsciousness
(Rajneesh Publications)

The Grass Grows by Itself
(Fumikura)

The Heart Sutra
(Merkmal)

Meditation: The Art of Ecstasy
(Merkmal)

The Mustard Seed
(Merkmal)

My Way: The Way of the White Clouds
(Rajneesh Publications)

The Orange Book
(Wholistic Therapy Institute)

The Search
(Merkmal)

The Beloved
(Merkmal)

Take It Easy (volume 1)
(Merkmal)

Tantra: The Supreme Understanding
(Merkmal)

Tao: The Three Treasures (volumes 1-4)
(Merkmal)

Until You Due
(Fumikura)

PORTUGUESE (BRAZIL)

TRANSLATIONS

O Cipreste No Jardim
(Soma)

Dimensões Além do Conhecido
(Soma)

O Livro Dos Segredos (volume 1)
(Maha Lakshmi Editora)

Eu Sou A Porta
(Pensamento)

A Harmonia Oculta
(Pensamento)

Meditacão: A Arte Do Extase
(Cultrix)

Meu Caminho:
  O Comainho Das Nuvens Brancas
(Tao Livraria & Editora)

Nem Agua, Nem Lua
(Pensamento)

O Livro Orange
(Soma)

Palavras De Fogo
(Global/Ground)

A Psicologia Do Esotérico
(Tao Livraria & Editora)

A Semente De Mostarda (volumes 1 & 2)
(Tao Livraria & Editora)

Tantra: Sexo E Espiritualidade
(Agora)

Tantra: A Supreme Comprensao
(Cultrix)

Antes Que Voce Morra
(Maha Lakshmi Editora)

SPANISH

TRANSLATIONS

Introducción al Mundo del Tantra
(Collección Tantra)

Meditación: El Arte del Extasis
(Collección Tantra)

Psicológia de lo Esotérico:
La Nueva Evolución del Hombre
(Cuatro Vientos Editorial)

¿Qué Es Meditación?
(Koan/Roselló Impresions)

Yo Soy La Puerta
(Editorial Diana)

Sòlo Un Cielo (volumes 1 & 2)
(Colección Tantra)

BOOKS ON BHAGWAN

El Riesgo Supremo
by Ma Satya Bharti
(Martinez Roca)

SWEDISH

TRANSLATION

Den Väldiga Utmaningen
(Livskraft)

RAJNEESH MEDITATION CENTERS, ASHRAMS AND COMMUNES

There are hundreds of Rajneesh meditation centers throughout the world. These are some of the main ones, which can be contacted for the name and address of the center nearest you. They can also tell you about the availability of the books of Bhagwan Shree Rajneesh — in English or in foreign language editions. General information is available from Rajneesh Foundation International.

A wide range of meditation and inner growth programs is available throughout the year at Rajneesh International Meditation University.

For further information and a complete listing of programs, write or call:

> Rajneesh International Meditation University
> P.O. Box 5, Rajneeshpuram, OR 97741 USA
> Phone: (503) 489-3328

USA

RAJNEESH FOUNDATION INTERNATIONAL
% Jesus Grove, P.O. Box 9, Rajneeshpuram, Oregon 97741.
Tel: (503) 489-3301

SAMBODHI RAJNEESH SANNYAS ASHRAM
Conomo Point Road, Essex, MA 01929. Tel: (617) 768-7640

UTSAVA RAJNEESH MEDITATION CENTER
20062 Laguna Canyon, Laguna Beach, CA 92651.
Tel: (714) 497-4877

DEVADEEP RAJNEESH SANNYAS ASHRAM
1430 Longfellow St., N.W., Washington, D.C. 20011.
Tel: (202) 723-2186

CANADA

ARVIND RAJNEESH SANNYAS ASHRAM
2807 W. 16th Ave., Vancouver, B.C. V6K 3C5.
Tel: (604) 734-4681

SHANTI SADAN RAJNEESH MEDITATION CENTER
1817 Rosemont, Montreal, Quebec H2G 1S5.
Tel: (514) 272-4566

AUSTRALIA

PREMDWEEP RAJNEESH MEDITATION CENTER
64 Fullarton Rd., Norwood, S.A. 5067. Tel: 08-423388

SATPRAKASH RAJNEESH MEDITATION CENTER
108 Oxford Street, Darlinghurst 2010, N.S.W.
Tel: (02) 336570

SAHAJAM RAJNEESH SANNYAS ASHRAM
6 Collie Street, Fremantle 6160, W.A.
Tel: (09) 336-2422

SVARUP RAJNEESH MEDITATION CENTER
169 Elgin St., Carlton 3053, Victoria. Tel: 347-6274

AUSTRIA

PRADEEP RAJNEESH MEDITATION CENTER
Siebenbrunnenfeldgasse 4, 1050 Vienna. Tel: 542-860

BELGIUM

VADAN RAJNEESH MEDITATION CENTER
Platte-Lo-Straat 65, 3200 Leuven (Kessel-Lo).
Tel: 016/25-1487

BRAZIL

PRASTHAN RAJNEESH MEDITATION CENTER
R. Paulos Matos 121, Rio de Janeiro, R.J. 20251.
Tel: 222-9476

PURNAM RAJNEESH MEDITATION CENTER
Caixa Postal 1946, Porto Alegre, RS 90000.

CHILE

SAGARO RAJNEESH MEDITATION CENTER
Golfo de Darien 10217, Las Condas, Santiago.
Tel: 472476

DENMARK

ANAND NIKETAN RAJNEESH MEDITATION CENTER
Strøget, Frederiksberggade 15, 1459 Copenhagen K.
Tel: (01) 139940

EAST AFRICA

ANAND NEED RAJNEESH MEDITATION CENTER
Kitisuru Estate, P.O. Box 72424, Nairobi, Kenya.
Tel: 582600

AMBHOJ RAJNEESH MEDITATION CENTER
P.O. Box 10256, Nairobi, Kenya

FRANCE

PRADIP RAJNEESH MEDITATION CENTER
23 Rue Cecile, Maisons Alfoet, 94700 Paris.
Tel: 3531190

GREAT BRITAIN

MEDINA RAJNEESH BODY CENTER
81 Belsize Park Gardens, London NW3.
Tel: (01) 722-8220, 722-6404

MEDINA RAJNEESH NEO-SANNYAS COMMUNE
Herringswell, Bury St. Edmunds, Suffolk 1P28 6SW.
Tel: (0638) 750234

HOLLAND

DE STAD RAJNEESH NEO-SANNYAS COMMUNE
Kamperweg 80-86 8191 KC Heerde. Tel: 05207-1261

GRADA RAJNEESH NEO-SANNYAS COMMUNE
Prins Hendrikstraat 64, 1931 BK Egmond aan Zee.
Tel: 02206-4114

INDIA

RAJNEESHDHAM NEO-SANNYAS COMMUNE
17 Koregaon Park, Poona 411 001, MS. Tel: 28127

RAJ YOGA RAJNEESH MEDITATION CENTER
C5/44 Safdarjang Development Area, New Delhi 100 016.
Tel: 654533

ITALY

MIASTO RAJNEESH NEO-SANNYAS COMMUNE
Podere S. Giorgio, Cotorniano, 53010 Frosini (Siena).
Tel: 0577-960124

VIVEK RAJNEESH MEDITATION CENTER
Via San Marco 40/4, 20121 Milan. Tel: 659-5632

JAPAN

SHANTIYUGA RAJNEESH MEDITATION CENTER
Sky Mansion 2F, 1-34-1 Ookayama, Meguro-ku, Tokyo 152.
Tel: (03) 724-9631

UTSAVA RAJNEESH MEDITATION CENTER
2-9-8 Hattori-Motomachi, Toyonaki-shi, Osaka 561.
Tel: 06-863-4246

NEW ZEALAND

SHANTI NIKETAN RAJNEESH MEDITATION CENTER
115 Symonds Street, Auckland. Tel: 770-326

PUERTO RICO

BHAGWATAM RAJNEESH MEDITATION CENTER
Calle Sebastian 208 (Altos), Viejo San Juan, PR 00905.
Tel: 725-0593

SPAIN

SARVOGEET RAJNEESH MEDITATION CENTER
C. Titania 55, Madrid, 33. Tel: 200-0313

SWEDEN

DEEVA RAJNEESH MEDITATION CENTER
Surbrunnsgatan 60, 11327 Stockholm. Tel: (08) 327788

SWITZERLAND

GYANDIP RAJNEESH MEDITATION CENTER
Baumackerstr. 42, 8050 Zurich. Tel: (01) 312 1600

WEST GERMANY

ANAND SAGAR RAJNEESH MEDITATION CENTER
Lutticherstr. 33/35, 5000 Cologne 1. Tel: 0221-517199

BAILE RAJNEESH NEO-SANNYAS COMMUNE
Karolinenstr. 7-9, 2000 Hamburg 6. Tel: (040) 432140

RAJNEESHSTADT NEO-SANNYAS COMMUNE
Schloss Wolfsbrunnen, 3446 Meinhard-Schwebda.
Tel: (05651) 70044

SATDHARMA RAJNEESH MEDITATION CENTER
Klenzestr. 41, 8000 Munich 5. Tel: (089) 269-077

DORFCHEN RAJNEESH NEO-SANNYAS
Urbanstr. 64, 1000 Berlin 61. Tel: (030) 691-7917